Ars musice

Medieval Institute Publications is a program of
The Medieval Institute, College of Arts and Sciences

 WESTERN MICHIGAN UNIVERSITY

Johannes de Grocheio

Ars musice

Edited and translated by

Constant J. Mews, John N. Crossley, Catherine Jeffreys,
Leigh McKinnon, and Carol J. Williams

TEAMS • Varia

MEDIEVAL INSTITUTE PUBLICATIONS
Western Michigan University
Kalamazoo

Library of Congress Cataloging-in-Publication Data

Johannes, de Grocheo, fl. 1300.
　[Ars musice. English]
　Ars musice / edited and translated by Constant J. Mews ... [et al.].
　　　p. cm. -- (Teams . varia)
　Includes bibliographical references and index.
　ISBN 978-1-58044-164-3 (clothbound : alk. paper) -- ISBN 978-1-
58044-165-0 (paperbound : alk. paper)
　1.　Music theory--Early works to 1800.　I. Mews, C. J. II. Title.
　ML171.J5913 2011
　781--dc23

　　　　　　　　　　　　　　　　　　　　　2011024658

1 2 3 4 5 C P 5 4 3 2 1

Contents

Acknowledgments

This project of editing and translating the *Ars musice* of Johannes de Grocheio was generated within an interdisciplinary medieval Latin reading group within the School of Historical Studies at Monash University (in Melbourne, Australia), that brought together specialists in intellectual history, musicology, and history of science. This was a collective endeavor that could not have been brought to fruition without the generous support of the Faculties of Arts and of Information Technology at Monash University and the Australian Research Council (Discovery Project 0555959). We are also profoundly grateful to a number of individuals who have helped us with this project, in particular Nancy van Deusen, Charles Burnett, and Rodney Thomson. Others who have given assistance in various ways include Alexander Fidora, Mary Wolinski, Margaret Bent, and librarians at the British Library, the Universitäts- und Landesbibliothek in Darmstadt, and St. John's College, Oxford. We have also benefited from the opportunity to present ideas about Grocheio and his milieu at a range of places, initially at a symposium of the International Musicological Society held at Monash University in 2004, at the seminar of Jean-Claude Schmitt at the Ecole des hautes études en sciences sociales, Paris, as well as at Johns Hopkins University and Texas A&M University and at a conference held at Monash University in July 2006 on the theme of Communities of Learning in medieval Europe. We are also profoundly grateful to TEAMS for venturing into new territory by accepting a treatise on music theory. An interdisciplinary project such as this necessarily involves learning from a wide range of people and fields of expertise. Responsibility for any errors is of course entirely our own.

Abbreviations

ALD1	Aristoteles Latinus Database 1. Turnhout: Brepols, 2003.
AM	Johannes de Grocheio, *Ars musice*
BL	British Library
BnF	Bibliothèque nationale de France
CS	Edmond de Coussemaker, ed., *Scriptores de musica medii ævi novam seriem a Gerbertina alteram*, 4 vols. (Paris: Durant, 1874–76; repr. Hildesheim: Olms, 1963)
CUP	Heinrich Denifle, ed., *Chartularium Universitatis Parisiensis*, 4 vols. (Paris, 1889–97; repr. Brussels: Culture and Civilisation, 1964)
GS	Martin Gerbert, ed., *Scriptores ecclesiastici de musica sacra potissimum*, 3 vols. (St. Blaise: Typis San-Blasianis, 1784; repr. Hildesheim: Olms, 1963)
JAMS	*Journal of the American Musicological Society*
MGG	*Die Musik in Geschichte und Gegenwart: Allgemeine Enzyklopädie der Musik*, ed. Friedrich Blume, 17 vols. (Kassel: Bärenreiter, 1949–86); rev. ed., ed. Ludwig Finscher, 29 vols. (Kassel: Bärenreiter, 1994–2007)
Rohloff 1943	Ernst Rohloff, *Der Musiktraktat des Johannes de Grocheo nach den Quellen neu herausgegeben mit Übersetzung* (Leipzig: Kommissionsverlag Gebrüder Reinecke, 1943)
Rohloff 1972	Ernst Rohloff, *Die Quellenhandschriften zum Musiktraktat des Johannes de Grocheio. In Faksimile herausgegeben nebst Übertragung des Textes und Übersetzung in Deutsche, dazu Bericht, Literaturschau, Tabellen und Indices* (Leipzig: Deutscher Verlag für Musik, 1972)

Introduction

The *Ars musice* of Johannes de Grocheio

> It is thus the intention of the present work, as much as we can, to explain to them music. . . . (*AM* 0.2) But it is not easy for us to divide music correctly. . . . The parts of music are many and diverse according to diverse uses, diverse idioms, or diverse tongues in diverse cities or regions. If, however, we divide it according to the use of the people in Paris . . . our intention will be seen to be sufficiently accomplished. (*AM* 6.1)

These comments of Johannes de Grocheio (Jean de Gruchy) about the difficulty of describing music illustrate a driving concern of a remarkable treatise, composed in Paris during the late thirteenth century, quite possibly in the 1270s.[1] Grocheio is aware of the enormous range of types of music performed in different ways in different places. How can he impose order on this enormous subject matter? He decided to resolve this question by structuring his discussion around the practice of music that he observed in the city of Paris, organized into three main "branches": music of the people (*musica vulgalis*),[2] composite or regular, "which they call measured music" (*musica mensurata*), and ecclesiastical music (*musica ecclesiastica*), which he claims derives from the other two (*AM* 6.2). The originality of Grocheio's treatise has attracted considerable scholarly interest.[3] It has long been recognized as a unique source of information about musical life in medieval Paris.[4] Through his treatise, Grocheio enables a modern reader to become aware of the complex auditory environment of that city in the late thirteenth century as well as of its intellectual vitality at a particularly vibrant moment in its history.

Grocheio provides a series of observations on the subject of *musica*, the theory of which, he complains, is little attended to "in our days" (*AM* 0.5). He discusses a variety of subjects, including theoretical fundamentals such as the "principles" (*principia*) of music and music notation, as well as theory specific to measured and ecclesiastical music. Early studies of Grocheio's treatise broached the main area of concern that has characterized much subsequent interest: *musica vulgalis*.[5] Grocheio's comments about measured music have received some attention, as have his comments about ecclesiastical music, particularly because of his comparison of ecclesiastical forms with the forms

1

of *musica vulgalis.*[6] Other points of interest in his treatise include discussion of the principles of natural scientific enquiry as elucidated in the works of Aristotle and criticism of the Boethian divisions of music into *mundana, humana,* and *instrumentalis.*[7] A detailed listing of the contents of the treatise follows this introduction.[8]

Grocheio's treatise survives in two medieval manuscripts: Darmstadt, Universitäts- und Landesbibliothek, MS 2663, fols. 56r–69r, and London, British Library, MS Harley 281, fols. 39r–52r. Darmstadt 2663 is a fourteenth-century miscellany of otherwise homiletic and liturgical commentaries, including works by David of Augsburg (d. 1272) and a French-language copy of the *Elucidarium* of Honorius Augustodunensis. BL Harley 281 is an early fourteenth-century anthology of music-theoretical tracts and tonaries, including works by Guido of Arezzo, Petrus de Cruce, and Guy of Saint-Denis. Grocheio's treatise was first edited in 1899 by Johannes Wolf, who knew only the Darmstadt copy.[9] Ernst Rohloff completed a dissertation on the treatise in 1925, also focusing on the Darmstadt copy, publishing a commentary and edition in 1930 and 1943.[10] Only in 1972 did Rohloff consider both manuscripts of the treatise in a new edition, *Die Quellenhandschriften zum Musiktraktat des Johannes de Grocheio,* that included facsimile reproduction of both manuscripts, even though his transcriptions may not always have been fully accurate.[11] The following year, Albert Seay produced the only complete English translation that has been available until now.[12] In 1993, Christopher Page edited afresh and translated excerpts of the treatise relating to secular music but left large sections untouched.[13]

We only know about Grocheio's name from the Darmstadt copy of his treatise, the final rubric on fol. 69r reading: "Explicit theoria magistri iohannis de grocheio." The spelling *Grocheo* is given in the table of contents to Darmstadt 2663 (fol. Tv: "Musica magistri joh de grocheo"); nonetheless, the spelling *Grocheio* is preferred here as the final rubric in the Darmstadt copy, although in a display script, is in the same hand as the text of Grocheio's treatise.[14] A colophon has also been added in this hand: "Scriptori flamen sacrum tribuat decus."[15] An enigmatic feature of the rubric on fol. 69r is that it is followed by the word *regens* (i.e., "teaching") in a different hand and not agreeing grammatically with "magistri iohannis de grocheio." In between the rubric and the colophon, and partially obscured by both, is a word construed as *Parisius* ("in Paris").[16]

The treatise has been given several titles. Johannes Wolf used the title *Theoria,* reproducing the rubric on fol. 69r of the Darmstadt copy ("Explicit theoria"). While no opening rubric is given to the work in this manuscript,

Rohloff preferred *De Musica*, claiming that it derived from Grocheio's words: "De tertia vero puta de musica est speculatio presens" (*AM* 22.5). Elsewhere, however, Grocheio refers to his own work as "de doctrina musicali" (*AM* 0.1) rather than as "de musica."[17] The table of contents to Darmstadt 2663 (fol. Tv) identifies the treatise as *Musica*. The author is not identified by name in BL Harley 281; the rubric "Incipit prologus in arte musice" precedes the prologue, "Incipit tractatus" (fol. 39r) introduces the treatise proper, and "Explicit tractatus musice" (fol. 52r) follows it. The title *Ars musice*, which is employed in the present edition, derives from the opening rubric to the Harley copy.[18]

Grocheio's Norman Background and Parisian Milieu

There can be little doubt about the Norman origin of Johannes de Grocheio, first identified by Christopher Page almost two decades ago.[19] Grocheio speaks as if from personal experience about a certain type of *cantilena* sung "in the West, namely in Normandy" ("versus occidentem puta in normannia"—*AM* 9.6). He also refers his audience to a discourse (*sermo*) that he had addressed to Clement, monk of the Norman abbey of Lessay ("ad clementem exaquiensem monacum"—*AM* 9.1). *Grocheio* ("Gruchy/Grouchy") itself is an established Norman name, although there are several places in Normandy called Gruchy/Grouchy and thus several possibilities for where Grocheio may have come from (see figure 1). Page speculated that Grocheio might have been related to the noble branch of the de Grouchy (*de Groci*) family, whose earliest known representative is identified in a mid-eleventh-century charter by Hugo *de Groci*.[20] Yet little is known about this branch of the family prior

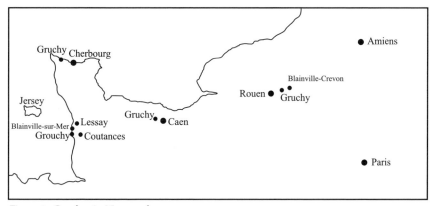

Figure 1. Gruchys in Normandy

to the fourteenth century, other than that two brothers, Robert and Henry de Grouchy, served Louis IX on crusade in 1248.[21] Settlements bearing the Gruchy name include one at the tip of the Cotentin peninsula, some thirty-five miles from Coutances, and another near Caen.[22] As Robert Mullally observed, however, Grocheio's acquaintance with Clement of Lessay makes it more likely that he was connected to the Gruchy on the western coast of the Cotentin, just south of Blainville-sur-Mer, thirteen miles from the Benedictine abbey at Lessay and less than eight miles from Coutances, the episcopal centre of the Cotentin.[23] This Gruchy, originally a Viking settlement from the ninth century, is likely to have been the site from where members of the de Gruchy family moved to different parts of Normandy, becoming a significant family in the Cotentin in the twelfth and thirteenth centuries.[24]

Grocheio's connection to Lessay may have been an old-standing family one, for in 1172 Richard and Thomas *de Groceio* witnessed a charter of the priory of Bohon (some twenty miles from Gruchy), alongside abbot Peter of Lessay.[25] The abbot was a significant figure in the region, from 1221 being a member of the cathedral chapter of Coutances.[26] In 1228, a William de Groceio, identified as a knight and royal servant, gave land to the Premonstratensian abbey of St. Nicolas de Blanchelande near Coutances, and thus was likely to have been from the Gruchy at Blainville-sur-mer.[27] In 1273, a Haretot de Grouceio bequeathed tithes to Jean d'Essay (Jean of Lessay), bishop of Coutances (1250–74).[28] Whatever his exact links to William and Haretot, the music theorist Johannes de Grocheio (Jean de Gruchy) inherited the name of a well-known Norman family. If he came from the Cotentin branch located in Gruchy near Blainville-sur-Mer, as seems likely because of his association with Clement of Lessay, his family may have been of only modest social standing within the duchy, but significant enough for him to have had familiarity with seigneurial culture in the region.

Recognizing that musical practice differed from region to region, Grocheio declared his intention to describe music as practiced by "the people in Paris" (*AM* 6.1) thereby suggesting the locale for the composition of his treatise. His role as a teacher is implied by his stated aim to "explain . . . something in brief about musical teaching" (*AM* 0.1) and the grammatically clumsy addition of *regens* to the rubric bearing his name in Darmstadt 2663. Norman allusions within Grocheio's treatise invite the proposal that he was a member of the Norman nation of the Faculty of Arts in Paris.[29] One college with which Grocheio could have been connected through his Norman background was the College of the Treasurer, established in 1266 by William de Saane, treasurer of the diocese of Rouen (ca. 1240/53–ca. 1280), specifically for students (twelve in arts and twelve in theology) from the diocese of Rouen.[30] Whereas the college founded in 1259 by Robert of Sorbonne (1201–74), a canon of the cathedral of Notre Dame, was uniquely for graduates studying theology, the College of the Treasurer deliberately covered students in both arts and theology. The College of the Treasurer, situated next to the Sorbonne, was endowed with a significant library that included the works of Aristotle and commentaries of Averroes.[31] Although Grocheio is more likely to have come from the diocese of Coutances, the possibility that he was connected through his family to the influential political and educational milieu of Rouen cannot be discounted.

Other evidence, however, suggests a link between Grocheio and another college in Paris: the College of Saint-Denis. This college was originally established before 1229 adjacent to the Dominican monastery of Saint-Jacques (founded 1217) to give a university education to a dozen monks destined for senior positions in the abbey.[32] As Sieglinde van der Klundert discovered, Grocheio's teaching was certainly known to Guy of Saint-Denis, who wrote his *Tractatus de tonis* probably around 1301.[33] Although Guy does not identify Grocheio by name, he cites the *Ars musice* directly and borrows key ideas otherwise particular to Grocheio, including his definition of *tonus* (*Tractatus de tonis* 1.1.11–19, cf. *AM* 26.1), his identification of consonances and concords as the principles of music (*Tractatus de tonis* 1.1.88–161, cf. *AM* 2.2ff.), and his explication of a threefold perfection in sound (*Tractatus de tonis* 1.1.300–322, cf. *AM* 3.3).[34] Although Grocheio never identifies himself as a monk, he does have familiarity with certain unusual liturgical practices described by Guy and presumably practiced at Saint-Denis.[35] Guy's intellectual debt to Grocheio's teaching raises the possibility that he had himself been taught by Grocheio at the College of Saint-Denis, either when it was still situated adjacent to the Dominican house of Saint-Jacques or in its new location on the Quai des Augustins, which could have been operational by the 1270s.

The account books of Saint-Denis first mention payment for an external teacher in 1229/30, recording payment of 43 *solidi* for "the robe of their teacher."[36] This was not a large amount, given that a single manuscript, such as a book of computus, could cost 60 *solidi* to copy and was much less than the sum given to a later *magister de Grecia* or visiting mendicant professors of theology.[37] Given that Grocheio opens his *Ars musice* by saying that he had been asked by certain *iuvenes* to explain something briefly about musical teaching, and that these friends had "for a long time given very great support for the necessities of [his] life" (*AM* 0.1), we can suggest that he composed his treatise as *magister iuvenum* at the College of Saint-Denis, and that these young monks were the people who had sustained him as a teacher. Even if his name suggests that he was related to a distinguished Norman family, he clearly relied on his friends in Paris for support.

The *Ars musice* and Scholastic Thought in Thirteenth-Century Paris

The *Ars musice* includes direct reference to authors and works that point to teachings in the Faculty of Arts in Paris from the second half of the thirteenth century. Nothing is known about Grocheio's education before—and activities after—his sojourn in Paris. Nonetheless, he appears to have been profoundly influenced by the wave of interest in the scientific works of Aristotle, the study of which had been prohibited by the bishop of Paris in 1210, and again by the papal legate in 1215 (on pain of excommunication), but which gradually became widely known in Paris during the course of the thirteenth century.[38] By 1245, these scientific texts were beginning to be used widely within the curriculum, and by 1255, the four nations of the Faculty of Arts had agreed on a complete curriculum of Aristotle's works on natural science.[39] Grocheio's own education seems to have taken place in the decade 1255–65, when Aristotelian scientific thinking was becoming fully established within the Faculty of Arts.

The method of enquiry Grocheio utilizes to describe music in the *Ars musice* draws on taxonomic systems outlined in Aristotle's *Physica* (*AM* 0.3) and *De animalibus* (*AM* 8.1). Grocheio also refers to the tenth book of the *First Philosophy* (*Prima philosophia*), or the *Metaphysica*, in relation to the concept of prime measure (*prima mensura*) (*AM* 16.1).[40] Two other works on natural science by Aristotle are alluded to but neither is named explicitly: Grocheio reiterates Aristotle's argument that celestial bodies in motion produce no sound (*AM* 5.6), as elucidated in *De caelo* 9.1, and he also maintains that all sound is produced by striking, "as has been shown in discourses about the soul" (*AM* 12.1), as found in *De anima* 2.8. The *Physica*, *Metaphysica* (books I–IV), and *De anima* were first translated into Latin from the Greek by James of Venice between 1125 and 1150. Gerard of Cremona (d. 1187) introduced *De caelo* to Latin readers through his translation from the Arabic, while Michael Scot (d. ca. 1234) pioneered translation of *De animalibus* from the Arabic before 1220 and also translated the *Metaphysica* (books II–X and XII) between 1220 and ca. 1234.[41] These translations were superseded by those prepared ca. 1260–71 by William of Moerbeke (ca. 1215–86), who either translated anew or revised the entire extant corpus of Aristotle's works on natural philosophy.[42] It is difficult to identify the translations of Aristotle that Grocheio used, because he elucidates Aristotle's ideas not through direct citation from any of the then-known Latin translations but through paraphrase, which often involves the conflation of otherwise disparate concepts. Grocheio's reference to Aristotle's *De animalibus* as a single book in the tripartite version (*De historiis animalium, De partibus*, and *De generatione*) as in Scot's translation, rather than the quinary version of Moerbeke, suggests that Grocheio may have been familiar with the former.[43]

Grocheio refers to other philosophers by name. Plato is mentioned several times in relation to notions about the reflection of the "world soul," the innateness of music in humans, and the demonstration of nature through number (*AM* 1.2, 2.5, and 4.9). In relation to the latter, Grocheio cites the *Timaeus*, which was widely known in the Middle Ages through the early fifth-century translation of Chalcidius.[44] Introductions to philosophy from the period 1230–40 confirm that the *Timaeus* and Boethius's *Consolatio philosophiae* were still studied in Paris.[45] Grocheio mentions John of Damascus's notion of the human soul as being in the image of the Creator (*AM* 3.4). One source for this is John's *De fide orthodoxa*, translated into Latin in the 1150s by Burgundio of Pisa.[46] Over one hundred manuscripts of Burgundio's translation survive, close to half of which were copied during the thirteenth century.[47] Grocheio also quotes verbatim (*AM* 9.5) from one of Seneca's *Epistolae morales ad Lucilium*, which circulated widely in the thirteenth century.[48]

The *Ars musice* contains a number of references to other intellectual disciplines, in particular, to quadrivial arts aside from *musica*. In *arithmetica* Grocheio assumes familiarity with cubic and perfect numbers (*AM* 17.1) and with five kinds of proportions (*AM* 2.8). Both of these are found in Chalcidius's version of the *Timaeus*, and they also occur in Boethius, to whom Grocheio explicitly refers. A knowledge of algorism, or at least the use of "figures" (*figurae*), is implied by the inclusion of Hindu-Arabic numerals in Grocheio's treatise—this is almost to the exclusion of roman numerals in BL Harley 281 while the Darmstadt copy uses arabic numerals only. Grocheio also mentions computus as one of three disciplines that churchmen "ought not to ignore" (*AM* 22.4). Sources for algorism and computus are *De arte numerandi* and *Computus*, the first two of three works that represent the Parisian teachings of John of Sacrobosco (ca. 1195–1236).[49] Within astronomy, Grocheio refers to the *aux* (*AM* 4.12), that is, the apogee in planetary motions, noting that there are many uses of this word. Such multiple uses are found in the *Theorica planetarum*, a summary of Ptolemaic astronomy sometimes attributed to Gerard of Cremona, often transmitted in the thirteenth century with the three works of Sacrobosco.[50]

Grocheio's familiarity with medical writings is indicated by his mention of Galen's *Tegni* as a book in which the "universal rules of the art of medicine are handed down" (*AM* 18.7). Several versions of the *Tegni* circulated in the Middle Ages, including one with the incipit "Tres sunt omnes doctrine qui ordine habentur . . . "[51] This version formed part of a collection of medical works known as the *Ars medicine*, which was collated in the twelfth century and widely circulated in the thirteenth.[52] The *Ars medicine* was also well established in the 1270s as a core text in the Paris "bacalarius in medicina licenciandorum."[53] Grocheio mentions Polykleitos's *Regula* (*AM* 16.3),[54] which is alluded to in several of Galen's treatises. One potential source for Grocheio is *De complexionibus* (*De temperamentis*), which was translated from Greek into Latin by Burgundio of Pisa and formed part of a corpus of Galenic works (known as the "New Galen") available in Paris from the 1240s.[55] Although the study of medicine in Paris was undertaken separately from the disciplines studied in the Faculty of Arts, this need not imply that Grocheio had undertaken formal study in the Faculty of Medicine, for which a degree in arts was a prerequisite.[56] A comparison may be made here with Engelbert of Admont (ca. 1250–1331), who also mentions Galen in his *De musica*, but for whom there is no evidence of his ever being a student of medicine.[57]

In the early sixth century, Boethius (480–524) composed his *De institutione musicae*—referred to by Grocheio as "de armonia musicali" (*AM* 1.2) and "de proprietatibus armonicis" (*AM* 2.5)—which introduced the reader to the numerical principles underlying the phenomena of musical sound. That Boethius was the dominant authority in Parisian expositions of *musica* in the 1230s is evident from the *Accessus philosophorum* composed during this decade by an anonymous master of the liberal arts.[58] One of many such guides from the thirteenth century, it provides a manual of basic knowledge about each of the disciplines taught in Paris at that time. This manual relies wholly on Boethius for the presentation of both *arithmetica* and *musica*. The section on *musica* declares that only the first two books of Boethius's *De musica* are *de forma* or formally prescribed.[59] Grocheio's references to Boethius (and to Pythagoras and Nicomachus of Gerasa) relate directly to these two books.

Grocheio draws explicitly on three thirteenth-century music theorists: Johannes de Garlandia, Franco of Cologne, and Lambert, each of whom is thought to have taught in Paris.[60] Some scholars have argued that the Johannes de Garlandia who wrote on music is a different person from John of Garland (ca. 1195–ca. 1270), who wrote extensively on grammar and rhetoric, as well as on liturgical and religious themes.[61] Although this John of Garland was born in England, he may have been part of the French nation—hence the epithet *Gallicus* given to him by Hieronymus de Moravia—as he taught in the *clos de Garlande* in Paris from around 1220 until his death, apart from a sojourn at Toulouse during 1229–32. Two tracts have been ascribed to the music theorist Garlandia: *De musica plana* and *De mensurabili musica.*[62] Grocheio alludes to Garlandia as an authority on both *musica plana* and *musica mensurabilis.* In particular, he refers to "Magister Johannes de Garlandia" by name as someone who advocates thirteen concords (*AM* 4.7, cf. *Musica plana*), who admits the ditone as a consonance (*AM* 4.14, cf. *De mensurabili musica*), who, like Boethius, divides music into *musica mundana, humana,* and *instrumentalis* in his treatise (*AM* 5.5, cf. *Musica plana*), and who distinguished measure by means of six modes (*AM* 17.7, cf. *De mensurabili musica*). Four manuscripts of the *Musica plana* survive, the earliest of which dates from the late thirteenth century.[63] *De mensurabili musica* survives in three manuscripts from the late thirteenth and early fourteenth centuries, including one that also preserves the *Musica plana.*[64]

Uncertainty also surrounds the theorist Franco of Cologne, to whom Grocheio refers in relation to the five modes of measure (*AM* 17.10) and the notational figures used by "very many of the moderns in Paris . . . as are taken up in the *Art* of Master Franco" (*AM* 18.7). Although Franco's *Ars cantus mensurabilis* has been dated variously to between 1240 and 1280, his treatise was probably composed ca. 1260, based on the musical examples therein, all from the early thirteenth century with none from after 1250.[65] Of the six surviving manuscripts of Franco's treatise, two were copied in France during the thirteenth century.[66] The other contemporaneous music theorist Grocheio refers to by name is Lambert (*AM* 17.8), whose identity has yet to be firmly established. Jeremy Yudkin has proposed that Lambert was a *magister* in Paris and dean of St. Vincent, Soignies, who, "healthy in mind, but weak in body," drew up his will in 1270.[67] This would imply that Lambert was active in the 1250s and perhaps the 1260s. Grocheio mentions Lambert in relation to his and others' extension of Garlandia's six modes to nine (*AM* 17.8), with the description of Lambert's first mode in the *Ars musice* matching that in Lambert's *Tractatus de musica.*[68] This work survives in four parchment copies, the earliest of which is of French origin and dates from the late thirteenth century.[69] Grocheio is one of only two theorists to mention Lambert by name.[70] While unraveling the confusion surrounding many decades of arguments about the lineage of thirteenth-century music-theoretical thought is beyond the scope of this introduction, it will be remarked that neither Johannes de Garlandia, Franco of Cologne, nor Lambert ever refer to each other; nor do any of these three theorists refer directly and exclusively to each other's treatises.[71]

The Dating of the *Ars musice*

Johannes Wolf, the first scholar to assess when the *Ars musice* might have been composed, argued that because Grocheio did not mention signs (*signa*) smaller in value than the semibreve and because he failed to mention Johannes de Muris or Philippe de Vitry despite being in Paris, he must have been working prior to them, estimating this to be "towards the turn of the century" at a time when the *ars nova* "initiated itself."[72] Ernst Rohloff repeated the argument in his 1943 edition, clarifying that the *Ars musice* was written before 1300.[73] In 1931, however, Heinrich Besseler affirmed that Grocheio was writing ca. 1300. Using arguments reiterated in 1949 in a review of Rohloff's edition, Besseler maintained that Grocheio's description of measure reflected rhythmic practice from 1300 to 1310 (thus contradicting Wolf), and that Grocheio's interests in natural science paralleled those of Johannnes de Muris (ca. 1290–95 to after 1344) without any close discussion of these scientific interests.[74] Rohloff in turn questioned this dating in 1972, putting forward arguments in favor of a date around 1275, including Grocheio's adherence to music theoretical principles from before 1275 and his failure to mention Petrus de Cruce's notational innovations.[75] Nonetheless, Besseler's date has been widely repeated in standard histories of music and has been evoked to inform the dating of other medieval theorists.[76]

Grocheio's remarks about measure form a principal basis upon which his treatise is dated to "ca. 1300,"[77] yet those remarks (*AM* 16.1–18.7) speak not to musical practice (as assumed by Besseler and others) but strictly to the *theory* of measure, more exactly, the theory expounded in Garlandia's *De musica mensurabilis*, Franco's *Ars cantus mensurabilis*, and Lambert's *Tractatus de musice*. Grocheio elucidates three aspects of mensural theory: the application of measure to sound (*tempus*), the modes of measure (*modi*), and the designation of measure (*figurae*). His summary of the modes of measure (*AM* 17.1–10) is based on Garlandia, Franco, and Lambert, and his description of figures (*AM* 18.2–7) corresponds exactly to the description in Franco's *Ars cantus mensurabilis*. Grocheio's position on *tempus*, however, takes into account Aristotle's position that time is a continuum and all continua are "divisible to infinity" (*AM* 16.4), as expounded in the *Physica*.[78] Grocheio describes the extent to which the "measure" (*mensura*) called *tempus* is divided by certain people into "2 equals, others into 3, and so on for others up to 6" (*AM* 16.4). For Grocheio, this division is unsatisfactory, not because he is aware of documented divisions of *tempus* that exceed six but because *tempus* applies to "sounds and voices" and therefore must be "divisible to the point that hearing can perceive a distinction" (*AM* 16.4), just as had long been the case for sound in general. Grocheio's description of the six modes of measure implies that the breve is the durational standard represented by *tempus*, although this is not stated explicitly. His description of a division of *tempus* "up to six" has thus provided the most compelling evidence of his knowledge of post-Franconian notational practices.[79] The interpretation of "up to six" (*usque ad 6*) as referring to the *minima* or its durational equivalent, however, ignores the implication that six is the *maximum* division of the breve known to Grocheio, whereas divisions of the breve associated with Franco's immediate successor, Petrus de Cruce, number up to *seven*.[80] There is another way of interpreting Grocheio's "up to six": if it is accepted that Grocheio is describing the division of the breve, "up to six" exactly matches the limits of division proposed by Franco, who states that for an altered breve, "it is not possible to admit less than four semibreves or *more than six*."[81] At the very least, Grocheio's remarks about measure, in particular his "up to six," do not provide the concrete evidence necessary to support a dating of his treatise to ca. 1300.

There is evidence to suggest that Grocheio was writing no earlier than 1271: if the Johannes de Garlandia to whom Grocheio refers was the famous grammarian and liturgical commentator known as John of Garland, Grocheio could well be writing after Garland's death (ca. 1271).[82] This was a turbulent time in the history of the University of Paris. On 10 December 1270, accusations were made by the bishop of Paris about "heretical opinions" circulating at the university, alluding to ideas associated with Siger of Brabant (ca. 1240–84) and his followers.[83] Although the papal legate forced Siger of Brabant to retire to Liège in 1275 (where he was summoned to face accusations of heresy the following year) and had installed in his place Peter of Auvergne (d. 1304) as rector of the university, Bishop Stephen Tempier and his theological advisers issued a list of 219 heretical doctrines circulating within the Faculty of Arts in 1277.[84] One statement in Grocheio's treatise suggests he was writing subsequent to some sort of intellectual restrictions being imposed, namely his lament that certain scholars "even now . . . conceal their activities and discoveries, not wanting to make them public to others" (*AM* 0.5). This statement readily reflects the intellectually volatile situation in Paris before 1277, a year in which factional conflict had heightened ecclesiastical suspicion towards the kind of Aristotelian discourse promoted by Siger of Brabant, Boethius of Dacia (fl. 1275), and even Thomas Aquinas (ca. 1225–74). Grocheio was shaped by a profound familiarity with Aristotelian science, as it emerged in the 1260s. His exposure to Aristotelian thinking reflects an intellectual shift permitted by the lifting of the traditional prohibition and led to one conclusion in particular that flew in the face of previous musical teachings: that "celestial bodies in movement do not make a sound" (*AM* 5.6).[85] Could this be the sort of finding that those who "conceal their activities and discoveries" are reluctant to reveal? Grocheio uses this finding as a basis to criticize Boethius, Johannes de Garlandia, and people who "designate harmony [as] caused by the motion of heavenly bodies" (*AM* 5.5–6).[86] Like Roger Bacon, writing in 1267, Grocheio makes no effort to find a compromise position between the teachings of Aristotle and Boethius (as is found in educational manuals from around 1250), but simply declares that Boethius was mistaken in his teaching about *musica mundana*.[87]

The extant repertoire of *cantus vulgalis* referred to by Grocheio also reflects a much earlier period than ca. 1300. Of the five songs named by Grocheio that have been identified, two are by Thibaut of Navarre, who died in 1253, and one has been variously attributed to Raoul de Ferrières (fl. 1200–1210) and Chastelain de Couci (d. 1203).[88] The remaining two (anonymous) songs are included in manuscripts prepared during the last quarter of the thirteenth century.[89] The epic *Girardo de Viana* (*AM* 10.2) is thought to be by Bertrand de Bar-Sur-Aube, who was active between 1190 and 1217.[90] Grocheio also mentions two names associated with instrumental forms: Tassin (*AM* 13.4) and Pierron (*AM* 13.3). Tassin has been identified as a musician in the court of John of Brabant (1252/3–94) in 1276–77 and in Paris in 1288.[91] His name is also found in the Montpellier codex, which includes three motet tenors identified as "chose Tassin."[92] The name Pierron surfaces in the motet *Entre copin*, again preserved in the Montpellier codex, a compilation of disputed date.[93] As Tassin was already a well-established minstrel in the 1270s, his presence in Paris in 1288 does not, therefore, necessarily imply a *terminus ante quem* later than the mid 1270s for Grocheio's treatise. Rohloff's dating of the *Ars musice* to around 1275 is supported here, as is the traditional dating of Franco of Cologne's treatise to 1250–65. These dates, however, remain a matter of debate, and further research is needed.

The Manuscripts

London, British Library, MS Harley 281 is an early fourteenth-century manuscript on parchment (fols. 5r–96v),[94] with ninety-six folios measuring 220 x 145 mm (written space 150 x 100 mm, with forty lead-ruled text lines) with front and rear flyleaves. The text on fols. 5r–96v is a unified anthology of musical treatises copied by a single scribe in a low-grade, gothic *rotunda* bookhand of Italianate influence; manuscript decoration and musical notation is distinctly Parisian, however. The anthology includes the corpus of writings by Guido of Arezzo, the anonymous *Dialogus de musica*, the Cistercian *Tonale* (attributed in the manuscript to Bernard of Clairvaux), the *Ars musice*, and the only known copies of Petrus de Cruce's tonary and the *Tractatus de tonis* of Guy of Saint-Denis. A second "scholar's" hand is responsible for editorial corrections throughout the manuscript. A good case can be made for identifying this scholar as Guy of Saint-Denis himself. The corrections in this hand are minor for most of the manuscript but extensive for Guy's *Tractatus*, resembling those found in an apograph, in particular, one made under the author's supervision and including the author's own corrections.[95] Guy's treatise is prefaced by a rubric that states, "You who read the name of the author [i.e., Guido] through the five first letters of the rubricist, pray this to be written from heaven,"[96] suggesting that Guy worked with the rubricator in the preparation of BL Harley 281. The musical illustrations in this manuscript are in the scholar's hand, indicating that they were written by someone who was musically literate. The likelihood that Guy sought out Grocheio's treatise for inclusion in BL Harley 281 increases the possibility of a personal connection between the two theorists.

References made by Guy of Saint-Denis in his *Tractatus de tonis* to the final quodlibetal disputation held by Peter of Auvergne in 1301 provide a *terminus post quem* for preparation of BL Harley 281.[97] Folio 4r bears the signature of a Jean Gosselin, who also entered marginal notes throughout the manuscript; notes on harmonic intervals on fols. 1r–4v are also in this hand. This Gosselin was probably Jean Gosselin de Vire (ca. 1505–1604), an astrologer and Guardian of the Royal Library of France from 1561 until his death.[98] If the manuscript was originally commissioned by Guy and housed at the abbey of Saint-Denis, it may have come into Gosselin's possession in 1567, when the abbey was sacked by Protestants and Saint-Denis monks were reported to have sold books from the abbey library.[99] A fourth hand from after 1784 gives the name "Mr Wren" on fol. 4r.[100] It is known that Christopher Wren the younger (1675–1747) presented Lord Harley (1661–1724) with BL Harley 281 sometime before 1709.[101] How the manuscript came into the possession of Wren the younger is unknown. The contents of the manuscript are outlined below.

fols. 1r–4v   [Notes in the hand of Jean Gosselin and Table of Contents (4r)]

fols. 5r–16v   Guido of Arezzo, *Micrologus*: "Gymnasio musas placuit revocare solutas . . ."[102]

fols. 16v–17r   "Nequaquam inquit tibi reor esse . . . "

fols. 17r–21r   Guido of Arezzo, *Regule rhythmice*: "Musicorum et cantorum magna est distantia . . . "[103]

fols. 21r–22v   Guido of Arezzo, *Prologus in Antiphonarium*: "Temporibus nostris super omnis . . . "[104]

fols. 23r–24v   Guido of Arezzo, *Epistola ad Martinum* [pro *Michaelem*] (*excerptum*): "Beatissimo atque dulcissimo fratri martino Guido . . . "[105]

fol. 24v   "Quicquid igitur auctoritate . . . "

fols. 25r–32r   Pseudo Odo, *Dialogus de musica*: "Quid est musica . . . "[106]

fols. 32r–33v   Guido of Arezzo, *Epistola ad Michaelem* (*excerptum*): "Omnes autem voces in tantum sunt . . . "[107]

fols. 33v–34r   "Ecce patet et non latet . . . "

fols. 34r–38v   *Tonale beati Bernardi*: "Quid est tonus . . . "[108]

fols. 39r–52r   Johannes de Grocheio, *Ars musice*: "Quoniam quidam iuvenum amici mei me . . . "

fols. 52v–58r   Petrus de Cruce, *Tractatus de tonis*: "Dicturi de tonis . . . "[109]

fols. 58v–96v   Guy of Saint-Denis, *Tractatus de tonis*: "Gaudere sciens brevitate modernos . . . "[110]

Darmstadt, Universitäts- und Landesbibliothek, MS 2663 is a thirteenth- and fourteenth-century parchment miscellany of works comprising five extant sections—each of which is distinct in terms of written space and text hand—totaling one hundred folios.[111] Grocheio's treatise is preserved on two discrete gatherings, the folios of which are unevenly cut and are slightly narrower (120 x 160 mm) than other gatherings (125 x 160 mm). The text on fols. 56r–69r is in a very small, neat, low-grade documentary script not found elsewhere in the manuscript. The scribe made numerous errors during the copying process and was particularly prone to misreading the text from which he copied.[112] Nonetheless, the Darmstadt copy of Grocheio's treatise is a professionally commissioned copy, most likely prepared in Paris,[113] the scribe providing examples of different scripts available for use on the final half-folio of the Grocheio gathering.[114] Despite the different contexts in which the two copies of the *Ars musice* survive, there are indications that they were copied from the same exemplar, the two copies including common abbreviations for approximately seventy percent of the text, with entire sentences abbreviated the same way.[115] There are also a number of variants that retain orthographic proximity; for example, we find *intimare* in BL Harley 281 for *ultimare* in Darmstadt 2663 (*AM* 0.2), *intentione* for *inventione* (*AM* 0.4), *proprietatibus* for *proportionibus* (*AM* 2.5), and *innata* for *inventa* (*AM* 3.4). Such proximity raises the possibility that these differences were the result of two scribes expanding the same abbreviation in different ways. A common exemplar is also implied by the example of the word *mathematica* in BL Harley 281 where the word *musica* appears in Darmstadt 2663 (*AM* 2.5 and *AM* 2.10); in both instances, the word is abbreviated in the same way (ma^ca/mu^ca), suggesting that the letters "a" and "u" were similar in appearance in the exemplar.

The Darmstadt manuscript originally belonged to the Charterhouse of Saint Barbara (founded in 1335) in Cologne and in 1451 survived a fire that destroyed much of the library. Presumably a monk at the monastery had the manuscript in his cell at the time. There are five hands in the table of contents on fol. Tv, representing different layers of additions to the miscellany. The majority of entries, including Grocheio's *Ars Musice*, are in hand 3, while hand 5 is that of John of Booze (near Liège), who claimed to have "written (*scripsit*) this book" but only added *ex libris* inscriptions to the manuscript.[116] As hand 3 is also found on the final half-folio of the Grocheio gathering (fol. 69v), it can be assumed that the Grocheio folios were already in Cologne prior to John of Booze's fourteenth-century "writing" of the manuscript. One possibility for how the Darmstadt copy may have found its way from Paris to Cologne is suggested by the presence—in the margins of several folios between 3r–51v—of a hand very similar to that of music theorist Heinrich Eger von Kalkar (1328–1408).[117] Von Kalkar studied in Paris during the 1350s, becoming a *baccalarius* in 1355 and a master teaching there in 1357–63. He spent a short spell as a canon at Cologne and Kaiserswerth before becoming a Carthusian monk at Saint Barbara in 1366, later serving as its prior (1377–84). In 1380, he wrote his music-theoretical tract, the *Cantuagium*, in which he refers back to the achievement "around fifty years ago, namely around thirteen hundred and thirty" of certain Parisian *artistae* in developing measured notation and alludes favorably to one, whom he says he has seen as a bishop (i.e., Philip de Vitry [1291–1361], appointed bishop of Meaux in 1351).[118] Von Kalkar is the only known medieval theorist to refer by name to "Hieronymus [de Moravia]," recommending his writings as well as those of "other ecclesiastical musicians, who correct chant."[119] Von Kalkar may have acquired the Darmstadt copy of Grocheio's treatise while in Paris, making him the medium through whom Grocheio's name is preserved in historical record. The contents of the Darmstadt miscellany are outlined below:

fol. T r	[Notes]
fol. T v	[Table of Contents]
fols. 1r–2r	"Confiteor deo et beate marie . . . "
fol. 2v	[Notes]
fols. 3r–13r	David of Augsburg, *Viginti passus*: "Quod nimis remissum regimen . . . "

About the Edition and Translation

The Latin text of the present edition is based on the copy of Grocheio's *Ars musice* preserved in BL Harley 281, fols. 39r–52r. This version of Grocheio's text has been chosen as it is superior to the Darmstadt version in terms of both readability and textual integrity. Only substantive variants in Darmstadt 2663 are indicated here. The Harley copy of the text also has the added aspect of most likely being edited by Guy of Saint-Denis, whose musical expertise is brought to bear upon the *Ars musice*. Particular attention is given to replicating scribal features of the Harley manuscript, such as orthography, capitalization, and the use of roman and arabic numerals. Three hands are identified for each copy. For BL Harley 281, **H1** denotes text copied by the main scribe; **H2** refers to the scholar-corrector hand, most likely that of Guy of Saint-Denis; and **H3** refers to the sixteenth-century marginal hand belonging to Jean Gosselin. For Darmstadt 2663, **D1** denotes the main scribe; **D2** refers to a contemporaneous margin hand; and **D3** refers to an additional explicit hand. The transcription takes the corrections made by **H2** into consideration. There are four punctuation signs, in addition to the *punctus*, utilized in BL Harley 281. The *virga suspensiva* (/) is rendered as a comma, the *punctus versus* (⸱/) as a colon, the *punctus elevatus* (⸴) as a semicolon, and the *punctus interrogativus* (*J*) is represented by the question mark. The ordinary *punctus* is retained. Capitalization follows the conventions in BL Harley 281, and a dash appears where a punctuation mark is missing before a capital letter. Both arabic and roman numerals are retained in the translation, the former often attracting Latin case endings, as in "3bus" for *tribus* (*AM* 4.11), "10o" for *decimo* (*AM* 16.1), and "8i" for *octavi*, among others (*AM* 26.5). Paragraph numbering follows the sections delineated by rubricated initials (numbered 0 to 43 in this edition) and paraphs in the manuscript.

The early stages of translation took into account Sandra Pinegar's transcription of BL Harley 281, fols. 39r–52r, prepared for the THEMA music-theory database.[123] There are considerable discrepancies between the Latin text presented in the present edition and Rohloff's edition, although these are not indicated here. The Latin text included in the present edition has been transcribed anew, which has led to the identification and correction of a number of erroneous expansions ultimately deriving from Johannes Wolf's 1899 transcription of Grocheio's text, based on Darmstadt 2663.

Any translation is necessarily a compromise between the demands of fidelity to Latin and of elegance and clarity of English expression. The translation provided here must be seen as no more than an interpretation (and not the final word) on the Latin text. Grocheio's text presents particular challenges for the modern translator, perhaps foremost is the prospect of translating the phrase *musica vulgalis*, which, since Wolf, has been erroneously rendered *musica vulgaris*. Grocheio uses the word *vulgalis* to describe music that is not measured (*mensurabilis*) nor ecclesiastical (*ecclesiasticus*), as a measure of demarcation from music that is. This latter interpretation of *vulgalis* is rendered here by the phrase "of the people."[124] Latin musical vocabulary is notoriously difficult to render into English, and there are a number of Latin terms in Grocheio's text for which there is no unambiguous English equivalent. The present translation includes a number of untranslated terms, many of which are not only defined by Grocheio but are also in common use in modern English-language musicological literature. Such terms include *gestualis*, *coronatus*, *versiculatus* (*versualis*, *versicularis*), *rotundellus*, *stantipes*, *ductia*, *diapason*, *diapente*, *diatessaron*, *diesis*, *puncta*, *nota*, *conductus*, *organum*, *motetus*, *triplum*, and *quadruplum*. Two terms not elucidated by Grocheio are *cantus* and *cantilena*. The term *cantus* is used to describe a wide variety of natural and artificial musical sounds produced in the voice. This use is not adequately captured by translations such as "song," "chant," or even "melody," which denote discrete items of sung music rather than varieties of sung sound. For this reason, the Latin *cantus* is by and large retained. The term *cantilena* has been used since antiquity to describe a less-elevated type of song and is also untranslated in the present edition.

NOTES

1. The treatise was dated to around 1275 by Ernst Rohloff in 1972, when he adopted the spelling Grocheio in place of Grocheo as in earlier literature; see Rohloff 1972, pp. 117–18. Grocheio's first editor, Johannes Wolf, had previously proposed a date of around 1300; see Wolf, "Die Musiklehre des Johannes de Grocheo," p. 67. Wolf's dating of Grocheio's treatise to around 1300, rather than that of Rohloff, has generally been followed in musicological literature and has led to the treatise being associated with fourteenth-century tracts, as for example, in the online *Thesaurus Musicarum Latinarum* database (<http://www.chmtl.indiana .edu/tml/>). Arguments for dating the treatise to the 1270s are outlined below.

2. Both manuscript sources of Grocheio's treatise read *vulgalis*, not the commonly cited term *vulgaris*.

3. See, for example, Haines and DeWitt, "Johannes de Grocheio and Aristotelian Natural Philosophy." Grocheio's treatise has not been well served in standard surveys of music theory. In her oft-cited survey of treatises that "sprang, directly or indirectly, from musical studies at the University of Paris," Nan Cooke Carpenter portrays Grocheio's treatise as a theoretical anomaly that failed to influence later music theorists; see *Music in the Medieval and Renaissance Universities*, p. 63. Grocheio surfaces only in passing in Eggebrecht et al., *Die Mittelalterliche Lehre von der Mehrstimmigkeit*. In his chapter "Die Musiklehre von Garlandia bis Franco," Max Haas refers to Grocheio as a problematic figure, difficult to classify ("der schwierig einzu-ordnenden Schrift des Johannes de Grocheio" [p. 119]). He is not mentioned at all in Christensen, *Cambridge History of Western Music Theory*.

4. See in particular Page, "Johannes de Grocheio on Secular Music," p. 17.

5. On Grocheio's *musica vulgalis*, often rendered as *vulgaris*, see for example, Aubry, *Estampies et danses royales*; Moser, "Stantipes und Ductia"; Sachs, *Eine Weltgeschichte des Tanzes*; Hibberd, "Estampie and Stantipes"; Inoue, "Johannes de Grocheo: Volkstümliche musikalische Formen"; Werf, *Chansons of the Troubadours and Trouvères*; DeWitt, "New Perspective on Grocheio's *Ars Musicae*," pp. 122–51; Stockmann, "Musica vulgaris bei Johannes de Grocheio (Grocheo)" and Stockmann, "'Musica vulgaris' im französischen Hochmittelalter"; Page, *Voices and Instruments of the Middle Ages*; McGee, "Medieval Dances"; Spanow, "*Ductia* und *cantus insertus* bei Johannes de Grocheio"; Page, *Owl and the Nightingale* and *Discarding Images*; Aubrey, *Music of the Troubadours*; Mullally, "Johannes de Grocheo's 'Musica Vulgaris'"; McGee, *Sound of Medieval Song*; and Haines, *Eight Centuries of Troubadours and Trouvères*.

6. On Grocheio's account of measure, see DeWitt, "New Perspective on Grocheio's *Ars Musicae*," pp. 152–88; Maddrell, "Grocheo and the Mensurability of Medieval Music: A Reply to Hendrik van der Werf." On Grocheio's account of ecclesiastical music, see DeWitt, "New Perspective on Grocheio's *Ars Musicae*," pp. 191–232, and Trout, "*Ars Musicae* of Johannes De Grocheio." On the relationship between ecclesiastical forms and the forms of *musica vulgalis*, see Handschin, "Über Estampie und Sequenz." In his revised Latin text and partial translation of Grocheio's treatise, Page omits the section on ecclesiastical music apart from those statements that include mention of the forms of *musica vulgalis*; see "Johannes de Grocheio on Secular Music," pp. 40–41.

7. On Grocheio's method of enquiry, see Bielitz, "Materia und Forma bei Johannes de

Grocheo"; Fladt, "Der artifizielle Prozess im Hochmittelalter," and *Die Musikauffassung des Johannes de Grocheo im Kontext der hochmittelalterlichen Aristoteles-Rezeption*; Eske, "Aristoteles Musicus"; Peraino, "Re-Placing Medieval Music." On Grocheio's views on Boethius, see Pietzsch, *Die Klassifikation der Musik von Boethius bis Ugolino von Orvieto*.

8. A breakdown of the treatise is also included in DeWitt, "New Perspective on Grocheio's *Ars Musicae*," pp. 20 and 23.

9. See Wolf, "Die Musiklehre des Johannes de Grocheo," pp. 65–130. In 1903, Hermann Müller gave further publicity to Wolf's achievement in "Zum Texte der Musiklehre des Johannes de Grocheo."

10. See Rohloff, "Studien zum Musiktraktat des Johannes de Grocheo," and *Studien zum Musiktraktat des Johannes de Grocheo*; Rohloff 1943. Johannes Wolf responded to Rohloff's 1943 edition in his review of the work in "Rezension von: E. Rohloff, Der Musiktraktat des J. de G., 1943."

11. The extent to which Rohloff's edition differs from the manuscripts was foreshadowed in DeWitt, "New Perspective on Grocheio's *Ars Musicae*," while Christopher Page in his 1993 partial edition identified a number of liberties taken by Rohloff; see, for example, Page, "Johannes de Grocheio on Secular Music," pp. 17 n. 2 and 19. Max Haas has also criticized Rohloff's edition, signaling the need for a new translation of the treatise; see *Musikalisches Denken im Mittelalter*, p. 107 n. 172.

12. Johannes de Grocheio, *Concerning Music* (*De musica*), trans. Seay. Although important for introducing Grocheio to the English-speaking world, Seay's translation is flawed in its lack of consistency of terminology and complete absence of editorial commentary.

13. See Page, "Johannes de Grocheio on Secular Music," pp. 19–41. The sections included in Page's edition (as numbered in the present edition) are: paras. 5.10–6.2, 7.7 (last two sentences)–7.8, 9.1–15.3, 19.1–21.8, 29.6, 32.4, 35.3–35.4 (first phrase), and extracts from 37.1.

14. The spelling *Grocheo* was taken up by Wolf for his edition of the treatise. More recently, Robert Mullally has argued that Wolf's spelling is preferred as it is the "traditionally accepted version"; see "Johannes de Grocheo's 'Musica Vulgaris,'" p. 1.

15. This colophon is not recorded in [Benedictines of Bouveret], *Colophons de manuscrits occidentaux des origines au XVIe siècle*.

16. The word in question is difficult to read and has been interpreted as *Parisius* by Wolf, Rohloff in 1972, and Page in 1993, although Page later expressed uncertainty about this; see Page, "Grocheio [Grocheo], Johannes de."

17. See Rohloff 1972, p. 171. Page reiterates Rohloff's claim in "Johannes de Grocheio on Secular Music," p. 17 n. 1.

18. This title was used by Heinrich Besseler in "Zur 'Ars musicae' des Johannes de Grocheo."

19. See Page, *Owl and the Nightingale*, pp. 171–72 and 246 n. 3, and "Johannes de Grocheio on Secular Music," p. 18.

20. Page, "Johannes de Grocheio on Secular Music," p. 18. Page draws on the very brief account given by Marquis Emmanuel-Henri de Grouchy (1839–1911) in *Mémoires du Maréchal de Grouchy*, 1:vi–vii. The Marquis de Grouchy confusingly reported, without supporting evidence, that the family split in 1300 into another branch at Monterolier. He mentions that a Gruchy accompanied William the Conqueror to England in 1066. He also reports that, according to a charter in the archives of St-Victor-en-Caux, two Gruchy brothers had endowed a Benedictine abbey in the diocese of Rouen in the eleventh century, making reference to Beaurepaire, "Recueil de chartes concernant l'abbaye de Saint Victor en Caux."

21. In 1888, the comte de Grouchy (presumably the same person as styled himself the Marquis de Grouchy in 1873), presented to the Bibliothèque nationale a detailed history of his family, correcting many points in an earlier account; see Comte de Grouchy, *Notes sur la Maison de Grouchy en Normandie* (BnF fr. 33237). In his account of Robert and Henry de Grouchy (fol. 8), he notes a reference to Favard, *Histoire du Palais de Versailles* ("où les armes des Grouchy d'or, figures dans la salle des croisades") and a Nicholas de Gruchy in 1297 (fol. 97). He drew on a *Mémorial servant à prouver la filiation et noblesse de François Jacques de Grouchy* (compiled in 1736), which was in his private possession but is apparently now in the Archives nationales. His history is significant because many records held at the Archives départementales at Saint-Lô were destroyed in June 1944, when Allied forces occupied Normandy.

22. The Gruchy near Cherbourg, now a picturesque Romanesque hamlet, was much painted by Jean-François Millet. In 1156, Henry II confirmed that Groceium was held by the abbey of St. Stephen at Caen (diocese of Bayeux) but part of it was given by Philippa, daughter of Hugh of Rosel, to the Premonstratensian church of St. Mary, Ardennes (diocese of Bayeux); see Round, *Calendar of Documents*, pp. 158 and 182.

23. Mullally, "Johannes de Grocheo's 'Musica Vulgaris,'" p. 1 n. 1. See also Morlet, *Dictionnaire étymologique des noms de famille et prénoms de France*, p. 484. On the Cotentin branch of the family, see Comte de Grouchy, *Notes sur la Maison de Grouchy*, fols. 66r–83v, esp. fol. 68r–v.

24. Le Quesne and Dixon, *De Gruchys of Jersey*, pp. 9–10, drawing on information about the ancestry of the family from Gruchy, *Medieval Land Tenures in Jersey*.

25. Abbot Peter of Lessay and Thomas and Richard de Groceio were among more than forty-five witnesses to a charter dated 10 March 1172 concerning the priory of Bohon in Normandy: "Notum vobis facimus quod Engerramus de Campo Rotundo contendebat adversus dominum suum Engelgerum de Bohun et calumpniabatur pro ecclesia de Capella. . . . Ipse etiam Engelgerus sepedictam ecclesiam quietavit et liberam reddidit, in presentia nostra, de auxilio regis et suo, in quibus computabatur pro XXX acris terre. Testibus: Petro abbate Exaquii, Willelmo abbate Sancti Laudi . . . de laicis: Ingelgro, Thoma et Ricardo de Groceio, fratribus, Radulfo de Bohun" (Delisle, *Recueil des actes de Henri II*). Hugh de Gournai (possibly the same person as Hugo de Groci, given the closeness of Gruchy to Gournay) was present at the foundation of Lessay in 1080; see Round, *Calendar of Documents*, p. 327. This may be the Hugh de Gruchy recorded as a *minister domini regis*, collecting taxes in 1089 from the island of Jersey, where there was a *ministerium de Groceio* by 1180; see Le Quesne and Dixon, *The De Gruchys of Jersey*, p. 10. In ca. 1181, a Richard de Groci witnessed a gift to monks of Longueville (diocese of Rouen); see Round, *Calendar of Documents*, p. 78. Le Quesne and Dixon report that a Richard de Grouchy went to England in 1204, while one brother (Jean or Guillaume) moved to Jersey and another (Eudes) settled near Gournay-en-Bray near Rouen; see Le Quesne and Dixon, *De Gruchys of Jersey*, p. 10.

26. Piolin, *Gallia Christiana*, Instrumenta, cols. 258–59. In 1198 a certain Johannes de Groceio was fined five *sous* for engaging in a "treaty of St. Paternus" (patron of the diocese of Vannes). Thomas and Robert de Groceio are referred to as *milites* in an 1197 charter originally in the Archives départementales of Saint-Lô and printed in the Archives d'Harfleur, *Preuves*, and Thomas de Groceio is mentioned in the *Exchiquier de Normandie* as a knight of Richard I of England in 1198; see Comte de Grouchy, Notes sur la Maison de Grouchy, fol. 68.

27. William de Groceio is mentioned again as a *miles* in a royal charter of 1247 issued to the royal representative in the region. Presumably this is the same William de Groceio as

mentioned as an *armiger* in a notice of his death on 5 March 1270. Upon his death, William bequeathed 15 *libras*, a bed, and some land to the abbey of the Trinitarians at St. Martin-du-désert in the south of the Cotentin; see *Recueil des historiens des Gaules et de la France*, p. 550: "Obitus Guillelmi de Grocheio, armiger, qui dedit Xvcim libras cum uno lecto fornito et Robertus, frater ejus, dedit triginta solidos." On 27 September 1270, an addition to this chronicle, made after 1316, records the death as a leper of another Guillelmus de Grocheio, who gave 20 *solidos* to the abbey; see *Recueil des historiens*, p. 551.

28. Fontanel, *Le cartulaire du chapitre cathédral de Coutances*, p. 358. While no immediate offspring of either William or Haretot have been identified, a Jean de Grouchy is mentioned in a royal missive from 1323; see Comte de Grouchy, *Notes sur la Maison de Grouchy*, fol. 68v. A Jean de Gruchy, born around 1300, is also remembered as the earliest known member of a branch of the family that settled in Jersey (part of the diocese of Coutances) in the early fourteenth century; see Le Quesne and Dixon, *De Gruchys of Jersey*, p. 21.

29. The other three nations are the French (including students from Spain and Italy), the Picard (covering those from northern France and the Low Countries), and the English (including Germans, Scandinavians, and others). These nations, rather than the Faculty itself, were the primary focus of loyalty of both masters and students within arts. On the bitterness of disputes between the nations, see Kibre, *Nations in the Mediaeval Universities*, esp. pp. 18–25. On tensions within the Norman archdiocese itself, see Davis, *Holy Bureaucrat*.

30. *CUP* no. 411, 1:458: "secularibus scolaribus civitatis et diocesis Rothomagensis, in theologia studentibus facultate." William clarified these provisions for twelve *artistas* and twelve students in theology from 1268; see *CUP* no. 423, 1–476–78: "duodecim scolares theologi . . . item quod alii duodecim artiste parvi, si aliquando esse possint . . . saltem ex tota diocesi Rothomagensi sint. Et tales eligantur quantum ad theologos, qui rexerint probabiliter in artibus quibusdam . . . " Statutes that William drew up in August 1280 laid down firm discipline at the College of the Treasurer, emphasizing that students in arts should graduate to theology and should only speak Latin, at least within the College; see *CUP* no. 499, 1:585: "Et volumus quod omnes, in domo ad minus, latinis verbis utantur." In January 1280, Philip III confirmed the possession of two houses for the twenty-four students; see *CUP* no. 494, 1:579–80. William de Saane, of noble family and the son of a priest, was a canon of Rouen since 1248 and elected archbishop by the canons of Rouen in 1275 but was forced to relinquish this post in 1278. On William de Saane and the disputed elections at Rouen, see Tabbagh, *Diocèse de Rouen*, pp. 86–90 and 209.

31. William lists books of theology that he was leaving to the college in 1268, including: "volumina plura sententiarum cum summis et scriptis pluribus de questionibus, item originalia plura, et multa alia scripta, quorum omnia nomina in quadam littera sigillo meo sigillata continentur." The 1437 catalogue is edited by Franklin, "Collège du Trésorier"; see esp. p. 340: "Secundum volumen textus Aristotelis Moralium. Incipiens in secundo folio: igitur perseuerandi et finiens in penultimo, respirat. Ethicorum, Rhetoricorum, Economica, Politicorum, Magna moralia, De vita Aristotelis, Decetorum, De secretis secretorum, Epistola Aristotelis ad Alexandrum. In isto volumine haec continentur. Aliud volumen commenti Averroys supra decem libros Phisicorum. Incipit secundo folio: Et oportet et finit in penultimo: immortales. Supra libros Phisicorum, Supra libros parvorum naturalium, Supra libros de anima. In isto volumine haec continentur. Aliud volumen commenti Politicorum supra decem libros."

32. In 1263, Matthew of Vendôme, abbot of Saint-Denis from 1258 until his death in 1278, decided to move the college away from its position adjacent to Saint-Jacques by purchasing land

from Saint-Germain closer to the royal palace, near the Quai des Augustins. Matthew was needing to reform much of the abbey's administration after the resignation of Henry Mallet, the previous abbot, and initiated production of a comprehensive cartulary for the abbey, a policy that would be continued by his successor, abbot Renaud Giffart (1287–1304); see Nebbiai-Dalla Guarda, "'Des rois et des moines': Livres et lecteurs à l'abbaye de Saint-Denis (XIIIe-XVe siècles)," esp. p. 359. Creating a new college to educate selected monks who would go on to hold senior posts, as well as completing the abbey itself, was an important way in which Matthew could develop educational standards at the abbey, as well as assert its traditional association with the Crown.

33. Michel Huglo has dated Guy's *Tractatus de tonis* to 1315–18, claiming that in the *Tractatus*, Guy refers to an "unknown chant for *Corpus Christi*" and therefore must have composed his treatise between 1315 (when the feast of Corpus Christi was introduced at Saint-Denis) and 1318 (when the Corpus Christi Office of Thomas Aquinas was introduced into Parisian usage); see Michel Huglo, "Guy de Saint-Denis," *Grove Music Online* (accessed 16 December 2006). Not only does Huglo not identify this "unknown chant" but none of the nontraditional chants cited by Guy is included in the feast of Corpus Christi; see Guido von Saint-Denis, *Tractatus de tonis*, 1:18 n. 19. A dating of Guy's *Tractatus* to 1301 is based on the presence of citations therein from a quodlibet held by Peter of Auvergne in 1301, the latest datable reference in the *Tractatus*.

34. On the identification of citations from Grocheio's treatise in the *Tractatus de tonis*, see Guido von Saint-Denis, *Tractatus de tonis*, 1:45–55.

35. The first plainchant item mentioned by Grocheio (*AM* 27.4) is the invitatory antiphon *Regem regum*, which he identifies as tone (*tonus*) one (i.e., mode one)—as does Guy of Saint-Denis in the tonary included in his *Tractatus*—although there are virtually no invitatory antiphons for modes one or eight. *Regem regum* was used as a mode one invitatory antiphon for the feast of Saint Denis (October 9) from the tenth century (see for example, Paris, BnF lat. 1085, fol. 90v) and was so used at Saint-Denis as indicated by Paris, BnF lat. 17296, a twelfth-century antiphonary of the abbey. The invitatory antiphon *Regem cui omnia vivunt* (usually identified as mode six) is similarly listed by both Grocheio (*AM* 27.4) and Guy as of the eighth tone (i.e., mode eight); see Guido von Saint-Denis, *Tractatus de tonis*, 2:104 and 133.

36. Nebbiai-Dalla Guarda, "Le collège de Paris de l'abbaye de Saint-Denis-en-France (XIIIe–VIIIe siècle)."

37. In 1284/85 and every year subsequently, the accounts specify that two external teachers were paid 32 *solidi* annually, one called *magister iuvenum*, the other *magister puerorum* (in 1287/88 the *magister puerorum de cantu*); see Nebbiai-Dalla Guarda, ed., *La Bibliothèque de l'abbaye de Saint-Denis en France du IXe au XVIIIe*, pp. 336–39: 1284/1285; 1285/86; 1287/88; 1288/89—raised to .XL. s. for the *magistro iuvenum* and .XXXII. s. for the *magistro puerum*, but back to .XXXII. s. in every year between 1289 and 1303, but raised to .XL.s in 1320/21 and still at that rate in 1342/43 ("Pro roba magistri eorum .XLIII s. [1229/30] . . . Magistro iuvenum .XXXI. s., Magistro puerorum .XXXII.") The reference "Pro uno Avicenna empto .XXIII. lib." (p. 337) evokes such a large sum, that one wonders if it was not a mistake for 23 *solidi*. In that year (1284/85), 14 *libri*, 2 *solidi*, and 3 *denarii* was spent on students' upkeep. The payment of 100 *solidi* in 1290 to a master from Greece (p. 340) may be connected to the practice of celebrating the feast of Saint-Denis at Pentecost in the Greek language; for comment, see Nebbiai-Dalla Guarda, "Des rois et des moines," pp. 360–362, also observing

that a certain Petrus de Sancto Dyonisio owned a collection of medical texts in the late thirteenth century (Paris, BnF lat. 8454).

38. *CUP* no. 11, 1:70, and *CUP* no. 20, 1:78–79. The prohibition on studying Aristotle's natural-scientific texts was reaffirmed by Pope Gregory IX on 13 April 1231, in a document in which he urged that students of theology should not present themselves as philosophers but explained that the banned writings could be studied once a commission "had purged these texts of error" (*CUP* no. 79, 1:138). In a separate document, the pope appointed three senior ecclesiastics to engage in this process: William of Auxerre (ca. 1140/50–1231), Stephen of Provins, and Symon of Authié. The text of the papal letter is given by Denifle, *CUP* no. 87, 1:143–44.

39. *CUP* no. 246, 1:278. Even as late as 1252, the English nation was laying down the curriculum its students should follow (only Aristotle's works of logic and *De anima*), although this would be supplanted by the 1255 statute; see *CUP* nos. 201 and 202, 1:227–32. Michel Huglo has summarized the information in this charter in tabular form in "Study of Ancient Sources of Music Theory in the Medieval Universities," see esp. p. 153.

40. This reference—"ut *in* 10°. *prime* philoso*phie* scriptum *est*"—has been hitherto unknown due to the failure of previous transcribers to correctly expand the relevant abbreviated text, with the passage consistently rendered as "ut *in* Io*hanne* po*sitione* philoso*phe* scriptum *est*," originating with Wolf, "Die Musiklehre des Johannes de Grocheo," p. 100. Rohloff even goes so far as to support this misreading with a cross-reference to the corpus of John of Salisbury; see Rohloff 1972, p. 139 n. 160. Writing ca. 1250, Robert Kilwardby also refers to the tenth book of the *Metaphysics* as being in the *Prima philosophia*, when alluding to Averroes as "Commentator super X Primae philosophiae"; see Kilwardby, *De ortu scientiarum* 30, pp. 94–95.

41. On the Latin translations of Aristotle's natural-scientific corpus, including a summary of the number of surviving manuscripts, see Bernard Dod, "Aristoteles latinus."

42. An overview of when Moerbeke completed his translations is given in Jozef Brams, "Guillaume de Moerbeke et Aristotle," pp. 317–36.

43. Moerbeke's translation includes two works not mentioned by Grocheio—*De motu animalium* and *De progressu animalium*—inserted between the *Historia animalium* and *De partibus animalium*. Siger of Brabant, writing between 1271 and 1275, was aware of *De motu animalium* and *De progressu animalium* in his *Quaestiones in Metaphysicam* 3.19, p. 145. The titles that Grocheio uses—*Historia animalium*, *De partibus animalium*, and *De generatione animalium*—may have been introduced by William of Moerbeke, as they either do not occur in manuscript sources of Michael Scot's translations or if they do are given as marginal entries; see Aristotle, *De animalibus: Michael Scot's Arabic-Latin Translation*, part 3: *Books XV–XIX: Generation of Animals*, p. viii. Of the approximately 240 surviving copies of Moerbeke's translation of *De animalibus*, only forty copies include all five works; see Dod, "Aristoteles latinus," p. 77. Copies of Scot's translation of *De animalibus* were also made after the appearance of Moerbeke's translation; see Aristotle, *De animalibus*, part 3, p. viii. A list of manuscripts of Scot's translation is given in part 2 of the series; see Aristotle, *De animalibus*, part 2: *Books XI–XIV: Parts of Animals*, pp. xiii–xxv. The first volume is yet to appear. See also Haines and DeWitt, "Johannes de Grocheio and Aristotelian Natural Philosophy."

44. On the manuscript tradition of Plato's *Timaeus*, see Waszink, *Timaeus a Calcidio translatus commentarioque instructus*, pp. cvi–cxxxi; see also Dutton, "Material Remains of the Study of the *Timaeus* in the Later Middle Ages."

45. See Lafleur, *Quatre Introductions à la philosophie au XIIIe siècle*, pp. 299–37, and

Le "Guide de l'étudiant" d'un maître anonyme de la faculté des arts de Paris au XIIIe siècle, pp. 69–71.

46. Buytaert, *De fide orthodoxa: Versions of Burgundio and Cerbanus*, p. ix. Burgundio's translation was revised by Robert Grosseteste in the 1230s; on Grosseteste's version, see Thomson, *Writings of Robert Grosseteste*, pp. 48–50. Sandra Pinegar has suggested that Grocheio may have known John's *Dialectica*, parts of which were translated by Robert Grosseteste— John Damascene, *Dialectica. Version of Robert Grosseteste*; see Pinegar, "Textual and Conceptual Relationships," p. 266.

47. On the manuscripts see Buytaert, *De fide orthodoxa: Versions of Burgundio and Cerbanus*, pp. xx–xli.

48. Two thirteenth-century manuscripts of Seneca's *Epistolae morales ad Lucilium* (one of books 1–13, the other of books 14–20) were included in Richard de Fournival's collection, which formed the basis of the early collection of the Sorbonne; see Richard H. Rouse, "Manuscripts Belonging to Richard de Fournival," p. 265. There was another at the College of the Treasurer; see Franklin, "Collège du Trésorier," p. 360. On the early transmission of Seneca in the Middle Ages, see Reynolds, *Medieval Tradition of Seneca's Letters*; see also Beddie, "Ancient Classics in the Mediaeval Libraries," p. 13.

49. The third work is a brief introduction to Ptolemy's *Almagest* known as *De sphera*. On Sacrobosco, see Pedersen, "In Quest of Sacrobosco."

50. This *Theorica planetarum*, with the incipit "Circulus eccentricus vel egresse cuspidis vel egredientis centri dicitur qui non habet centrum suum cum centro mundi," survives in approximately 210 manuscripts. On different interpretations of *aux* in this work, see "Theory of Planets," pp. 452–54. On the transmission of the *Theorica planetarum* with the works of Sacrobosco, see "Theory of Planets," p. 451; see also Pedersen, "Origins of the 'Theorica Planetarum,'" pp. 113–14. The *Theorica planetarum* does not mention Aristotle, which Grocheio alludes to in *AM* 5.6, where he implies that Aristotle's "idea and hypothesis" ought to be related in the *Theorica planetarum*.

51. The *Tegni* was also known as the *Ars parva*, *Ars medica*, and the *Microtegni*; see Thorndike and Kibre, *Catalogue of Incipits of Mediaeval Scientific Writings in Latin*, cols. 1376 and 1585.

52. This group of texts included Johannitius's *Isagoge*, the Hippocrates' *Aphorism* and *Prognostics*, Theolphilus's *Urines*, Philaretus's *Pulses*, and Galen's *Tegni*; see O'Boyle, *Art of Medicine*, p. 83.

53. *CUP* no. 453, 1:517; see also O'Boyle, *Art of Medicine*, p. 124.

54. Grocheio's allusion to the "Rule of Polykleitos" (fifth century BCE) could be interpreted as a reference to Polykleitos's fragmentary treatise entitled *Canon* or to Polykleitos's statue the Doryphoros, which was known as the "rule" (*regula, canon*) because its proportions epitomized (male human) anatomical perfection. Comprehensive treatment of Polykleitos's Rule is given in Moon, *Polykleitos, the Doryphoros, and Tradition*.

55. On Galen's allusions to the rule, see Leftwich, "Polykletos and Hippokratic Medicine," pp. 38–40. On the transmission of Galen's medical treatises during the Middle Ages, see Jacquart, "Principales étapes dans la transmission des textes de médecine (XIe–XIVe siècle)." On the "New Galen" and its availability in Paris, see O'Boyle, *Art of Medicine*, pp. 6–7 and 121.

56. The earliest traces of a medical "faculty" [*facultas*] in Paris date from the 1250s; see O'Boyle, *Art of Medicine*, p. 19.

57. "Musica humana consistit et consideratur in proportionibus contrariarum qualita-

tum et diversarum ac dissimilium partium humani corporis inter se, et rursus unionis animae ad ipsum. Da qua harmonia, Aristoteles in libro I. de Anima, et in libro de Animalibus, et Galenus, et Avicenna in suis libris medicinalibus, et Algazel in suis naturalibus, et constabulus in libro de Spiritu et Anima multipliciter sunt locuti" (Engelbertus Admontensis, *De musica* 1.2, GS 2:287–98 at p. 288). Engelbert studied at the University of Padua, where, as in Paris, medicine was undertaken as an advanced discipline; see Wingell, "*De musica* of Engelbert of Admont," p. 127.

58. Lafleur, *Quatre Introductions à la philosophie au XIIIe siècle*, pp. 147–51. On the relationship of music to other parts of the curriculum in the thirteenth century and before, see for example Max Haas, "Studien zur mittelalterlichen Musiklehre I," and "Die Musiklehre im 13. Jahrhundert von Johannes de Garlandia bis Franco"; Weijers, "La place de la musique à la faculté des arts de Paris"; Weijers acknowledges the studies of Maître, "La place d'Aristote dans l'enseignement de la musique à l'Université," and Vellekoop, "La place de la musique"; see also Hentschel, *Musik, und die Geschichte der Philosophie und Naturwissenschaften im Mittelalter*.

59. Lafleur, *Quatre Introductions à la philosophie au XIIIe siècle*, p. 204: "Sunt autem in Musica .V. libri partiales, set de forma tantum duo."

60. On Johannes de Garlandia, see Waite, "Johannes de Garlandia"; on Lambert, see Anderson, "Magister Lambertus and Nine Rhythmic Modes"; on Franco, see Huglo, "Recherches sur la personne et l'oeuvre de Francon."

61. William Waite identified a number of musical concerns in the writing of the John of Garland; see Waite, "Johannes de Garlandia." Erich Reimer argued that because the music theorist was described as Johannes Gallicus, and not Anglicus, by Hieronymus de Moravia, he had to be a different person from the John of Garland who was born in England but settled in France to teach; see Reimer, *De mensurabili musica*, 1:13–17. Hieronymus, however, clearly equated Johannes Gallicus with Johannes de Garlangia, a point omitted from Reimer's argument; see Hieronymus de Moravia, *Tractatus de musica*, p. 10: "Est et alius Johannes dictus de Garlangia, qui musicae definitionem sic venatur dicens . . . Musica est veraciter canendi scientia et facilis ad canendi perfectionem via. Haec Johannes Gallicus. Rationem autem diversitatis omnium definitionum, quae potest colligi ex sequentibus, non ponimus prolixitatem operis evitantes." Rudolf Rasch noted the parallels between the grammatical writings of John of Garland and those of the *Plana musica* attributed to Johannes de Garlandia but argued the grammarian's comments about music were those of a dilettante, while the music theorist was more advanced in his thinking (disregarding the point that in writing on grammar one would not be expected to go into detail on music); see Rasch, *Johannes de Garlandia en de ontwikkeling van de voor-Franconische notatie*, pp. 85–116, summarized at p. 321.

62. Christian Meyer has edited four *reportationes* of the *Musica plana* representing four redactions of oral lectures delivered by Johannes de Garlandia; see Johannes de Garlandia, *Musica plana*, pp. 3–62. Another related treatise of uncertain attribution—*Introductio musicae planae secundum magistrum Johannem de Garlandia*—has also been edited by Meyer, who argues that it is by a disciple of Johannes de Garlandia; see Johannnes de Garlandia, *Musica plana*, pp. 123–30. The title *De musica mensurabili positio* is used to distinguish early redactions of *De musica mensurabili* from the version of the text in the compendium of Hieronymus de Moravia; see *Tractatus de musica*, pp. 194–230.

63. On the manuscript sources of the *Musica plana*, see Johannes de Garlandia, *Musica plana*, pp. xi–xiv.

64. Vatican City, Biblioteca Apostolica Vaticana, MS Vat. lat. 5325, copied in France in

the late thirteenth or early fourteenth century; see Johannes de Garlandia, *Musica plana*, p. xii. On the manuscripts of *De mensurabili musica*, see Reimer, *De mensurabili musica*, pp. 19–29.

65. See in particular Huglo, "Recherches sur la personne et l'oeuvre de Francon," p. 16. See also Leitmeir, "Types and Transmission of Musical Examples in Franco's *Ars cantus mensurabilis musicae*." Biographical testimony about Franco in some fifteenth-century manuscripts (of uncertain value) led to suggestions that he was the Franco who died at Cologne in 1247; see Rieckenberg, "Zur Biographie des Musiktheoretikers Franco von Köln," pp. 280–82. In 1970, Wolf Frobenius proposed a date of 1280 for Franco, challenging the traditional assumption that Franco was active 1250–65, on the rather fragile grounds that because the Anonymous of St. Emmeram did not mention Franco by name in his defense of traditional music theory completed in 1279, Franco must have written his treatise subsequently; see Frobenius, "Zur Datierung von Francos *Ars cantus mensurabilis*." These arguments are summarized in Reaney and Gilles, *Ars cantus mensurabilis*, pp. 10–11; see also Frobenius, "Der Musiktheoretiker Franco von Köln," pp. 345–56.

66. One of these sources is the compendium of Hieronymus de Moravia (Paris, BnF lat. 16663). On the manuscripts of Franco's treatise, see Reaney and Gilles, *Ars cantus mensurabilis*, pp. 12–19.

67. Yudkin, *De musica mensurata*, p. 341; see also Yudkin, "Anonymous Music Treatise of 1279."

68. Lambert, *Tractatus de Musica*, CS 1:269.

69. This manuscript is described in Everist, "Music and Theory in Late Thirteenth-Century Paris."

70. The other theorist to mention Lambert is the Anonymous of St. Emmeram (fl. 1279); see Yudkin, *De musica mensurata*. Jacques of Liège also refers to Lambert but uses the name "Aristotle"; see Jacobus Leodiensis, *Speculum musicae* 1.6, p. 27: "De mensurabili autem musica multi tractaverunt, inter quos amplius florere videntur quidam, qui Aristoteles in titulo libri sui nominatur, et Franco Teutonicus." Lambert's ideas are reproduced in a treatise, preserved alongside a summary of Franco's teachings, by the late thirteenth-century master Johannes de Ballox (Paris, BnF lat. 15128, fols. 124–127); see Gilles, "*De musica plana breve compendium* (un témoignage de l'enseignement de Lambertus)."

71. The relationship between Garlandia, Franco, and Lambert has been approached from the perspective of conceptual concordances, the most comprehensive study being that in Pinegar, "Textual and Conceptual Relationships." The lack of consensus about when Garlandia, Franco, and Lambert were active lies in part with the assumption that each forms a point of development in a linear evolution of music-theoretical ideas. It might be suggested that all three theorists belonged to the same era, with both Lambert and Franco following Garlandia, who in turn foreshadowed certain elements of their theories, but no contact between Franco and Lambert can be conclusively demonstrated.

72. Wolf, "Die Musiklehre des Johannes de Grocheo," p. 67: "Da er nun einerseits kleinere Noten als die Semibrevis nicht kennt und andererseits, obgleich er von den Musikverhältnissen in Paris ausgeht, Johannes de Muris nicht erwähnt, so ist er vermutlich früher als dieser und Philipp de Vitry anzusetzen, das heißt er wird gegen die Wende des 13. Jahrhunderts gewirkt haben, eine Zeit, in der die ars nova sich anbahnte."

73. Rohloff 1943, p. 15.

74. Besseler, "Zur 'Ars Musicae' des Johannes de Grocheo." Heinrich Besseler had already dated Grocheio's treatise to 1300 in his influential discussion in the *Handbuch der Musikwis-*

senschaft; see *Die Musik des Mittelalters und der Renaissance*, p. 135; Robert Haas, in the same series, simply describes Grocheio as in the late thirteenth century; see *Aufführungspraxis der Musik*, pp. 70–75.

75. Rohloff 1972, pp. 171–72.

76. Besseler's dating of Grocheio was not questioned by Gilbert Reaney in his influential discussion in *Die Musik in Geschichte und Gegenwart*; see Reaney, "Johannes de Grocheo." This dating is repeated in turn by Ellinore Fladt in her 2003 revision of Reaney's entry (*MGG* 9:1094–98). Christopher Page also supports a date of around 1300 in his various writings, including his entry in the *New Grove Dictionary of Music and Musicians*—"Grocheio, Johannes de." A 1300 date for Grocheio was taken for granted in 1970 by Wolf Frobenius in his argument that Franco of Cologne's discussion of mensural notation should be assigned to 1280; see Frobenius, "Zur Datierung von Francos *Ars cantus mensurabilis*."

77. See for example Besseler, "Zur 'Ars musicae'," p. 230; DeWitt, "New Perspective on Grocheio's *Ars Musicae*," pp. 6–7; Page, "Johannes de Grocheio on Secular Music," p. 17.

78. Aristotle, *Physica* 6.1–2 (231b21–233b31).

79. Besseler argued that Grocheio description of the division of the breve into six parts indicates his familiarity with the *minima* and therefore matches rhythms used in motets in the *Roman de Fauvel*, even though Grocheio does not mention the *minima*; see Besseler, "Zur 'Ars musicae' des Johannes de Grocheo," p. 230: "In der Musik, von der die Rede ist, war also die Longa perfekt und enthielt 3 Breven. Die Brevis dagegen bestand aus 2, 3 und weiter bis zu 6 gleichen Teilen. Anders ausgedrückt: de Grocheo kennt in der Motette, um die es sich hier praktisch handelt, nur perfekten *Modus*, aber sowohl perfektes wie imperfektes *Tempus*, und zwar mit insgesamt höchstens 6 *Minimen*. Das sind genau die Rhythmen, die noch in der Mehrzahl der Motetten des *Roman de Fauvel* von 1316 vorliegen." Grocheio goes on to describe a "fuller measure" called a perfection (*perfectio*) by which the moderns measure "all their *cantus*" (*AM* 16.5). Grocheio's application of a *tempus perfectum* to *all cantus* is a clear indication that the theory of the *tempus imperfectum* associated with the *ars nova* was unknown to him, making it very unlikely that he would have any knowledge of the *minima*. Besseler's argument about the meaning of Grocheio's "up to six" as referring to the *minima* is refined in DeWitt, who accounts for Grocheio's failure to describe the *minima* by arguing that he describes the "value" of the *minima*, not the *minima* itself; see DeWitt, "New Perspective on Grocheio's *Ars Musicae*," pp. 6–7: "[s]ince [Grocheio] mentions the division of the breve into six parts . . . he must have written after the *value* of the *minima* was in use," going on to explain that division of the breve with such *value*—but utilizing the semibreve—is consistent with the divisions of the breve associated with Petrus de Cruce as found in the Montpellier codex and the *Roman de Fauvel*.

80. A comparison may be drawn with Walter Odington's description of the division of the breve. Odington notes that the breve was previously divided into two breves but "the moderns" sometimes divide it into two, sometimes into three. Like Grocheio, Odington avers that "because a continuum is divisible to infinity and *tempus* is a continuum, certainly voices [that] are measured in *tempora* will hence be divisible into infinity" ("quia continuum est divisible in infinitum, et tempus continuorum est, voces quidem sunt mensuratae temporibus quare divisibiles erunt in infinitum"); see Odington, *Summa de speculatione musice*, p. 128. Unlike Grocheio, however, Odington notes that the breve is divided into *six or seven* parts "which they rightly call minor semibreves," thus reflecting the Petronian division of the breve: "Brevis vero apud priores resoluta est in duas semibreves, sic vocatas a re: apud modernos, aliquando

in tres, aliquando in duas. Cum autem in duas, dicitur prima minor et secunda major, quia duas minores continet, quarum figura accipitur secundum species quadranguli . . . Rursumque invenitur brevis divisa in sex vel septem partes, quas adhuc semibreves vocant minus iuste" (Odington, *Summa de speculatione musice*, p. 128). Odington's treatise has been variously dated to between 1217 and 1346, although Odington himself is named in a document dated to 1298; see *Summa de speculatione musice*, p. 26.

81. Franco, *Ars cantus mensurabilis* 5, "Pro altera autem brevi minus quam quatuor semibreves accipii non possunt . . . nec plures quam sex . . . "

82. Grocheio refers to Johannes de Garlandia in the imperfect tense ("distinguebat") in *AM* 17.7, implying that the *magister* to whom he refers was no longer active.

83. These accusations involved claims that heretical doctrines were being taught about the eternity of the world and the mortality of the human soul; see *CUP* no. 432, 1:487.

84. The condemnations of 1277 (*CUP* no. 473, 1:543–55) have been the subject of enormous literary and philosophical investigation, summarized most recently in Aertsen, *Nach der Verurteilung von 1277*. They have been reedited and commented on by Piché, *La condemnation Parisienne de 1277*.

85. Aristotle *De caelo* 290b30. See also Rico, "'Auctoritas cerum habet nasum.'"

86. The earliest *reportatio* of the *Musica plana* is included in Paris, BnF lat. 18514, fols. 85r–94r copied in either the thirteenth or fourteenth centuries and from southwest France; see Johannes de Garlandia, *Musica plana*, p. xi. This *reportatio* begins: "Tractatus de musica collectus ex hiis quae dicta sunt a Boetio supra, atque declaratio musice practice" (Johannes de Garlandia, *Musica plana*, p. 3). The *supra* refers to the glossed text of Boethius's *De musica*, preserved immediately before the *reportatio prima* in this manuscript. He repeats Boethian doctrine about the music of the spheres in each of these reports; see Johannes de Garlandia, *Musica plana*, pp. 3, 25, 39, and 55.

87. Bacon, *Opus Tertium* 59, p. 229, and *Communia mathematica* 1.4, pp. 52–53. The compromise position, which Bacon rejects, is developed in *Philosophica disciplina* (Lafleur, *Quatre Introductions à la philosophie au XIIIe siècle*, p. 267).

88. *Ausi com l'unicorne* (*AM* 9.4) and *Chanter m'estuet quer ne m'en puis tenir* (*AM* 9.5) are attributed to Thibaut of Navarre. *Quant il rousignol* (*AM* 9.4) is attributed to Raoul de Ferrières and Chastelain de Couci; see Raynaud, *Bibliographie des Chansonniers Français des XIIIe et XIVe siècles*, p. 165.

89. The anonymous *Au repairier que je fis de prouvence* (*AM* 9.5) is included in the *Chansonnier de l'Arsenal* (Paris, BnF Arsenal 5198) redacted during the 1270s, and *Toute sole passerai le vert boscage* (*AM* 9.6) is included in Bamberg Staatsbibliothek, MS lit. 115 (fol. 58), prepared during the last quarter of the thirteenth century.

90. Holmes, *History of Old French Literature*, pp. 259–60. See also "Chansons de geste— Girart de Viane."

91. Heinrich Besseler does not identify his sources for Tassin in his article "Ars antiqua." Tassin is mentioned as a minstrel in the court of Flanders in 1276–77 according to a document identified by Mary Wolinski (to whom we are indebted for this information), Rijksarchief Gent, Gaillard 12 (22 Dec. 1276–13 June 1277): "Adonc as menestrels le Duch de Brabant. Tassin, Boid, et Estuol le sot, vi lb. 10 s." Tassin is also mentioned among a list of minstrels in the court of Philip IV in 1288; see Lalou, *Les comptes sur tablettes de cire de la chambre au deniers de Philippe III le hardi et de Philippe IV le Bel*, p. 855: "Robertus de Berneville, Guillelmus de Baudreceni, Rex heraudorum, Rex flajoletorum, Henricus de Lauduno, Tassinus,

Guillelmus trompator, Guyots de Bremireil, Guillelmus le Ber." There were close ties between the French court and the court of Brabant. In 1270, John of Brabant married Marguerite of France (1255–71), daughter of Louis IX, while John's sister, Maria of Brabant (1256–1321), was the second wife (married in 1274) of Louis's son, Philip III of France (1245–85). Catherine Parsoneault notes a correlation between Grocheio's description of the audience for motets and Guillaume de Nangis's description of Marie of Brabant's coronation in 1275. See Parsoneault, "Montpellier Codex," pp. 178–79.

92. Montpellier, Faculté de Médecine, MS 196, fol. 298v: *Amours dont je sui epris*, fol. 331v: *De chanter me vient talens*, and fol. 336v: *Entre Jehan et Philippet*.

93. Montpellier 196, fol. 277v: "Entre Copin, et Bourgois, Hanicot et Charlot et Pierron, sont a Paris Demourant, mout loial compaignon . . . " On the disputed date of the Montpellier codex, see Wolinski, "Compilation of the Montpellier Codex"; see also Everist, "Motets, French Tenors, and the Polyphonic Chanson," esp. n. 18, and Parsoneault, "Montpellier Codex," pp. 130–52.

94. The modern foliation, 1–96, supersedes a seventeenth-century pagination of ninety-two parchment folios. This earlier pagination is recorded in the 1808 catalogue of Harleian manuscripts; see *Catalogue of the Harleian Manuscripts*, 1.104. Folio references to BL Harley 281 follow the modern pagination.

95. On the anthology in Harley 281, see Mews et al., "Guy of Saint-Denis and the Compilation of Texts about Music." On apographs, see Pollard, "Pecia System in the Medieval Universities," p. 151. Facsimile reproduction of Guy's tonary is included in Guido von Saint-Denis, *Tractatus de tonis*, 2:139–74.

96. BL Harley 281, fol. 58v: "Qui legis auctoris nomen per quinque priora Gramata pictoris, hoc scribi celitus ora."

97. Klundert has identified passages from Peter's *continuatio* to Thomas Aquinas's commentary on Aristotle's *Politics* in Guy's *Tractatus*; see Guido von Saint-Denis, *Tractatus de tonis*, 1:152–201. Closer inspection indicates that Guy also drew from Peter's final quodlibital disputation.

98. On Jean Gosselin see Pattison, *Isaac Casaubon*, pp. 173–80.

99. See Carolus-Barré, "Pillage et dispersion de la bibliothèque de l'abbaye de Saint-Denis."

100. This same hand gives cross-references to the works in BL Harley 281 included in Martin Gerbert's *Scriptores ecclesiastici de musica sacra potissium* published in 1784.

101. Wright, *Fontes Harleiani—A Study of the Sources of the Harleian Collection of Manuscripts*, p. 363.

102. Guido Aretinus, *Micrologus*, pp. 80–233.

103. Guido d'Arezzo, "Regule rhythmice."

104. Guido d'Arezzo, "Prologus in Antiphonarium."

105. Guido d'Arezzo, "Epistola ad Michahelem," pp. 438–72 (even).

106. [Pseudo] Odo, *Dialogus*, GS 1:252–64.

107. Guido d'Arezzo, "Epistola ad Michahelem," pp. 490–530 (even).

108. Meyer, "Le tonaire cistercien et sa tradition."

109. Petrus de Cruce Ambianensi, *Tractatus de tonis*, pp. vi–xxv

110. Guido von Saint-Denis, *Tractatus de tonis*, 2:2–137.

111. Cf. Knaus, "HS 2663. Johannes de Grocheo: Ars musicae."

112. Some of the errors made by this scribe include the omission of abbreviation elements,

poorly expanded abbreviations, omitted words, and skipped lines of text, not all of which are corrected.

113. On the book trade in Paris, see Richard H. Rouse and Mary A. Rouse, *Manuscripts and Their Makers*. See also Mary A. Rouse and Richard H. Rouse, *Authentic Witnesses*, esp. chap. 8, "The Book Trade at the University of Paris, ca. 1250–ca. 1350," pp. 259–338.

114. This folio, 69v, includes the incipit to the *Ars musica* ("Quoniam quidam Juvenum amici mej") in one script, the words "sal ar mara ra" in another, and the word "Intentionem" with a decorated "I" in the script used for the text. Other notes on this half-folio were added in a later, St. Barbara hand as indicated by its presence in other parts of the miscellany.

115. For example, the opening sentences of para. 1.3, "Ductus enim fuit ut narrat boethius quasi divino spiritu ad fabrorum officia. Et ibi audiens mirabilem armoniam ex ictibus malleorum," are abbreviated in the exact same way in both manuscripts, excepting the words *enim* (which is transcribed using a specific abbreviation in each manuscript) and "boethius quasi." Examples of scribal conventions particular to BL Harley 281 include: *in* typically abbreviated "i", *enim* "ei," and *autem* "aut"; the same words are rendered "in," ".n.," and "a" in Darmstadt 2663.

116. Darmstadt 2663, fol. Tv: "Istum librum scripsit dominus Iohannes de Bocis monachus domus sancte Barbare Colonensis ordinis Cathusianesis requiescat in pace." John de Booze also added "Iste liber . . . Colonia" (with the entry between *liber* and *Colonia* crossed out) on fol. 1r, and "Iste liber est Carthusie in Colonia" on fol. 55v. On John of Booze, see Marks, *Medieval Manuscript Library of the Charterhouse of St Barbara*, 1:44.

117. This assessment is based on a comparison of a sample of von Kalkar's handwriting from Darmstadt, Universitäts- und Landesbibliothek, MS 610 as reproduced in Marks, *Medieval Manuscript Library of the Charterhouse of St Barbara*, 1:45, with margin entries between fols. 3v–50r of Darmstadt 2663.

118. Von Kalkar, *Cantuagium*, pp. 44–45: "Sed quia ex notulis his non redactis ad mensuram cantari contigit olim satis discorditer, ideo quidam magni artistae Parisius, quorum nomina in quodam discantu ponuntur, qui incipit 'Zodiacus,' si bene recolo, et <quorum unum> vidi episcopum, ante annos circiter quinquaginta, circa annum videlicet Domini millesimum trecentesimum tricesimum." The *Cantuagium* consciously parallels von Kalkar's *Loquagium*, a treatise on rhetoric; see Rüthing, *Der Kartäuser Heinrich Egher von Kalkar*, pp. 82–87. Six manuscripts survive of the *Cantuagium* and seven of the *Loquagium* (still unedited).

119. Von Kalkar, *Cantuagium*, pp. 39–40: "Hostium musicae praecipue ecclesiasticae, si cui autem placuerit, intrare longius ad musicam speculativam vel practicam, legat libros et studeat Boetii, Augustini, Hieronymi [de Moravia] et aliorum musicorum ecclesiasticorum, qui cantus corrigunt, qui differentias tonorum in diversis tonis dividunt et multa exempla de cantibus ecclesiasticis ponunt."

120. David de Augusta, *De exterioris et interioris hominis compositione secundum triplicem statum incipientium, proficientium et perfectorum libri tres*.

121. Hugo of St. Cher, *Hugonis a St. Charo Tractatus super missam seu speculum ecclesiae*.

122. Honorius Augustodunensis, *Lucidaire*.

123. URL: <www.uga.edu/theme/gro-har.html> (accessed 17 November 2005).

124. The editors owe a debt of gratitude to Charles Burnett for suggesting this rendering. Page's translation of *vulgaris* as "of the lay public" is not dissimilar, although Page argued that the contrasting term *litterati* should be taken "in its traditional sense of 'the clergy'"; see Page, "Johannes de Grocheio on Secular Music," p. 36 n. 72. This implies that the laity and clergy

constitute two distinct categories of musical audience, although this is not evidenced in the treatise; moreover, Grocheio uses the terms *ecclesiastici* (*AM* 4.12) and *vir ecclesiasticus* (*AM* 22.4, 22.5) to allude to non-secular persons. In the present edition, *litterati* is interpreted as "educated," which is both comparable to the appositive "those who are seeking out subtleties in the arts" (*AM* 19.2) and a counterpoint to the *vulgalis* or "common people."

Outline of the *Ars musice*

These headings are not the work of Grocheio, but serve to indicate the structure of the *Ars musice* by noting its various sections and subsections.

Prologue on the art of music

0.1 Request for the work
0.2 Intention of the work
0.3 The way of proceeding
0.4 Concerning principles
0.5 Petition to the audience
0.6 Conclusion to the prologue

Beginning of the treatise

1.1 The fabled discoverers of music
1.2 Boethius's opinion on the discovery of music
1.3 Boethius's description of Pythagoras's discovery of music
1.4 Pythagoras's discovery of the material of music
1.5 Conclusion to the discovery of music

2.1 Introduction to the principles of music
2.2 Definition of consonance and concord
2.3 Introduction to consonances
2.4 On consonances being infinite
2.5 Limiting the number of consonances to three
2.6 On proportion
2.7 Proportion as a cause of consonance
2.8 The species of proportion
2.9 Only man recognizes consonances
2.10 Consonance as a natural phenomenon

3.1 Introduction to the three perfections in sounds
3.2 The perfect threefold harmony in sound
3.3 The most perfect consonance in metaphor
3.4 The human soul and the threefold perfection in sound

33

Explicit to the treatise on music

Ars musice:
Text and Translation

[39r] Incipit prologus in arte musice.[1]

[0.1] QUoniam quidam iuvenum amici mei me cum affectu rogaverunt,[2] quatinus eis aliquid de doctrina musicali sub brevibus explicarem: Eorum precibus mox acquiescere volui. Eo quod in eis inveni maximam fidelitatem, amicitiam et virtutem. Et per longum tempus ad necessaria vite mee maximum tribuerunt iuvamentum.

[0.2] Et ideo presentis operis intentio est pro posse nostro eis musicam intimare.[3] Cuius cognitio est necessaria volentibus habere completam cognitionem de moventibus et motibus.[4] videtur enim esse magis de sono qui inter sensibilia propria reperitur, et potentie apprehensive obiectum est.[5] Valet etiam ad opus. nam mores hominum corrigit et meliorat si modo debito usi sint. In hoc etiam excellit alias artes, quod immediatius ad creatoris laudem et gloriam totaliter ordinatur.

[0.3] Modus autem procedendi erit primo considerare communia que dicuntur principia. et postea ex illis orientia sigillatim secundum subiecte materie facultatem.[6] Sic enim vadit tota cognitio humana sive sensitiva sive intellectiva, ut ait aristoteles in prohemio physicorum.

[0.4] Adhuc autem circa principia primo contingit querere de eorum intentione.[7] postea autem de quiditate. quantitate. et qualitate. et que circa principia sunt querenda. Sicut enim videns modum inveniendi distantiam corporis solis a centro terre non admirabitur sed factus erit sciens. Sic videns inventionem principiorum musice magis erit dispositus ad sciendum.

[0.5] Non increpent autem nos quidam dicentes scientiam corrumpere eo quod scriptorum diversitas et opinionum pluralitas impediat veritatem. videmus enim diligenter considerantes pluralitatem opinionum querere et ex illis extrahere quod est verum: Circa vero artes humanas est opinionum diversitas. ut in mecanicis. Diversitas in edificiis et in vestimentis homini ad sensum manifestat. Semper enim potest ars humana et eius opus meliorari, cum nunquam naturam vel artem divinam attingat. Que semper quod melius est in omnibus operatur. Licet enim plures diebus istis practicam huius artis querant. pauci tamen de eius speculatione sunt curantes. Et adhuc quidam speculativi suas operationes et inventiones abscondunt nolentes aliis publicare. Cum tamen quilibet vir debeat in talibus veritatem manifestare ad laudem et manifestationem veritatis increate.

---

1 Incipit prologus in arte musice] *om* **D1**
2 rogaverint **D1**
3 ultimare **D1**
4 moti **D1**
5 nota quod item, significat es *in marg.* **H3**
6 ordo disciplinæ *in marg.* **H3**
7 inventione **D1**

Here begins the prologue on the art of music.

[0.1] Since certain young men, my friends, have affectionately asked me to explain to them something in brief about musical teaching, I wanted to accede to their requests presently, for I have found in them the greatest loyalty, friendship, and virtue, and over a long time they have given very great support for the necessities of my life.

[0.2] It is thus the intention of the present work, as much as we can, to explain to them music, a knowledge of which is necessary for those wishing to have a complete knowledge of moving things and of movements,[1] for it seems to be more concerning sound, which is found among the proper sensibles,[2] and is the object of our apprehensive ability. It is also worthwhile for the work, for it corrects and improves the behavior of men if they use it in the way they ought. In this it also surpasses the other arts, for it is more immediately and wholly ordained for the praise and glory of the Creator.

[0.3] The way of proceeding will be first to consider commonalities, which are called principles, and then, one by one, issues arising from them according to the nature of the subject matter. For thus all human knowledge proceeds, whether sensory or intellectual, as Aristotle says in the preface to the *Physics*.[3]

[0.4] Further, concerning principles, it is appropriate first to ask about their intention, then afterwards, about the quiddity, quantity, and quality,[4] and what should be investigated about principles. For just as one seeing the method of finding the distance of the body of the sun from the center of the earth will not be surprised but will be made knowledgeable, so one seeing the discovery of the principles of music will be more disposed to knowing.

[0.5] Let certain people not rebuke us, saying that we corrupt knowledge in that diversity of writings and a plurality of opinions might impede the truth. For we see that those considering carefully the plurality of opinions inquire after and extract from them what is true. But there is a diversity of opinions about human arts, as in the mechanical arts.[5] A diversity in buildings and in clothes is evident to man through the senses. For human art and its work can always be improved, since it never reaches divine nature or art, which always produces what is better in everything. For although these days many people seek out the practice of this art, few, however, pay attention to its theory. Even now, certain theorists conceal their activities and discoveries, not wanting to make them public to others, although any man ought, however, to reveal the truth of such matters to the praise and revelation of truth uncreated.

[0.6] Que quidem[8] igitur sit intentio et cuius gratia et quis modus procedendi prohemialiter sic sit dictum.

Incipit tractatus.[9]

[1.1] FAbulose loquentes dixerunt musicam inveniri a musis iuxta aquas habitantibus. Et inde nomen accipere. Et alii dixerunt **[39v]** eam inveniri a viris sanctis et prophetis.

[1.2] Sed boetius vir valens et nobilis alium tenet modum. Cuius sententie magis est adherendum. eo quod nisus fuit ostendere ea que dixit per demonstrationem. Ait enim in libro suo de armonia musicali. quod pictagoras principia musice adinvenit. Licet enim homines semper quasi a principio cantaverint: eo quod musica sit eis naturaliter innata ut vult plato et boetius: Principia tamen cantus et musice ignorabant usque ad tempus pytagore. que sic adinvenit.

[1.3] Ductus enim fuit ut narrat boetius quasi divino spiritu ad fabrorum officia. Et ibi audiens mirabilem armoniam ex ictibus malleorum. Ad eos[10] accedens fecit malleos in manibus percutientium alternari. Et sic vidit armoniam ex viribus percutientium non causari. Et tunc scivit hoc ex proportione malleorum provenire: examinansque[11] et ponderans eos. Invenit unum in dupla proportione ad alterum sicut sunt .12. ad .vi.[12] Et isti adinvicem reddebant consonantiam que dyapason appellatur. Ille idem malleus ad duos alios medios in sexquialtera proportione et sexquitertia se habebat pondere— Ita quod ad unum in sexquialtera sicut 12 ad [8][13] qui dyapente reddebant. Et ad[14] alium se habebat in sexquitertia proportione sicut .12. ad .9. qui dyatessaron resonabant. Similiter etiam isti duo cum subduplo in proportione sexquialtera et sexquitertia se habebant et consonantiam dyatessaron et dyapente resonabant. Sed isti duo in proportione sexquioctava se habebant sicut .9. ad .8. et tonum adinvicem resonabant. Quintus autem malleus omnibus improportionalis erat. Et ob hoc nullam reddebat armoniam. sed potius corrumpebat.

8 quidam **D1**
9 Incipit tractatus] *om* **D1**
10 eam **D1**
11 examinansque] *post corr.* **H2**; Examinans **D1**; examinans **H1**

12 .6. **D1**
13 12 ad [8]] .12. ad. 6. **D1**; *infra rasuram* . .
ad. 9. **H1**
14 ad] *om* **D1**

[0.6] Let this suffice by way of introduction, therefore, about what is our intention, and by whose grace, and about what [is our] manner of proceeding.

Beginning of the *tractatus*.

[1.1] Those speaking in fables have said that music was discovered by the Muses dwelling near the waters and took the name thence.[6] And others have said that it was discovered by holy men and prophets.[7]

[1.2] But Boethius, a worthy and noble man, holds to another way. His opinions are more to be followed, since he strove to show those things which he said through demonstration. For he says in his book on musical harmony that Pythagoras discovered the principles of music.[8] For although people have always sung, as if from the very beginning, since music is naturally innate to them as Plato and Boethius would have it,[9] nevertheless they did not know the principles of *cantus* and music up to the time of Pythagoras, which he discovered thus:

[1.3] For he was led, as Boethius relates,[10] as if by divine inspiration to the workshops of blacksmiths. And there, hearing the wonderful harmony made by hammer blows [and] approaching them, he had the hammers in the hands of those striking swapped around. And thus he saw that the harmony was not caused by the strength of those striking. And then he knew that it came from the proportions of the hammers, and examining and weighing them, he discovered one in duple proportion to another, just as 12 is to 6. And these together gave forth a consonance which is called the *diapason*. That same hammer was found to be in sesquialter and sesquitertian proportion when compared to two other intermediary ones; with the result that for the one in sesquialter as 12 is to 8, which rendered the *diapente*, and for the other in sesquitertian proportion as 12 is to 9, which resounded the *diatessaron*. Also, these two were likewise in sesquialter and sesquitertian proportion with the subduple and resounded the consonance of the *diatessaron* and *diapente*. But these two taken together were found in sesquioctave proportion, as 9 is to 8, and resounded a tone in relation to each other. The fifth hammer was not in proportion to all the others, and because of this it returned no harmony, but rather corrupted it.

[1.4] Et sic invenit pytagoras quid esset. Dyesis. Tonus. Ditonus. Semiditonus.[15] Dyatessaron. Dyapente. Dyapason. Et ex hiis composita. Ista autem
principia sunt et materia qua utitur omnis musicus. Et in ea formam musicam introducit. Licet enim in naturalibus efficiens dicatur principium plus
quam materia. In artificiatis tamen materia principium potest dici. Eo quod
sit in[16] actu. Et forma artis sit ei accidentalis.

[1.5] De inventione igitur principiorum musice et de modo inveniendi hec
dicantur.

[2.1] REliquum est temptare dicere. Que et quot sint principia.[17] et propter
quam causam. Quod non potest bene a musico fieri. eo quod debet principia sue artis ut alii artifices supponere. Et ex illis conclusiones per ordinem
demonstrare.

[2.2] Principia autem musice solent consonantie et concordantie appellari.
Dico autem concordantiam quando unus sonus cum alio armonice continuatur. Sicut una pars temporis vel motus cum alia continua est. Consonantiam
autem dico quando duo soni vel plures simul uniti et in uno tempore unam
perfectam armoniam reddunt.

[2.3] Primum vero de consonantiis disserendum est eo quod per **[40r]** consonantias concordantias invenerunt.

[2.4] Quidam autem vulgaliter loquentes dixerunt esse consonantias infinitas. Sed sue positionis nullam assignaverunt rationem.

[2.5] Alii autem rationabiliter loquentes tres[18] consonantias esse asserunt.
volentes per numeros sui dicti rationem ostendere. Sicut magister pytagoras primus inventor, et nichomacus arismeticus. Et plato studiosus, qui per
matematica[19] voluit naturalia demonstrare. unde in libro qui thimeo intitulatur numerum elementorum declaravit. eo quod inter duo cubica est semper duo media proportionalia invenire. Et boetius vir latinus istos sequens in
libro de proprietatibus[20] armonicis istas consonantias[21] per numeros nisus est
declarare.

15 Semiditonus] *post corr.* **H2**; Semitonus **D1, H1**   19 musicam **D1**
16 sit in] sit ens in **D1**   20 proportionibus **D1**
17 principia] *om* **D1**   21 consonas **D1**
18 .3. **D1**

[1.4] And thus Pythagoras discovered what was *diesis*, tone, ditone, semiditone, *diatessaron*, *diapente*, *diapason*, and ones composed from these. These are the principles and the material which every musician uses, and he introduces the musical form into these. For although in natural things the agent is called the principle rather than material, in artificial things, however, the material can be said to be the principle, because it is actual, and the form of the art may be accidental to it.[11]

[1.5] Let these suffice, therefore, about the discovery of the principles of music and about the manner of discovering them.

[2.1] It now remains to try to say what and how many principles there are and for what reason. This cannot be done well by the musician since he ought to apply the principles of his art like other artists, and establish conclusions from them through order.

[2.2] The principles of music are usually called consonances and concords. I say "concord" when one sound is continued harmonically by another, just as one part of time or motion is continuous with another. I say "consonance" when two or more sounds united at the same moment and in one time give one perfect harmony.

[2.3] But consonances are to be discussed first, for it is through consonances that concords are found.

[2.4] Certain people, speaking commonly, have said that consonances are infinite,[12] but they have given no rationale for their position.

[2.5] Others speaking in a reasoned way have asserted that there are three consonances,[13] wishing to show the reasoning of their statements through numbers, just like Master Pythagoras the first discoverer,[14] and Nicomachus the arithmetician,[15] and studious Plato, who wished to demonstrate natural things through mathematics, whence he stated the number of the elements in the book entitled the *Timaeus*,[16] since between two cubes, two intermediate proportions are always to be found.[17] And Boethius, a Latin man following these, strove to define these consonances through numbers in the book of harmonic properties.[18]

[2.6] Omnes autem isti fundamentum sue positionis accipiunt in hoc quod proportio ut dicunt primo et per se in numeris invenitur, et per numeros est aliis attributa: Sed istud fundamentum apud discipulos aristotelis. non est certum. Dicerent enim forte proportionem primo esse inter primas qualitates et formas naturales si vox sit imposita ad hoc signandum. Quis[22] autem istorum verum dicat non est huius negotii pertractare sed ubi prima scientiarum principia[23] pertractantur.

[2.7] Adhuc autem, supponentes proportionem esse primo inter numeros per hoc non potuerunt causam reddere de consonantiis et de numero consonantiarum. Si enim proportio consonantie causa esset[24] ubi esset talis proportio ibi esset talis consonantia. Quod[25] non videtur intuenti sonum tonicus cum alio ei habenti proportionem. Non enim armoniam faciunt. sed potius organum auditus corrumpunt.

[2.8] Adhuc autem, cum sint .v.[26] species proportionis vel inequalitatis .scilicet. multiplex. Superparticularis. Superpartiens. multiplex superparticularis. multiplex superpartiens.[27] Tres .scilicet. simplices. et due composite: Querendum est ab eis quare non sunt tot consonantie. Et adhuc ab eis[28] est querendum, cur in multiplici est[29] una tantum consonantia .scilicet. dyapason. In superparticulari due .scilicet. dyapente et dyatessaron. et in superpartiente nulla: Et mirandum quare boetius qui sententiam aristotelis senserat, in talibus se fundavit: Sed forte aliud per proportionem sensit. volens per eam causas occultas et non nominatas circumloqui.

[2.9] Adhuc autem querendum est cur alia animalia ab homine consonantias non cognoscunt. Licet enim quedam in sonis delectentur inclinatione naturali sicut aves in suo cantu. et equi in sono tube vel tympani. Et canes[30] in sono cornuum et fistularum. Solus tamen homo consonantias tres[31] apprehendit: et cognoscit, et in eis delectatur.[32]

22 Qui **D1**
23 prima scientiarum principia] *post corr.* **H2**; prima principia scientiarum **D1, H1**
24 essent **D1**
25 eidem **D1**
26 .5. **D1**

27 Multiplex superparticularis. Multiplex superpartiens.] *om* **D1**
28 adhuc ab eis] *post corr.* **H2**; adhuc eis **D1, H1**
29 et **D1**
30 carnes **D1**
31 .3. **D1**
32 delectantur **D1**

[2.6] All these have taken the foundation for their position in this, that proportion, as they say, is found firstly and in itself in numbers and is attributed through numbers to other things.[19] But this foundation is not certain among the disciples of Aristotle.[20] For they would say perhaps that proportion is first among prime qualities and natural forms if an utterance is assigned in order to signify this. It does not belong to this work to consider who of these may be speaking the truth, but where the first principles of the sciences are considered.

[2.7] Still, assuming that proportion is first among numbers, they could not provide by this a cause of consonances and for the number of consonances. For if proportion were the cause of consonance, wherever there was such a proportion, there would be such a consonance. This is not evident to someone considering the sound of a thunderous blow with another having a proportion to it. For they do not make harmony, but rather corrupt the organ of hearing.

[2.8] Still, there are 5 species of proportion or inequality,[21] namely multiplex, superparticular, superpartient, multiplex superparticular, and multiplex superpartient,[22] namely three simple and two compound; it must be sought by them why there are not the same number of consonances. And further, it must be sought by them why there is only one consonance in a multiplex, namely the *diapason*, two in a superparticular, namely the *diapente* and the *diatessaron*, and none in a superpartient. And one must wonder why Boethius, who understood the opinion of Aristotle, based himself on such [notions].[23] But perhaps he understood something else by proportion, wishing to allude through it to occult and not-named causes.

[2.9] It must still be asked why other animals apart from man do not recognize consonances. For although certain ones delight in sounds by natural inclination, as birds in their song and horses in the sound of the trumpet or drum, and dogs in the sound of horns and pipes. But only man grasps and knows the three consonances and delights in them.

[2.10] Adhuc autem si consonantia sit naturalis, ex[33] fine cognosci habet. Naturalis enim potius ex fine demonstrat. ut ait aristoteles. secundo[34] physicorum. finis enim primo movet efficientem, et ultimo complet opus: Si vero matematica:[35] eius cognitio sufficiens est per formam: Propter hec itaque et propter talia plura difficile videtur assignare propter quid de numero consonantiarum.

[3.1] TEmptemus tamen aliquid probabile de hoc dicere—Cuius difficultas est in duobus. In hoc .scilicet. quod tres[36] sunt tantummodo in sonis perfectiones, [**40v**] et in hoc quod solum ab homine cognoscuntur.

[3.2] Dicamus igitur quod omnium sublimis creator, a principio in sonis trinam armoniam inseruit[37] perfectam, ut in eis suam bonitatem ostenderet, et per illos nomen suum laudaretur. unde[38] david. Laudate dominum in sono tube. et cetera: Et etiam ut nullus possit se excusare a laude divina. Sed omnis lingua in sonis nomen glorie fateatur.

[3.3] Et forte sicut est in trinitate gloriosa. Ita quodam modo in hac experientia docet. Est enim una prima armonia quasi mater, que dyapason ab antiquis dicta est: Et alia quasi filia in ista contenta dyapente dicta. Et tertia ab eis procedens que dyatessaron appellatur. Et iste tres[39] simul ordinate[40] consonantiam perfectissimam[41] reddunt. Et forte hoc senserunt quidam pytagorici naturali inclinatione ducti non ausi tamen sub talibus verbis exprimere sed in numeris sub methaphora loquebantur.

[3.4] Dicamus ergo[42] quod anima humana immediate a primo creata speciem vel ymaginem retinet creatoris.[43] Que ymago a Iohanne damasceno. ymago trinitatis dicitur: mediante qua naturalis cognitio est ei innata.[44] Et forte ista naturali cognitione in sonis trinam perfectionem apprehendit. Que anime brutorum propter suam imperfectionem non debetur.

[3.5] Quot igitur sint consonantie et propter quid. sic sit dictum. Que autem sit unaqueque nunc dicatur.

[4.1] DEscribunt autem sic dyapason in sonis duplam proportionem dicentes[45] esse. ut si corda alii comparata in dupla proportione extendatur[46] dyapason consonantiam resonabit.

---

33 in **D1**

34 .2. **D1**

35 musica **D1**

36 .3. **D1**

37 inserunt **D1**

38 ut **D1**

39 .3. **D1**

40 ordinante **D1**

41 perfectissima **D1**

42 etiam **D1**

43 creatori **D1**

44 inventa **D1**

45 dicentes] *post corr.* **H2**; videntes **D1**, **H1**

46 extenditur **D1**

[2.10] Further, if consonance is natural, it has to be known from the end. For natural philosophy demonstrates rather from the end, as Aristotle says in the second [book] of the *Physics*;[24] for first the end moves the agent and finally completes the work. But if we are dealing with mathematics, knowledge of it is sufficient through form.[25] Therefore, because of these things, and because of many other such things, it seems difficult to assign a reason for the number of consonances.

[3.1] Nevertheless, let us say something demonstrable about this. Its difficulty lies in two [points]: namely, that there are only three perfections in sounds, and that they are recognized only by man.

[3.2] Let us say, therefore, that the sublime Creator of all things has, from the beginning, introduced a perfect threefold harmony in sounds so that He may show His goodness in them, and through them His name may be praised; hence David: "Praise the Lord in the sound of the trumpet" etc.,[26] and also so that no one may be able to absent himself from divine praise, but every tongue may confess the name of glory in sounds.

[3.3] And perhaps just as is in the glorious Trinity, so in a certain way experience teaches in this. For there is one first harmony, like a mother, which is called the *diapason* by the ancients, and another, like a daughter, contained in it, called the *diapente*, and a third proceeding from them which is named the *diatessaron*, and these three ordered together produce the most perfect consonance. And perhaps certain Pythagoreans led by natural inclination sensed this, not having dared, however, to express it in such words but used to speak of it in numbers through metaphor.

[3.4] Let us say, therefore, that the human soul, created from the outset without mediation, retains the species or image of its Creator. This image is called by John of Damascus the image of the Trinity,[27] by whose mediation natural awareness is innate to it. And perhaps by this natural awareness it perceives a threefold perfection in sounds, which is not pledged to the soul of brutes because of their imperfection.

[3.5] Let this suffice, therefore, concerning how many consonances there are and the reason for them. What each of them is must now be discussed.

[4.1] They describe the *diapason* in this way, saying there is a duple proportion in sounds, so that if a string is extended in duple proportion compared to another, it will resound a *diapason* consonance.

[4.2] Dyapente autem sexquialteram proportionem.

[4.3] Sed dyatessaron in sexquitertia proportione dicunt[47] esse.

[4.4] Istarum autem proprietates[48] posterius apparebunt.

[4.5] De principiis autem musice in quantum[49] sunt consonantie nunc dictum sit. De ipsis autem ut concordantie sunt nunc dicatur.

[4.6] Quibusdam vero videtur concordantias infinitas esse. Sed ad hoc nullam probabilitatem adducunt.

[4.7] Alii finitas esse dicunt et sub numero determinato. plures tamen quam .7. puta .13. qui volunt dictum suum per experientiam declarare. sicut magister .Iohannes. de garlandia.

[4.8] Alii autem omnes ad .7. reducunt. Qui modo subtiliori investigant. Melius enim est pauca principia supponere, cum pluralitas principiis contradicat.[50] Isti autem ex dictis poetarum originem sui dicti capiunt. et cum hoc rationes probabiles adducunt. dicentes esse .7. dona spiritus. et in celo .7. planetas. et in[51] septimana .7. dies. quibus multotiens resumptis totus annus mensuratur. Et similiter[52] in sonis esse concordantias .7. dicunt.

[4.9] Istorum autem opinioni assentimus, dicendo quod homo ut ait plato et aristoteles. est quasi mundus. unde et microcosmus .idest. minor mundus ab eis dicitur. unde et leges[53] et operationes humane debent[54] legem divinam ut possibile est penitus imitari. Ad diversitatem autem generationum et corruptionum totius universi .vii.[55] stelle cum earum virtutibus suffecerunt. Et ideo rationabile fuit ponere in arte **[41r]** humana .vii.[56] principia que omnium diversitatum[57] sonorum cum armonia cause essent, que quidem cause concordantie appellantur.

[4.10] Antequam autem aliorum experientia dissolvatur, oportet videre quid unaqueque istarum sit. et qualiter sic dicatur. Dicimus autem eas. Unisonum. Tonum. Semitonum. Dytonum. Semiditonum vel dyatessaron. Dyapente, et dyapason.

---

47 dicuntur **D1**

48 autem proprietates] autem consonantiorum proprietates **D1**

49 quam **D1**

50 contradicit **D1**

51 in] *om* **D1**

52 generaliter **D1**

53 et leges] et eius leges **D1**

54 operationes humane debent] *post corr.* **H2**; op[p]erationes debent **D1, H1**

55 .7. **D1**

56 .7. **D1**

57 diversitarum **D1**

[4.2] The *diapente* is in sesquialter proportion.

[4.3] But they say the *diatessaron* is in sesquitertian proportion.

[4.4] The properties of these will appear later.

[4.5] Let this suffice concerning the principles of music as much as they are consonances. Concerning these as concords, let it now be said.

[4.6] But for some people, it seems that concords are infinite, yet they offer no demonstration for this.[28]

[4.7] Others say that they are finite and below some fixed number, more, however, than 7, such as 13; these people wish to establish their view through experience, just like Master Johannes de Garlandia.[29]

[4.8] Others reduce them all to 7. These people investigate in a more subtle way. For it is better to posit few principles, since plurality contradicts principles. These people take the source of their saying from the sayings of the poets, and with this they advance demonstrable reasons, saying that there are 7 gifts of the spirit and 7 planets in heaven and 7 days in a week, by the multiple repetition of which the whole year is measured. And they say that similarly there are 7 concords in sounds.

[4.9] We agree with their opinion, saying, as Plato and Aristotle do,[30] that man is like the world, hence he is said by them to be a microcosm, that is, a lesser world;[31] hence both human laws and operations ought to imitate divine law as completely as possible. For the 7 stars, with their forces, have sufficed for the diversity of generation and decay of the whole universe. And therefore it was reasonable to posit 7 principles in human art, which would be the causes of all diversities of sounds with harmony; these causes, indeed, are called concords.

[4.10] Before the experience of others is refuted, we ought to see what each of these is and how it is so called. We call these unison, tone, semitone, ditone, semiditone or *diatessaron*,[32] *diapente*, and *diapason*.

[4.11] Est[58] autem unisonus cum unus sonus alii continuus equalis est ei in acuitate vel gravitate. ut in numeris duo sunt equalia duobus et .3. 3bus.[59]

[4.12] Tonus autem multipliciter dicitur velud aux in motibus.[60] uno enim modo dicitur de elevatione, depressione, et fine cantus, ut ecclesiastici accipiunt: Alio modo dicitur de concordantia que consistit in aliqua proportione. et isto modo tonus est cum unus sonus alii continuatus[61] eum in acuitate vel gravitate excedit vel exceditur[62] ab eo in sexquioctava proportione sicut .9. se habet ad .8. vel econtrario.

[4.13] Semitonus autem vel dyesis dicitur non quia medietatem toni contineat. Sed quia ab eius perfectione deficit. Est enim quasi tonus remissus vel imperfectus, qui alii comparatus sic[63] forte ei proportionatur sicut .256. ad .243. Eius autem proprietas est cum tono omnem cantum et omnem concordantiam[64] aliam mensurare et melodiam in cantu facere.

[4.14] Dytonus autem est concordantia continens .2. tonos que sono precedenti comparata sic proportionari videtur sicut .81. ad .64. Hec autem ab aliquibus consonantia dicitur et in numero consonantiarum reponitur. puta a magistro .Iohanne. de guerlandia.[65] Quia tamen imperfectam est eam dimisimus. et quia eius mixtio auribus dure sonat.

[4.15] Semidytonus autem vel dyatessaron est concordantia .2. tonos cum uno semitonio continens que precedenti sono comparata eum in sexquitertia proportione excellit. In qua proportione se habent .4. ad .3. vel .12. ad .9.

[4.16] Dyapente autem est concordantia .3. tonos cum uno semitonio continens, que precedenti sono comparata eum superat in sexquialtera proportione sicut .3. 2. superant. vel .6. 4.

[4.17] Dyapason autem est concordantia continens .5. tonos et duo semitonia, que ex coniunctione dyatessaron cum dyapente resultat. Que sono immediate precedenti comparata eum in dupla proportione excellit sicut .4. 2. vel .6. 3. Ista autem concordantia omnes precedentes in se includit et ab hoc nomen[66] habere videtur.

58 Et **D1**
59 .3. **D1**
60 montibus **D1**
61 continuatur **D1**
62 excedetur **D1**

63 si **D1**
64 concordiam **D1**
65 garlandia **D1**
66 nomen] *om* **D1**

[4.11] It is a unison when one sound continuous with another is equal to it in height or depth, as in numbers two are equal to two and 3 to 3.[33]

[4.12] Tone is spoken of in many ways, just like apogee in [planetary] motions,[34] for in one way it is spoken of by the elevation, the depression, and the end of a *cantus*, as churchmen accept.[35] In another way it is said of a concord that it consists in some proportion, and in this way a tone is when one sound continued with another exceeds it in height or depth or is exceeded by it in sesquioctave proportion, as 9 is to 8 or conversely.[36]

[4.13] A semitone or *diesis* is so called not because it contains half of a tone, but because it lacks the latter's perfection.[37] For it is like a diminished or imperfect tone which, compared to the other in this way, is perhaps in proportion to it as 256 to 243.[38] Its property is with the tone to measure every *cantus* and every other concord and to make melody in *cantus*.

[4.14] A ditone is a concord containing 2 tones which, compared to a preceding sound, seems to be in proportion as 81 to 64.[39] This is called a consonance by some and is placed among the number of consonances as, for example, by Master Johannes de Garlandia.[40] Since it is imperfect, however, we have put it aside, since its mixing sounds harsh to the ears.

[4.15] A semiditone or *diatessaron* is a concord containing 2 tones with one semitone. This compared to the preceding sound exceeds it in sesquitertian proportion. In that proportion are 4 to 3 or 12 to 9.[41]

[4.16] A *diapente* is a concord containing 3 tones with one semitone, which compared to the preceding sound surpasses it in sesquialter proportion just as 3 surpasses 2 or 6 [surpasses] 4.[42]

[4.17] A *diapason* is a concord containing 5 tones and two semitones which results from the conjunction of a *diatessaron* with a *diapente*. This compared to the immediately preceding sound exceeds it in duple proportion just as 4 to 2 or 6 to 3.[43] This concord includes all the preceding ones in itself and seems to take its name from this.[44]

[4.18] Manifestato igitur quid unaqueque harum sit. apparet non esse necessarium plures quam[67] .7. ponere. Et ideo ad experientiam aliarum[68] solutio
est. Qui enim scit quid tonus. quid dytonus. potest de levi per additionem
toni tritonum efficere. Et qui cognoscit quid dyapente potest ex additione
toni tonum cum dyapente efficere. que concordantie composite et non simplices debent dici. Nos autem solum hic intendimus de hiis ut sunt simplices
et principia aliarum.[69]

[4.19] De principiis itaque musicalibus que consonantie et concordantie
dicuntur quibus omnis sonus et tota musica efficitur, ad presens[70] dicta sufficiant. **[41v]** Quid igitur sit musica et que eius partes, sequens est pertractare.

[5.1] DEscribunt autem[71] musicam quidam ad formam et materiam considerantes. Dicentes eam esse de numero relato ad sonos. Alii autem ad eius
operationem considerantes, dicunt eam artem ad cantandum deputatam.

[5.2] Nos autem utroque modo notificare intendimus eandemque.[72] sicut
notificatur instrumentum, et quelibet ars notificari debet. Sicut enim calidum naturale est primum instrumentum mediante quo anima exercet suas
operationes: Sic ars est instrumentum principale sive regula mediante qua
intellectus practicus suas operationes explicat et exponit.

[5.3] Dicamus igitur quod musica est ars vel scientia de sono numerato
armonice sumpto ad cantandum facilius deputata. Dico autem scientiam in
quantum principiorum tradit cognitionem. Artem vero in quantum intellectum practicum regulat operando. De sono vero armonico quia est materia
propria circa quam operatur. per numerum etiam eius forma designatur. Sed
per cantare tangitur operatio ad quam est proprie deputata.

[5.4] Quid igitur sit musica sic sit dictum.

[5.5] Quidam vero musicam in .3. genera dividunt, puta boetius. magister
.Iohannes. de. guerlandia in suis tractatibus, et eorum sequaces. Unum autem
genus dicunt de musica mondana. Aliud vero de humana. Sed tertium de
instrumentali. Per mundanam musicam signant armoniam ex motu corpo-
rum celestium causatam. Per humanam vero temperamentum complexionis
in corpore humano existens propter optimam mixtionem elementorum in eo.
Sed per instrumentalem signant illam que est de sonis instrumentorum, sive
naturalium sive artificialium.

67 quam **D1**; quod **H1**
68 aliorum **D1**
69 aliorum **D1**
70 presens] *post corr.* **H2**; prius **D1, H1**

71 autem] *om* **D1**
72 eandemque] *post corr.* **H2**; eamdem **D1**; eandem **H1**

[4.18] Having now revealed what each of these is, it does not seem necessary to posit more than 7. And therefore there is a solution for the experience of the others. For he who knows what a tone is, [and] what a ditone is, can easily make the tritone by the addition of a tone. And he who grasps what a *diapente* is can make the tone plus *diapente* by the addition of a tone, which ought to be called compound concords and not simple ones. We intend here to concern ourselves only with these, since they are simple and the principles for the others.

[4.19] Thus let this suffice for the present concerning musical principles which are called consonances and concords by which every sound and all music is made. What, therefore, music is and what are its parts is to be considered as follows.

[5.1] Certain people describe music considering it according to form and material, saying that it is about number related to sounds.[45] Others, considering its operation, say it is an art applied to singing.[46]

[5.2] We intend to examine this, indeed, both ways, just like any instrument is examined and any art ought to be examined. For just as natural heat[47] is the first instrument through which the soul carries out its operations, so art is the principal instrument or rule through which the practical intellect articulates and sets out its operations.[48]

[5.3] We may therefore say that music is the art or science concerning numbered sound taken harmonically, used for singing more easily. I say "science," in as much as it treats the knowledge of principles, but "art" in as much as it rules the practical intellect in operation. But it concerns harmonic sound because this is the proper material around which it operates; its form is also designated through number. And through singing, the operation to which it is properly applied is taken up.

[5.4] Let this suffice, therefore, for what music is.

[5.5] But certain people, such as Boethius,[49] Master Johannes de Garlandia in their treatises,[50] and their followers, divide music into 3 kinds. They say that one kind is *musica mundana*, but another is *humana*, and the third is *instrumentalis*. By *musica mundana* they designate the harmony caused by the motion of heavenly bodies. But by *humana* [they designate] the moderation of the constitution existing in the human body through the best mixing of elements in it. And by *instrumentalis* they designate that music which concerns the sounds of instruments, either natural or artificial.[51]

[5.6] Qui vero sic dividunt, aut dictum suum fingunt: aut volunt pytagoricis vel aliis magis quam veritati obedire. aut sunt naturam et logicam ignorantes. Prius enim dicunt universaliter musicam esse de sono numerato. Corpora vero celestia in movendo sonum non faciunt, quamvis antiqui hoc[73] crediderunt. nec findunt orbes secundum aristoteles. Cuius ymaginatio et possibilitas debet tradi in libro de theoria planetarum.

[5.7] Nec etiam in complexione humana sonus proprie reperitur. Quis enim audivit complexionem sonare?

[5.8] Genus autem tertium quod de instrumentali musica dicitur. In .3. distribuunt. puta in dyatonicum. Cromaticum. et enarmonicum. secundum que .3. concordantias monocordi procedere dicunt. Dyatonicum autem appellant quod procedit per tonum et tonum et semitonum, secundum quod fiunt ut plurimum cantilene. Cromaticum quod procedit per dyesim et semitonia .3. incomposita. et dicunt planetas uti tali cantu. Enarmonicum autem dicunt quod per dyesim et dyesym atque tonum procedit, quod dulcissimum dicunt eo quod angeli eo utuntur.

[5.9] Istam[74] autem divisionem non intelligimus. eo quod solum de instrumentali prosequuntur, membra alia dimittentes. **[42r]** Nec etiam pertinet ad musicum de cantu angelorum tractare nisi forte cum hic fuerit theologus aut propheta. Non enim potest aliquis de tali cantu experientiam habere nisi inspiratione divina. Et cum dicunt planetas cantare, videntur ignorare quid sit sonus sicut in divisione particularia dicebatur.

[5.10] Alii autem musicam dividunt in planam sive immensurabilem et mensurabilem. per planam sive immensurabilem[75] intelligentes ecclesiasticam, que secundum gregorium pluribus tonis determinatur. Per mensurabilem intelligunt illam que ex diversis sonis simul mensuratis et sonantibus efficitur. sicut in conductibus et motetis. Sed si per immensurabilem intelligant musicam nullo modo mensuratam immo totaliter ad libitum dictam: Deficiunt. eo quod quelibet operatio musice et cuiuslibet artis debet illius artis regulis mensurari. Si autem per immensurabilem non ita precise mensuratam intelligant, potest ut videtur ista divisio remanere.

[5.11] Quomodo igitur quidam dividunt musicam sic[76] sit dictum.

---

73 hoc] *om* **D1**
74 Ista **D1**
75 per planam sive immensurabilem] *om* **D1**

76 dividunt musicam sic] *post corr.* **H2**; dividunt sic **D1**, **H1**

[5.6] But those who divide in this way either construct their claim or wish to submit to the Pythagoreans or others more than to the truth, or are ignorant of nature and logic. For first they say universally music is concerning numbered sound. But celestial bodies in movement do not make a sound,[52] although the ancients believed this, nor do they plow through the orbs according to Aristotle, whose idea and hypothesis ought to be followed in the book *On the Theory of the Planets*.[53]

[5.7] Nor is sound properly to be found in the human constitution.[54] For who has heard a constitution sounding?

[5.8] The third kind, which is spoken of concerning instrumental music, they distribute into 3, namely into diatonic, chromatic, and enharmonic, according to which 3 they say the concords of the monochord proceed.[55] They call diatonic that which proceeds by tone and tone and semitone, according to which *cantilenae* are made for the most part.[56] Chromatic [is that] which proceeds by a *diesis* and 3 semitones in any order,[57] and they say that the planets use such *cantus*. They call enharmonic that which proceeds by a *diesis* and a *diesis* and a tone,[58] which they say is the sweetest in that the angels use it.[59]

[5.9] We do not understand this division since they only pursue the instrumental, leaving out the other branches. Nor does it pertain to a musician to discuss the *cantus* of the angels unless perchance when he is a theologian or a prophet. For no one can have experience of such *cantus* except by divine inspiration. And when they say "the planets sing," they seem to be ignorant of what a sound is, as was said in the particular division.

[5.10] Others divide music into plain or unmeasured, and measured, understanding by plain or unmeasured the ecclesiastical, which, according to Gregory, is determined by many tones. By measured they understand that which is made out of diverse sounds measured and sounding simultaneously, just as in *conducti* and motets. But if by unmeasured they understand music not measured in any way but rather uttered completely at will, they are wrong, since any operation of music and of any art ought to be measured by the rules of that art. If by unmeasured they understand not so precisely measured, it is possible that this division seems to remain.

[5.11] Let this therefore suffice for how certain people divide music.

[6.1] NObis vero non est facile musicam dividere recte, eo quod in recta divisione membra dividentia debent totam naturam totius divisi evacuare. Partes autem musice plures sunt et diverse secundum diversos usus: diversa ydiomata, vel diversas linguas in civitatibus vel regionibus diversis. Si tamen eam diviserimus secundum quod homines parisius ea utuntur, et prout ad usum vel convictum civium est necessaria, et eius membra ut oportet pertractemus, videbitur sufficienter nostra intentio terminari. Eo quod diebus nostris principia cuiuslibet artis liberalis diligenter parisius inquiruntur,⁷⁷ et usus earum et fere omnium mechanicarum inveniuntur.

[6.2] Dicamus igitur quod musica qua utuntur homines parisius, potest ut videtur ad .3. membra generalia reduci. Unum autem membrum dicimus de simplici musica vel civili, quam vulgalem musicam appellamus. Aliud autem de musica composita vel regulari vel canonica, quam appellant musicam mensuratam. Sed tertium genus est quod ex istis duobus efficitur et ad quod ista duo tamquam ad melius ordinantur:⁷⁸ Quod ecclesiasticum dicitur: Et ad laudandum⁷⁹ creatorem deputatum est.

[7.1] ANtequam autem de quolibet membro pertractemus sigillatim: Oportet nos illud quod est commune cuilibet pertractare.

[7.2] Hoc autem est modus describendi. Sicut enim grammatico fuit ars scribendi necessaria et inventio litterarum, ut dictiones inventas et ad signandum impositas mediante⁸⁰ scriptura reservaret: Sic musico est ars scribendi necessaria, ut diversos cantus ex diversis concordantiis compositos, ea mediante reservet.

[7.3] Et ideo quidam attendentes quod cantus penes acuitatem et gravitatem differebat, cordam unam vel lineam depingebant, respectu cuius gravitatem et acuitatem signabant. Secundum enim quod cantus magis acuebatur, secundum hoc notulas superponebant. Et secundum quod [**42v**] magis gravabatur, magis signa vel notulas supponebant.

[7.4] Isti autem per istum modum⁸¹ describendi inter diversas concordantias non potuerunt ponere differentiam.

[7.5] Et ideo alii considerantes ad numerum .15. cordarum cithare in quibus omnes consonantie et omnes concordantie tam simplices quam composite secundum eos inveniebantur cantum⁸² per .15. lineas depingere voluerunt.

---

77 inquirunt **D1**
78 ordinatur **D1**
79 laudandem **D1**
80 mediate **D1**

81 istum modum] modum istum **D1**
82 inveniebantur cantum] *post corr.* **H2**; inveniebantur. Sic cantum **D1, H1**

[6.1] But it is not easy for us to divide music correctly, since in a correct division the dividing branches ought to exhaust the full nature of the divided whole. The parts of music are many and diverse according to diverse uses, diverse idioms, or diverse tongues in diverse cities or regions. If, however, we divide it according to the use of the people in Paris, and just as is necessary for the use or community life of the citizens, and we consider its branches as is proper, our intention will be seen to be sufficiently accomplished. Because in our days the principles of any liberal art are carefully investigated in Paris, and the uses of these and of almost all mechanical arts are found.

[6.2] Let us say, therefore, that the music that people make use of in Paris can, as is evident, be reduced to 3 general branches. We say that one branch concerns simple or civil music, which we call music of the people. Another concerns composed or regulated or canonic music, which they call measured music. But the third kind is what is effected from these two and to which these two are, as it were, ordered for the better. This is called ecclesiastical, and it is assigned for the praise of the Creator.

[7.1] Before we consider any branch separately, we should consider what is common to any of them.

[7.2] This is our method of description. For just as for the grammarian the art of writing and the finding of letters was necessary, so that, by means of writing, he could preserve terms found and put in place to signify, so the art of writing is necessary for the musician, so that he may preserve diverse *cantus* composed from diverse concords by this means.

[7.3] And so certain people noticing that a *cantus* differed in its possessing height and depth drew one string or line with respect to which they indicated the depth and height. For as the *cantus* went up higher, so they placed the little marks higher. And as it went down lower, they placed the signs or little marks lower.

[7.4] These people were not able to establish a differentiation between diverse concords by this means of description.

[7.5] Others, therefore, considering the number, 15, of strings of the cithara in which were found—according to them—all consonances and all concords, both simple and compound, wished to depict *cantus* by means of 15 lines.[60]

[7.6] Sed adhuc intuenti apparet quod per istum modum omnes variationes depingere non potuerunt.[83] nec eis signa distinctiva tribuerunt.

[7.7] Et ideo alii subtiliori modo considerantes .19. dictiones ex .7. litteris et .6. vocibus compositas invenerunt quas gamaut. are. bemi. vocaverunt. In istis enim .19. dictionibus duplicem dyapason cum tono et dyapente invenerunt que omnes concordantias et consonantias tam simplices quam compositas comprehendebant: quibus etiam organum auditus contentum esse videtur. Istas autem dictiones in superficie monocordi extenderunt et ibi suas concordantias acuendo et gravando cordam per elongationem et abreviationem probaverunt. Dictiones autem predictas ex .7. litteris .scilicet. abcdefg. componebant ad numerum concordantiarum attendentes. Sed[84] ex .6. vocibus .scilicet. ex. ut re.[85] mi. fa. sol. la. forte rationem a pythagora vel ab arismeticis trahentes. Est enim numerus senarius primus in genere perfectorum. Isti[86] autem non potuerunt .19. dictiones ex .7. litteris et .6. vocibus efficere nisi easdem litteras et voces multotiens repeterent. Et ideo ab a. inceperunt usque[87] ad .6. continuantes[88] et iterum easdem litteras repetentes usque ad .19. unam autem litteram primo cum una sillaba addiderunt .scilicet. Gut. ut prime .scilicet. in subdupla proportione resonaret. Septem autem voces tono sunt[89] ad se invicem differentes: mifa exceptis, que semitonio differunt. Quas ita ordinaverunt in dictionibus ut in[90] hiis transcursis, iterum resumerentur. Et in una dictione oportuit plures voces esse, ut in eodem tono fieret vocum mutatio propter earum continuationem puta in una .2. ut in cfaut. dsolre. In alia[91] vero .3. ut in Gsolreut. alamire. ubi vero tantum due voces inveniuntur. et due mutationes inveniuntur, quia non possunt pluribus modis combinari. ut in cfaut. faut. et utfa. ubi vero .3. inveniuntur .6. mutationes sunt. ut in Gsolreut. solre. et resol. solut. et utsol. reut. et utre.[92] quia tot combinationes inter .3. voces possibiles sunt. Sed in bfabmi nullam dixerunt esse mutationem. eo quod mi. et fa. in eodem tono concordare non possint.[93] Sibi tamen duo signa sive .2. litteras attribuerunt. per unam autem tonum completum per aliam semitonum signaverunt. Et quia in istis dictionibus eedem littere et eedem voces pluries repetebantur, oportebat eos signa diversitatis inter easdem litteras et easdem voces invenire. Litteras igitur diversa

---

83 poterunt **D1**
84 scilicet **D1**
85 .scilicet. ex. ut re.] scilicet ut. re. **D1**, scilicet ex. re. **H1**
86 Istis **D1**
87 us **H1**; usque **D1**
88 .6. continuantes] .6. cum continuantes. **D1**

89 voces tono sunt] *post corr.* **H2**; voces sunt **D1**, **H1**
90 in] *om* **D1**
91 alio **D1**
92 ure **H1**; utre **D1**
93 possit **D1**

[7.6] But it is still obvious to anyone contemplating this that they could not depict all the variations by this means. Nor did they assign distinctive signs to them.

[7.7] Therefore others, considering this in a more subtle way, found 19 terms composed from 7 letters and 6 syllables which they called Gamma-ut, A-re, B-mi.[61] For in these 19 terms, they found a double *diapason* plus a tone and *diapente* which included all the concords and consonances, both simple and compound. And with these, the organ of hearing seems to be content. They extended these expressions to the surface of the monochord, and there they tested their concords by tightening and slackening the string by stretching or contracting it. They put together the above mentioned terms from 7 letters namely a b c d e f g, paying attention to the number of concords, but from 6 syllables, namely ut, re, mi, fa, sol, la, perhaps taking their reasoning from Pythagoras or from the arithmeticians. For the hexad number is the first in the genus of perfect numbers.[62] They could not make 19 terms from 7 letters and 6 syllables unless they repeated the same letters and syllables many times. And so they started from A, continuing for 6 [letters], and repeating the same letters again up to 19, they added one letter first with one syllable, namely Γ-ut, so that it resounds first, namely in subduple proportion. The seven voices are different from each other by a tone, save mi-fa, which differ by a semitone. They therefore arranged these in expressions, so that having run through them, they would start again. And it was necessary for there to be several syllables in one expression, so that there would be a mutation of syllables on the one tone on account of their overlapping, for example on one [there are] 2, as on C-fa-ut, D-sol-re. But on another, [there are] 3, as on G-sol-re-ut, a-la-mi-re. But where two syllables are found, and two mutations are found, [this is] because they cannot be combined in more ways, as on C-fa-ut: fa-ut and ut-fa. But where 3 are found, there are 6 mutations as on G-sol-re-ut: sol-re and re-sol, sol-ut and ut-sol, re-ut and ut-re, because all the combinations amongst these 3 syllables are possible. But on b-fa-b-mi they said there is no mutation since mi and fa cannot agree on the same tone. So they assigned for them two signs or 2 letters; through one they designated a complete tone, through the other a semitone. And since in these terms the same letters and the same syllables were repeated many times, it was necessary for them to find diversifying signs between the same letters and the same syllables. They therefore distinguished letters by diverse figuring and diverse naming, saying certain ones were grave, and figuring them one way, namely

figuratione et diversa nominatione distinxerunt. Quasdam dicentes graves et secundum unum modum eas figurantes. puta illas que sunt a primo .a. **[43r]** usque ad secundum. Alias vero acutas et secundum alium modum figurantes. puta illas que sunt a secundo .a. usque ad tertium. Residuas vero superacutas dixerunt figuram diversam omnimode tribuentes: Voces similiter per triplicem differentiam distinxerunt. quam. bquarre, naturam, bmolle, vocaverunt. Bequarre vero a primo ut inceperunt .scilicet. a Gut usque ad secundum continuantes. A secundo vero usque ad tertium naturam dixerunt. A tertio usque ad .4. bemolle vocaverunt. Et iterum bequarre naturam et bemolle resumentes usque ad ultimum continuaverunt. Et adhuc ut istas in superficie describerent alium modum diversitatis invenerunt dicentes unum lineam et aliud spatium. Incipientes a.[94] Gut. usque ad delasol procedentes, sic itaque apparet quod ponendo signa vel notas in lineis et spatiis omnes concordantias et omnem cantum sufficienter describere potuerunt.[95]

[7.8] Moderni vero propter descriptionem consonantiarum et stantipedum et ductiarum aliud addiderunt quod falsam musicam vocaverunt. quia illa duo signa .scilicet. ♭. et ♮. que in bfabmi tonum et semitonum designabant: In omnibus aliis faciunt hoc designare. Ita quod ubi erat semitonus per ♮. illud ad tonum ampliant ut bona concordantia vel consonantia fiat. Et similiter ubi tonus inveniebatur illud per ♭. ad semitonum restringunt.

[7.9] Ex hiis itaque universaliter apparere potest, qualiter cantus potest scribi, et in scriptis postea reservari.

[7.10] Quidam autem istam artem depingunt in superficie. et alii in .19. iuncturis manuum .19. dictiones cum suis litteris et sillabis figurant ut facilius novi auditores et pueri comprehendant.

[7.11] Hiis itaque tractatis[96] ad propositum redeamus quod erat notificare et pertractare sigillatim unumquodque membrum in divisione musice prius datum.

---

94 autem **D1**   96 itaque tractatis] itaque per tractatis **D1**
95 voluerunt **D1**

those that are from the first "A" up to the second, but others were acute, figuring them in another way, namely those that are from the second "a" up to the third. But they said the remaining ones were superacute, defining a different figure altogether. Similarly, they distinguished syllables through a threefold differentiation, which they called b-*quarre*, natural, b-*molle*.[63] But they began b-*quarre* from the first ut, namely continuing from Γ-ut to the second. But from the second to the third, they called natural. From the third to the 4th, they called b-*molle*. And again they continued taking b-*quarre*, natural, and b-*molle* up to the end. And further, so that they could describe these on a surface, they found another way of diversification, calling one a line and the other a space. Beginning from Γ-ut proceeding up to ^d_d-la-sol, so in this way by placing signs or notes on the lines and spaces, they were able to write out adequately all concords and every *cantus*.

[7.8] But the moderns have added something else which they have called false music, for the sake of writing down consonances, *stantipedes*, and *ductiae*, because those two signs—namely ♭ and ♮, which indicated the tone and the semitone on b-fa-b-mi—make them indicate this in all the others. As a result, where there was a semitone, they extend that to a tone through "a ♮," so that there may be a good concord or consonance. And similarly, where a tone was found, they reduce that to a semitone through "a ♭."

[7.9] From these it can therefore be seen universally how *cantus* can be written and subsequently be preserved in writing.

[7.10] Certain men represent this art on a surface, and others figure on the 19 joints of the hands 19 terms with their letters and syllables, so that new listeners and boys may understand more easily.

[7.11] So, having dealt with these things, let us return to the matter at hand, which was to make known, and deal individually with, each branch in the division of music given earlier.

[8.1] NOtificatio vero omnium istorum ex tribus est. primo enim ex cognitione universali que per diffinitionem vel descriptionem habetur. Secundo vero ex cognitione perfecta que in distinguendo et cognoscendo partes consistit. Sed tertio ex ultima que per cognitionem compositionis habetur. Sic enim cognoscuntur res naturales sive fuerint corpora simplicia sicut ignis. aer. aqua. terra. sive fuerint mixta vel mineralia sicut lapides et metalla. sive etiam fuerint animata sicut plante et animalia. unde aristoteles. in libro qui de[97] animalibus intitulatur sic notitiam de animalibus tradit. Primo enim ea notificavit confuse et universaliter et per anathomisationem et mores et proprietates eorum in libro qui de hystoriis dicitur. Secundo vero ea magis perfecte et determinate notificavit per partium cognitionem in libro qui de partibus appellatur. Sed tertio maxime notificavit ea per generationem vel eorum factionem. In quo cognitionem de animalibus ultimavit.

[9.1] DIcamus igitur quod forme musicales vel species contente sub primo membro quod vulgale dicebamus. ad hoc ordinantur, ut eis mediantibus mitigentur adversitates hominum innate **[43v]** quas magis particulavimus in sermone ad clementem exaquiensem[98] monacum. Et sunt duobus modis. Aut enim in voce humana. aut in instrumentis artificialibus exercentur.

[9.2] Que autem in voce humana fiunt .2. modis sunt. Aut enim dicimus cantum. Aut cantilenam. Cantum autem et cantilenam triplici differentia distinguimus. Aut enim gestualem. aut coronatum. aut versiculatum. Et cantilenam. rotundam. aut stantipedem. aut ductiam appellamus.

[9.3] Cantum vero gestualem dicimus in quo gesta heroum[99] et antiquorum patrum opera recitantur. Sicuti vita et martyria sanctorum, et prelia et[100] adversitates quas antiqui viri pro fide et veritate passi sunt. Sicuti[101] vita beati stephani prothomartyris. Et hystoria regis karoli: Cantus autem iste debet antiquis et civibus laborantibus et mediocribus ministrari dum requiescunt ab opere consueto. Ut auditis miseriis et calamitatibus aliorum suas facilius sustineant. Et quilibet opus suum alacrius agrediatur. Et ideo cantus iste[102] valet ad conservationem totius civitatis.

---

97 libro qui de] **D1**, *post corr.* **H2**; libro de **H1**
98 exaquiansem **D1**
99 herorum **D1**

100 prelia et] *om* **D1**
101 Sicut **D1**
102 cantus iste] iste cantus **D1**

[8.1] But awareness of all these is from three things: first from universal knowledge, which is had through definition or description; secondly from perfect knowledge, which consists in distinguishing and knowing the parts. But thirdly it is had from the last, which is had through knowledge of composition. For thus natural things are known whether they be simple bodies, such as fire, air, water, earth, or whether they be mixtures or minerals, such as stones and metals, or even if they be animated, such as plants and animals. In this way Aristotle passes on knowledge about animals in the book which is called *De animalibus*. For first he made those things known imprecisely and universally and through describing their parts and their behavior and properties, in the book which is called *De historiis*. Secondly, he made these things more perfectly and precisely known through knowledge of parts, in the book which is called *De partibus*. But thirdly, he made these things known most fully through their generation or making, in which he has finalized the knowledge of animals.[64]

[9.1] Let us therefore say that musical forms or species contained under the first branch, which we called [music] of the people, are ordained for this, so that through their mediation, the innate trials of humanity may be softened, which we have made out in more detail in a discourse to Clement, monk of Lessay.[65] And these are of two types. For they are realized either by the human voice or by artificial instruments.

[9.2] Those made with the human voice are of 2 types: for we speak of either *cantus* or *cantilena*. We differentiate *cantus* and *cantilena* in a threefold way: for we call the former either *gestualis* or *coronatus* or *versiculatus* and a *cantilena* either *rotundus* or *stantipes* or *ductia*.

[9.3] But we call *cantus gestualis* that in which the deeds of heroes and the achievements of our ancient fathers are recited, such as the life and martyrdom of saints, and the struggles and adversities that men of old suffered for faith and truth, such as the *Life of Blessed Stephen, Protomartyr,* and the *History of King Charlemagne.* That *cantus* ought to be provided for the aged and working citizens and ordinary people while they rest from their usual labor, so that, having heard about the miseries and disasters of others, they may more easily bear their own, and each one may approach his work more eagerly. And therefore this *cantus* is beneficial for the preservation of the whole city.

[9.4] Cantus coronatus ab aliquibus simplex conductus dictus est. Qui propter eius bonitatem—In dictamine et cantu a magistris et[103] studentibus circa
sonos coronatur. Sicut gallice. Ausi com lunicorne. vel Quant li roussignol.
Qui etiam a regibus et nobilibus solet componi. Et etiam coram regibus et
principibus terre decantari. ut eorum animos ad audaciam et fortitudinem
magnanimitatem et liberalitatem commoveat. Que omnia faciunt ad bonum
regimen. Est enim cantus iste de delectabili materia et ardua, sicut de amicitia
et karitate. Et ex omnibus longis et perfectis efficitur.

[9.5] Cantus versualis est qui ab[104] aliquibus cantilena dicitur respectu coronati et ab eius bonitate[105] in dictamine et concordantia deficit. Sicut gallice.
Chanter mesteut quer ne men puis tenir. vel. Au repairier que je fis de prouvence. Cantus autem iste debet iuvenibus exhiberi. Ne in otio totaliter sint
reperti. Qui enim refutat laborem et in otio vult vivere: ei labor et adversitas
est parata. unde seneca. Non est viri timere sudorem. Qualiter igitur[106] modi
cantus describuntur sic apparet.

[9.6] Cantilena vero quelibet rotunda vel rotundellus a pluribus dicitur eo
quod ad modum circuli in seipsam reflectitur et incipit et terminatur[107] in
eodem. Nos autem solum illam rotundam vel rotundellum dicimus cuius
partes non habent diversum cantum a cantu responsorii. vel refractus et longo
tractu cantatur velud cantus coronatus. Cuiusmodi est gallice. Toute sole
passerai levert boscage. Et huiusmodi[108] cantilena versus occidentem puta in
normannia solet decantari a puellis et iuvenibus in festis[109] et magnis conviviis
ad eorum **[44r]** decorationem.

[9.7] Cantilena que dicitur stantipes est illa in qua est diversitas in partibus
et refractu tam in consonantia dictaminis quam in cantu, sicut gallice. A lentrant damors. vel. certes mie ne cuidoie. Hec autem facit animos iuvenum et
puellarum propter sui difficultatem circa hanc stare et eos a prava cogitatione
divertit.

[9.8] Ductia vero est cantilena levis et velox et[110] ascensu et descensu que in
choreis[111] a iuvenibus et puellis decantatur. sicut gallice. Chi encor querez
amoretes. Hec enim ducit corda puellarum et iuvenum. et a vanitate removet.
et contra passionem que dicitur amor hereos valere dicitur.

103 et] *om* **D1**
104 ab] *om* **D1**
105 bonitatem **D1**
106 igitur] *om* **D1**
107 terminatus **D1**

108 huius **H1**; huiusmodi **D1**
109 festiis **D1**
110 in **D1**
111 choris **D1**

[9.4] *Cantus coronatus*[66] is called simple *conductus* by some, which, because of its excellence in text and *cantus*, is crowned by masters and students with sounds, as in the French *Ausi com l'unicorne*[67] or *Quant li rousignol.*[68] Indeed, it is normally composed by kings and nobles, and also sung before kings and princes of the earth, so that it may move their spirits to boldness and bravery, magnanimity, and liberality, which all make for good government. For this *cantus* is about delightful and lofty material, such as friendship and love. And it is made entirely from longs and perfects.

[9.5] *Cantus versualis* is what is called *cantilena* by some in comparison with *coronatus*, and it lacks the latter's excellence in text and concord, as in the French, *Chanter m'estuet, quer ne m'en puis tenir*[69] or *Au repairier que je fis de prouvence.*[70] This *cantus* ought to be performed for the young lest they fall completely into idleness. Labor and adversity has been prepared for him who rejects labor and wishes to live in idleness. Hence Seneca says, "It is not for a man to fear sweat."[71] Let this suffice, therefore, for how the types of *cantus* are described.

[9.6] But any round or *rotundellus*[72] is called a *cantilena* by many in that it turns back on itself like a circle and begins and is terminated at the same place. We only call it a round or *rotundellus* the parts of which do not have a *cantus* different from the *cantus* of the response or refrain and is sung in drawn-out longs, like the *cantus coronatus.* Of this type is in the French *Toute sole passerai le vert boscage.*[73] And a *cantilena* of this type is usually sung in the west, namely in Normandy, by girls and young men at feasts and at great celebrations for their enhancement.

[9.7] A *cantilena* which is called a *stantipes* is that in which there is diversity between the parts and the refrain, as much in the consonance of the text as in the *cantus*—as in the French *A l'entrant d'amors*[74] or *Certes mie ne cuidoie.*[75] This makes the spirits of young men and girls focus on it because of its difficulty and diverts them from depraved thought.

[9.8] But a *ductia* is a *cantilena* light and swift in both ascent and descent, which is sung in *caroles* by young men and girls, as in the French *Chi encor querez amoretes.*[76] For this draws the hearts of girls and young men and takes them away from vanity and is said to be effective against the passion which is called love sickness.

[9.9] Est autem[112] alius modus cantilenarum quem cantum insertum vel cantilenam entatam vocant. qui ad modum cantilenarum incipit et earum fine clauditur vel finitur. Sicut gallice. Je mendormi el sentier. Sic igitur apparet descriptio istorum tam cantuum quam cantilenarum.

[10.1] PArtes autem eorum multiplices dicuntur. ut versus. refractorium. vel responsorium. et additamenta.

[10.2] Versus autem in cantu gestuali qui ex pluribus versiculis efficitur et in eadem consonantia dictaminis cadunt. In aliquo tamen cantu clauditur per versum ab aliis consonantia discordantem. Sicut in gesta que dicitur de Girardo de viana. Numerus autem versuum in cantu gestuali non est determinatus sed secundum copiam materie et voluntatem compositoris ampliatur. Idem etiam cantus debet in omnibus versibus reiterari.

[10.3] Versus vero in cantu coronato est qui ex pluribus punctis et concordantiis ad se invicem armoniam facientibus efficitur. Numerus vero versuum in cantu coronato ratione .7. concordantiarum determinatus est ad .7. Tot enim versus debent totam sententiam materie nec plus nec minus continere.

[10.4] Versus vero in cantu versiculari illi de cantu coronato secundum quod potest assimilatur. Numerus vero versuum in tali cantu non est determinatus. sed in aliquibus plus in aliquibus minus secundum copiam materie et voluntatem compositoris ampliatur.

[10.5] Responsorium vero est quo omnis[113] cantilena incipit et terminatur.

[10.6] Additamenta vero differunt in rotundello ductia et stantipede. In rotundello vero consonant et concordant in dictamine cum responsorio. In ductia vero et stantipede differunt quedam et alia consonant et concordant. In ductia etiam et stantipede responsorium cum additamentis versus appellatur. Quorum numerus non est determinatus. sed secundum voluntatem compositoris et copiam sententie augmentatur.

[10.7] Hec itaque sunt partes cantus et cantilene diverse. De modo igitur componendi cantum et cantilenam nunc dicamus.

[11.1] MOdus autem componendi hec generaliter est unus quemadmodum[114] in natura. Primo enim dictamina loco materie preparantur. Postea vero cantus unicuique dictamini proportionalis loco forme introducitur. [44v] Dico autem unicuique proportionalis, quia alium cantum habet cantus gestualis et coronatus et versiculatus ut eorum descriptiones alie sunt quemadmodum[115] superius dicebatur.

112 etiam **D1**

113 omni **D1**

114 quamadmodum **D1**

115 quamadmodum **D1**

[9.9] There is another type of *cantilena* which they call *cantus insertus* or *cantilena entata*,[77] which begins, and at their end is closed or finished, in the way of *cantilenae*, such as in the French *Je m'endormi el sentier*.[78] Let this therefore suffice as a description of these, as much of *cantus* as of *cantilenae*.

[10.1] Multiple parts of these are spoken of, such as verse, refrain or response, and supplements.

[10.2] A verse in a *cantus gestualis* is what is constructed from several versicles; and they fall in the same consonance of text. In some *cantus*, however, it is closed by a verse discordant from the others in consonance [of text], as in the epic which is called *De Girardo de Viana*.[79] The number of verses in a *cantus gestualis* is not fixed but is extended according to the abundance of material and the will of the composer. Also, the same *cantus* ought to be repeated in all verses.

[10.3] But the verse in a *cantus coronatus* is that which is constructed of many *puncta* and concords making harmony with each other. But the number of verses in a *cantus coronatus*, by reason of the 7 concords, is fixed at 7. For so many verses ought to contain the whole statement of the material—neither more nor less.

[10.4] A verse in a *cantus versicularis* is as much like that of a *cantus coronatus* as it can be. But the number of verses in such a *cantus* is not fixed, but in some is extended more, in others less, according to the abundance of the material and the will of the composer.

[10.5] The response is that by which every *cantilena* begins and is terminated.

[10.6] The supplements are different in a *rotundellus*, a *ductia*, and a *stantipes*. But in a *rotundellus*, they are consonant and concordant in text with the responsory. But in a *ductia* and a *stantipes*, some things differ and others are consonant and concordant. Also in a *ductia* and a *stantipes*, the response with supplements is called a verse. Their number is not fixed but is increased according to the will of the composer and the abundance of the message.

[10.7] Thus these are the different parts of a *cantus* and a *cantilena*. So let us now discuss the way of composing a *cantus* and a *cantilena*.

[11.1] This way of composing is generally uniform just as in nature. For first texts are prepared as the material. A *cantus* suiting each text is subsequently introduced as form. I say "suiting each," because a different *cantus gestualis*, *coronatus*, and *versiculatus* has a different *cantus*, since their descriptions are different, just as was said above.

[11.2] De formis igitur, musicalibus que in voce humana exercentur hec dicta sint. De instrumentalibus vero nunc prosequamur.

[12.1] INstrumenta vero a quibusdam dividuntur divisione soni artificialis in eis generati. Dicunt enim sonum in instrumentis fieri afflatu. puta in tubis. calamis. fistulis. et organis. vel percussione. puta in cordis. tympanis. cymbalis et campanis. Sed si hec omnia subtiliter considerentur inveniuntur a percussione fieri cum omnis sonus percutiendo causetur. prout in sermonibus de anima comprobatum[116] est.

[12.2] Nos autem hic non intendimus instrumentorum compositionem vel divisionem nisi propter diversitatem formarum musicalium que in eis generantur. Inter que instrumenta cum cordis principatum optinent. Cuiusmodi sunt. psalterium. Cythara. lira. Quitarra sarracenica et viella. In eis enim subtilior et melior soni discretio[117] propter abreviationem et elongationem cordarum. Et adhuc inter omnia instrumenta cordosa visa a nobis, viella videtur prevalere. Quemadmodum[118] enim anima intellectiva alias formas naturales in se virtualiter includit ut[119] tetragonum trigonum et maior numerus minorem: Ita viella in se virtualiter alia continet instrumenta. Licet enim aliqua instrumenta[120] suo sono magis moveant animos hominum puta in festis, hastiludiis et torneamentis tympanum et tuba: In viella tamen omnes forme musicales subtilius discernuntur. Et ideo de hiis tantummodo nunc dicatur.

[12.3] Bonus autem artifex in viella omnem cantum et cantilenam et omnem formam musicalem generaliter introducit. Illa tamen que coram divitibus in festis et ludis fiunt communiter ad .3. generaliter reducuntur, puta cantum coronatum. ductiam et stantipedem.

[12.4] Sed de cantu coronato prius dictum est. De ductia igitur et stantipede nunc dicendum.

[12.5] Est autem ductia sonus illiteratus cum decenti percussione mensuratus. Dico autem illiteratus. quia licet in voca humana fieri possit et per figuras representari, non tamen per litteras scribi potest. quia littera et dictamine caret. Sed cum recta percussione, eo quod ictus eam mensurant et motus[121] facientis: Et excitant animum hominis ad ornate movendum secundum artem quam balare vocant, et eius motum mensurant in ductiis et choreis.

116 comprobantum **D1**
117 descriptio **D1**
118 Quamadmodum **D1**

119 ut] *post corr.* **H2**; et **D1, H1**
120 instrumenta] *om* **D1**
121 motum **D1**

[11.2] Therefore let these things be said of musical forms that are exercised in the human voice. But let us now pursue instrumental ones.

[12.1] But instruments are divided by certain people through division of the artificial sound generated in them. For they say that sound in instruments is made by blowing, as in trumpets, reed-pipes, pipes, and organs,[80] or by beating, as in strings, drums, cymbals, and bells.[81] If all these be considered carefully, they are found to be made by beating, since all sound is caused by beating, as has been shown in discourses about the soul.[82]

[12.2] Here we are not concerned with the composition or division of instruments except on account of the diversity of the musical forms that are generated in them. And amongst these, instruments with strings have primacy. Of this type are the psaltery, the cithara, the lyre, the Saracen guitar,[83] and the vielle. For in these the discernment of sound is more subtle and better on account of the shortening and lengthening of strings. And further, amongst all stringed instruments seen by us, the vielle is seen to prevail. For just as the intellective soul[84] contains other natural forms virtually in itself as the square the triangle and the greater number the lesser, so the vielle contains other instruments virtually in itself. Although some instruments move the spirits of men more by their sound, such as the drum and trumpet in feasts, spear games, and tournaments, in the vielle, however, all musical forms are more subtly discerned. And now in this way sufficient is said on these matters.

[12.3] The good artist generally introduces every *cantus* and *cantilena* and every musical form on the vielle. Those that commonly take place at feasts and games in the presence of the rich, however, are generally reduced to 3, namely *cantus coronatus*, *ductia*, and *stantipes*.

[12.4] But there has already been discussion about *cantus coronatus*. Therefore, the *ductia* and *stantipes* are now to be discussed.

[12.5] A *ductia* is an unlettered sound measured with an appropriate beat. I say "unlettered," because, although it can be made in the human voice and represented through figures, it cannot, however, be written in letters because it lacks letter and text. But with the correct beat insofar as the *ictus* measure it and the movement of the performer. And they arouse the spirit of man to move decorously according to the art which they call dancing, and they measure its movement in *ductiae* and *caroles*.

[12.6] Stantipes vero est sonus illiteratus habens difficilem concordantiarum discretionem per puncta determinatus. Dico autem habens difficilem et cetera. propter enim eius difficultatem facit animum facientis circa eam stare et etiam animum advertentis. Et multotiens animos divitum a prava cogitatione divertit. Dico etiam per puncta determinatus eo quod percussione que est in ductia[122] caret, et solum punctorum distinctione cognoscitur.

[13.1] **[45r]** PArtes autem ductie et stantipedis puncta communiter dicuntur.

[13.2] Punctus autem est ordinata agregatio concordantiarum armoniam facientium ascendendo et descendendo, duas habens partes in principio similes in fine differentes que[123] clausum et apertum communiter appellantur.[124] Dico autem duas habens partes et cetera, ad similitudinem duarum linearum, quarum una sit maior alia: maior enim minorem claudit, et est fine differens a minori.

[13.3] Numerus vero punctorum in ductia ad numerum .3. consonantiarum perfectarum[125] attendentes ad .3. posuerunt. Sunt tamen alique note vocate .4. punctorum que ad ductiam vel stantipedem imperfectam reduci possunt. Sunt etiam alique ductie .4. habentes puncta puta ductia pierron.

[13.4] Numerum vero punctorum in stantipede quidam ad .6. posuerunt ad rationes vocum inspicientes. Alii tamen de novo inspicientes forte ad numerum .7. concordantiarum vel naturali inclinatione ducti. puta tassynus, numerum ad .7. augmentant.[126] Huiusmodi autem stantipedes sunt res[127] cum .7. cordis. vel difficiles res tassyni.

[14.1] COmponere ductiam et stantipedem est sonum per puncta et rectas percussiones in ductia et stantipede determinare: quemadmodum[128] enim materia naturalis per formam naturalem determinatur. ita sonus determinatus per[129] puncta et per formam artificialem ei ab artifice attributam.

[14.2] Quid igitur sit ductia et stantipes.[130] Et que earum partes. et que earum compositio sic sit dictum. In quo propositum de simplici seu vulgali musica terminatur.

[14.3] De musica igitur composita et regulari sermonem perquiramus.

122 est in ductia] **D1**, *post corr.* **H2**; est ductia **H1**
123 qui **D1**
124 appellatur **D1**
125 consonantiarum perfectarum] consonantiarum et perfectarum **D1**
126 augmentat **D1**

127 stantipedes sunt res] *post corr.* **H2**; stantipedes res **D1, H1**
128 quamadmodum **D1**
129 determinatus per] determinatus est per **D1**
130 stantipedes **D1**

[12.6] A *stantipes* is an unlettered sound, having a difficult distinction of concords determined through *puncta*. I say "having a difficult" etc., since, because of its difficulty, it makes the spirit of the performer and also the spirit of the observer focus on it. And often it diverts the minds of the rich from depraved thought. I also say "determined through *puncta*" in that it lacks the beating that is in the *ductia*, and it is recognized through the distinction of *puncta* alone.

[13.1] The parts of a *ductia* and *stantipes* are in general called *puncta*.

[13.2] A *punctus* is an ordered assemblage of concords making harmony by ascending and descending, having two parts similar in the beginning, different at the end, which are commonly called closed and open. I say "having two parts" etc., in the likeness of two lines, of which one may be greater than the other; for the greater encloses the lesser and it is different from the lesser at the end.

[13.3] But the number of *puncta* in a *ductia* they placed at 3, paying attention to the number, 3, of perfect consonances. There are some called *notae*, however, with 4 *puncta* that can be rendered as a *ductia* or an imperfect *stantipes*. There are also some *ductia* having 4 *puncta* such as the *ductia Pierron*.[85]

[13.4] But the number of *puncta* in a *stantipes* certain people placed at 6, looking at the rationale of the syllables. Others, however, perhaps considering afresh the number of concords, 7, or led by natural inclination, raise the number to 7, for example Tassinus.[86] *Stantipedes* of this type are pieces with 7 "strings," or the difficult pieces of Tassinus.

[14.1] To compose a *ductia* and a *stantipes* is to determine sound in a *ductia* and a *stantipes* through *puncta* and correct beating. For just as natural material is determined through natural form, so sound is determined through *puncta* and through the artificial form given to it by the artist.

[14.2] Let this suffice, therefore, for what a *ductia* and *stantipes* are and what their parts and composition are. In this, the subject of simple [music] or music of the people is concluded.

[14.3] Let us therefore pursue a discussion about composed and regulated music.

[15.1] QUidam autem per experientiam attendentes ad consonantias tam perfectas quam imperfectas cantum ex duobus compositum invenerunt. Quem quintum et discantum seu duplum organum appellarunt. Et de hoc plures regulas invenerunt. ut apparet eorum tractatus aspicienti. Si tamen aliquis predictas consonantias sufficienter cognoverit, ex modicis regulis poterit talem cantum et eius partes et eius compositionem cognoscere. Sunt enim aliqui qui ex industria naturali et per usum, talem cantum cognoscunt, et componere[131] sciunt.

[15.2] Sed alii ad .3. consonantias perfectas attendentes cantum ex .3. compositum uniformi mensura regulatum invenerunt. quem[132] cantum precise mensuratum vocaverunt. Et isto cantu moderni parum[133] utuntur. quem[134] antiqui pluribus modis diviserunt.

[15.3] Nos vero secundum usum modernorum in .3. generaliter dividimus puta motetos. organum. et cantum abscisum. quem hoquetos vocant.

[15.4] Et quoniam mensurari et modus mensurandi cum arte describendi vel signandi commune est omnibus hiis, oportet de hiis dicere antequam de singulis tractemus.

[16.1] OMne[135] autem mensurans[136] prima mensura utitur aut eius virtute operatur, quemadmodum[137] **[45v]** omne movens in virtute primi moventis. Primum enim in unoquoque genere causa est omnium posteriorum. ut in .10o.[138] prime philosophie scriptum est. Prima autem mensura tempus dicitur sive in re fuerit sive secundum intellectum[139] tantum. Est enim tempus mensura motus et est[140] primi motus et primi mobilis et ex consequenti[141] cuiuslibet alterius prout a philosopho[142] subtiliter perscrutatur.

[16.2] Istam autem mensuram antiqui consideratores ad sonos et voces applicaverunt, quam tempus communi nomine vocaverunt.

[16.3] Est autem tempus prout hic specialiter accipitur illud spatium in quo minima vox vel minimus sonus plenarie profertur seu proferri potest. Dico autem spatium in quo et cetera. quia pausa quemadmodum[143] sonus mensuratur. Ista autem mensura totum cantum mensurat quemadmodum[144] una revolutio totum tempus. Est enim tamquam regula policleti.

131 compositionem **D1**
132 quam **D1**
133 parisius **D1**
134 quam **D1**
135 Omnem **D1**
136 omne autem mensurans *in marg.* **D2**
137 quamadmodum **D1**

138 .10. **D1**
139 intellectu **D1**
140 etiam **D1**
141 sequenti **D1**
142 phisico **D1**
143 quamadmodum **D1**
144 quamadmodum **D1**

[15.1] Certain people paying attention through experience to consonances, as much to perfect as to imperfect,[87] have found *cantus* put together from both of them, which they called fifthing and *discant* or *organum duplum*.[88] And they have discovered many rules about this, as is apparent to one considering their treatises. If, however, anyone knows the aforementioned consonances sufficiently, he will be able to recognize such *cantus* and its parts and its composition through modest rules, for there are some people who recognize and know how to compose such *cantus* out of natural effort and through practice.

[15.2] But others paying attention to the 3 perfect consonances found *cantus* put together from 3 of them, regulated by a uniform measure, which they have called precisely measured *cantus*. And the moderns little use that *cantus* which the ancients divided in several ways.

[15.3] But we generally divide into 3 according to the practice of the moderns, namely motets, *organum*, and *cantus abscisus*, which they call hockets.

[15.4] And since being measured and the way of being measured with the art of writing down or notating is common to all these, it is appropriate to speak about these before we treat each one in turn.

[16.1] All that measures uses a prime measure, or works by virtue of it,[89] just as all that moves does so by virtue of a prime mover.[90] For in each genus, the first thing is the cause of all that follows, as has been written in the 10th [book] of the *First Philosophy*.[91] The first measure is called *tempus*, whether it be in the thing itself or in the intellect only. For *tempus* is the measure of motion,[92] both of the first motion and of the *primum mobile* and of whatever else that follows, just as is investigated carefully by the Philosopher.

[16.2] Ancient thinkers applied this measure to sounds and voices, which they called by a common name *tempus*.

[16.3] *Tempus*, as specifically accepted here, is that space in which the smallest voice or the smallest sound is fully articulated or can be articulated. I say "space in which" etc., because a pause is measured just like a sound.[93] This measure measures all *cantus* just as one rotation [measures] all time. For this is just like the Rule of Polykleitos.[94]

[16.4] Istam vero mensuram quidam in .2. equalia dividunt. Alii in .3. et sic de aliis. usque ad .6. Nos autem dicimus eam in infinitum divisibilem. eo quod rationem continui participat. Quoniam tamen sonis et vocibus applicatur dicimus eam[145] divisibilem usque ad hoc quod auditus discretionem percipere possit.

[16.5] Isti autem mensure alii ampliorem addiderunt, quam perfectionem appellarunt. Est autem perfectio mensura ex .3. temporibus constans. Quemadmodum enim in corporibus ex trina dimensione attenditur perfectio: Ita in sonis ex tribus temporibus perfectionem vocaverunt.[146] Ista autem mensura moderni utuntur. et hac[147] totum suum cantum et cantando et figurando mensurant. Quemadmodum enim .3. linee extense una communi mensura mensurantur[148] et eadem adinvicem coequantur. Ita .3. cantus vel plures predicta mensura intendimus mensurare.[149]

[17.1] IStam autem mensuram diversi per diversos modos distinxerunt. Quidam enim per .6. distinxerunt, rationem[150] a numero vocum accipientes qui senarius dicitur. Est enim inter perfectos primus, prout ab arismetico declaratur.

[17.2] Primum autem modum dixerunt quando .2. tempora in eodem tono et in[151] eadem figura representantur[152] et post, unde sequitur una figura designatum.

[17.3] Secundum vero econtrario.

[17.4] Sed tertium dixerunt cum .3. tempora una figura eodem tono designantur. et postea figuris similibus et disiunctis similiter perfectio designatur.

[17.5] Quartum vero econtrario.

[17.6] Et quintum cum[153] tempus post tempus diversis tonis eadem figura designatur.

[17.7] Sed sextum cum perfectio in eodem tono eadem figura designatur. et ei perfectio continuatur in eodem tono vel alio figura consimili designata. Et sic distinguebat magister .Iohannes. de guearlandia.[154]

---

145 autem **D1**
146 vocaverat **H1**; vocaveru[n]t **D1**
147 hic **D1**
148 mensuratur **D1**
149 mensurari **D1**

150 ratione **D1**
151 in] *om* **D1**
152 representatur **D1**
153 cum] *post corr.* **H2**; cum **D1**; quod **H1**
154 guerlandia **D1**

[16.4] But certain people divide this measure into 2 equals, others into 3, and so on for others up to 6. We say it is divisible to infinity, in that it shares the quality of a continuum.[95] Since, however, it is applied to sounds and voices, we say that it is divisible to the point that hearing can perceive a distinction.[96]

[16.5] To this measure others added a fuller one, which they called a perfection. A perfection is a measure consisting of 3 *tempora*. For just as in bodies a perfection is reached from a threefold dimension, so in sounds they have called it a perfection from three *tempora*. The moderns use this measure, and by this they measure all their *cantus* both in singing and in figuring. For just as 3 extended lines are measured by one common measure and by the same are made equal to each other, so we intend to measure 3 or more *cantus* by the aforesaid measure.

[17.1] Different people have distinguished this measure through different modes. For some have distinguished it through 6, which is called the hexad, taking their reasoning from the number of syllables. For it is the first among perfect numbers, just as is declared by the Arithmetician.

[17.2] They have called the first mode when 2 *tempora* are represented on the same tone and in the same figure and subsequently, whence follows [a *tempus*] designated by one figure.

[17.3] But the second is the reverse.

[17.4] But they have called the third when 3 *tempora* are designated on the same tone by one figure, and afterwards a perfection is similarly designated by figures similar and distinct.

[17.5] But the fourth is the reverse.

[17.6] And the fifth is when *tempus* after *tempus* on diverse tones is designated by the same figure.

[17.7] But the sixth is when a perfection is designated on the same tone by the same figure, and a perfection follows it designated on the same tone or another by a similar figure. And this is how Master Johannes de Garlandia used to distinguish them.[97]

[17.8] Sed lambertus et alii istos modos ad .9. ampliaverunt ex .9. instrumentis[155] naturalibus fantasiam adsumentes. Primum enim dixerunt qui ex perfectionibus continuatur figura simili designatis. **[46r]** Et alios ex tempore et eius partibus composuerunt.

[17.9] Sed forte si aliquis tempus ad perfectionem comparaverit vel econtrario, et tempus ad suas partes inveniet multo plures.

[17.10] Alii autem istos modos ad .5. per reductionem posuerunt. puta magister franco. Reductio tamen ut videtur pluralitatem non impedit. Quamquam enim omnis sillogismi ad .4. primos reducuntur: propter hoc non est eorum pluralitas impedita. Et forte qui .6. modos posuerunt melius dixerunt. plurimi enim modernorum adhuc eis utuntur et ad illos omnes suos cantus reducunt. Si vero fuerint tantum .6. sive plures sive pauciores parum differt. quia eadem mensura utrobique reservatur.

[17.11] Postquam itaque de mensura et modo mensurandi diximus. Dicamus qualiter cantus designatur et per que signa representatur.

[18.1] YMaginatur autem cantus unus vel plures quemadmodum[156] una linea determinata quantitate uniformi regula mensurata vel plures linee sic adinvicem coequate.

[18.2] Sed sonus in voce humana non potest diu continuari immo oportet pausare et pausam aliquo modo designare. quam antiqui per lineam ex transverso[157] positam designaverunt: et adhuc ista moderni utuntur. sive pausa universalis sit quam finem punctorum appellant. sive sit unius perfectionis vel plurium sive .2. temporum sive unius, sive alicuius partis temporis maioris vel equalis.

[18.3] Et ad sonum representandum quedam signa generalia et figuras indeterminatas inveniebant, per quas non potuerunt sufficienter cantum vel sonum representare. Et ideo alii determinationem addiderunt: posuerunt enim unam figuram quadratam habentem lineam recte descendentem et[158] ascendentem a parte dextra. Quam longam appellaverunt. Et eam per duplicem longam perfectam et imperfectam diviserunt.

[18.4] Aliam autem posuerunt quadratam[159] simplicem quam brevem vocaverunt. Et eam per rectam brevem[160] et alteram brevem diviserunt.

155 instrumentibus **D1**

156 quamadmodum **D1**

157 transverso] *post corr.* **H2**; traverso **D1, H1**

158 vel **D1**

159 quadrata **D1**

160 rectam brevem] brevem rectam **D1**

[17.8] But Lambertus and others have extended these modes to 9 basing their conjecture on the 9 natural instruments.[98] For they called the first that which is extended from perfections designated by a similar figure. And they composed the others from *tempus* and its parts.

[17.9] But if anyone happens to compare a *tempus* to a perfection or the reverse and a *tempus* to its parts, he will find many more.

[17.10] Others have put these modes at 5 through reduction, like Master Franco.[99] But, as is apparent, reduction does not prevent plurality. For although all syllogisms are reduced to 4 basic ones,[100] their plurality is not prevented because of this. And perhaps those who have posited 6 modes have spoken better. For many of the moderns still use these and reduce all their *cantus* to these. But if there are only 6 or more or less, it makes little difference, because the same measure is kept in both instances.

[17.11] And so after we have spoken about measure and the way of measuring, let us speak of how *cantus* is designated and by what signs it is represented.

[18.1] One *cantus* or several is imagined just as one line, fixed in quantity, measured by a uniform rule, or as several lines made commensurable with each other in this way.

[18.2] But sound in the human voice cannot be sustained for long; on the contrary, it is necessary to pause and to designate a pause in some way. This the ancients designated with a line placed crosswise; and the moderns still use this, whether it be a universal pause which they call *finis punctorum* or whether it is of one perfection or of several, or of 2 *tempora* or of one or of any part of a *tempus*, greater or equal.[101]

[18.3] And they used to invent certain general signs and indeterminate figures in order to represent sound, by which they were not able to represent *cantus* or sound adequately. And so others added a specification. For they placed one square figure, having a line correctly descending or ascending from the right-hand part, which they called a long, and they divided it in a twofold way: a perfect and an imperfect long.[102]

[18.4] They posited another simple square, which they called a breve, and distinguished it into a proper breve and an altered breve.[103]

[18.5] Tertia vero figura fuit habens angulos ex opposito se respicientes equales. Adinvicem autem inequales.[161] quam semibrevem vocaverunt. Et quemadmodum[162] gramaticus ex paucis litteris earum coniunctione et situatione potest dictionem quamlibet designare: Et artificialiter numerans ex paucis figuris earum prepositione et postpositione numerum quemlibet infinitum designare: Ita musicus ex .3. figuris cantum quemlibet[163] mensuratum. Per longam enim potest perfectionem vel .2. tempora significare: puta per perfectam perfectionem: et per imperfectam .2. tempora. Sed per brevem tempus vel .2. tempora. Per dictam vero semibrevem partes temporis designantur.[164]

[18.6] Et ulterius cum cantus aliquotiens sit sine dictamine et discretione sillabarum: ut signum signato responderet oportuit hec [**46v**] ligatione figurarum representare. unde et ex bonitate artis que breviora querit, superflua eiciens, regulam acceperunt. quod ubicumque potest poni figura ligata non debet apponi pluralitas figurarum. Fecerunt igitur figuras ligatas[165] ex .2. vel .3. vel pluribus quas per diversas differentias tam a parte principii quam a parte finis distinxerunt. A parte vero principii per lineas descendentes et ascendentes tam a dextra quam a sinistra. Quas cum proprietate et cum opposita proprietate et suas oppositas vocaverunt.

[18.7] Istis autem figuris diversimode significationem tribuerunt. unde sciens cantare et exprimere cantum secundum quosdam. secundum[166] alios non est sciens: Omnium autem istorum diversitas apparebit diversos tractatus aliorum intuenti. Nos vero hic non intendimus istorum diversitates enarrare nec ad omnia particularia descendere. sed secundum posse nostrum sicut in libro galieni qui dicitur tegni traduntur canones universales artis medicine. Nimius enim descensus circa particularia fastidium generat et plures revocat a cognitione veritatis: Plurimi tamen modernorum parisius utuntur figuris prout in arte magistri franconis sumuntur.

[18.8] De mensura itaque et modo mensurandi[167] et modo designandi vel describendi cantum, universaliter hec dicantur. Sequens igitur est dicere de mensuratis quid unumquodque[168] sit et que partes eorum et qualiter componantur.

---

161 equales **D1**
162 quamadmodum **D1**
163 quamlibet **D1**
164 desig[n]atur **D1**
165 figuras ligatas] ligatas figuras **D1**

166 quosdam. secundum] quosdam et secundum **D1**
167 item significat es *in marg.* **H3**
168 unumque **D1**

[18.5] But there was a third figure which they called a semibreve, having opposite angles equal to each other, adjacent unequal.[104] And just as the grammarian is able to designate any term out of a few letters by their conjunction and placement, and someone numbering by artifice any unbounded number with a few figures by placing them before and after, so a musician [can designate] any measured *cantus* from 3 figures. For with a long it is possible to signify a perfection or 2 *tempora*, namely through the perfect perfection, or through the imperfect 2 *tempora*. But through the breve, a *tempus* or 2 *tempora*; but through the breve, a *tempus* or 2 *tempora*; but through the said semibreve, parts of a *tempus* are designated.

[18.6] And further, since a *cantus* is sometimes without a text and a separation of syllables, it is necessary to represent these things by a binding of figures, in order that the sign correspond to what is signified. Whence, rejecting superfluous things, from the goodness of the art that seeks brevity, they accepted the rule that wherever a ligated figure can be put,[105] a plurality of figures should not be put. Therefore, they made ligated figures from 2 or 3 or more which they distinguished into diverse differentiations, as much from the part of the beginning as from the part of the end, but from the part of the beginning through ascending and descending lines as much on the right as on the left. These they called with propriety and with opposite propriety and their opposites.[106]

[18.7] They assigned signification to these figures in diverse ways, whence according to some one knows how to sing and proclaim *cantus*; according to others, one does not know. The diversity of all these will be evident to anyone considering the diverse treatises of others. But we do not intend to expound their diversities here, nor to go into all the details, but [intend to expound] according to our ability, just as the universal rules of the art of medicine are handed down in the book of Galen, which is called *Tegni*.[107] For too much descent into details generates scorn and restrains many from knowledge of the truth. But very many of the moderns in Paris use figures just as are taken up in the *Art* of Master Franco.[108]

[18.8] Therefore, let these suffice universally about measure, the way of measuring and the way of designating or writing down *cantus*. What follows, therefore, is a discussion about the measured, what each might be, and what are their parts and how they are composed.

[19.1] MOtetus[169] vero est cantus ex pluribus compositus habens plura dictamina vel multimodam discretionem sillabarum. utrobique armonialiter consonans. Dico autem ex pluribus compositus eo quod ibi sunt .3. cantus vel .4: Plura[170] autem dictamina. quia quilibet debet habere discretionem sillabarum tenore excepto. Qui in aliquibus habet dictamen et in aliquibus non: Sed dico utrobique armonialiter consonans eo quod quilibet debet cum alio consonare secundum aliquam perfectarum consonantiarum puta secundum dyatessaron. vel dyapente. vel dyapason. De quibus superius diximus cum de principiis tractabamus.

[19.2] Cantus autem iste non debet coram vulgalibus propinari. eo quod eius subtilitatem non advertunt nec in eius auditu delectantur. Sed coram litteratis et illis qui subtilitates artium sunt querentes. Et solet in eorum festis decantari ad eorum decorationem,[171] quemadmodum[172] cantilena que dicitur rotundellus in festis vulgalium laycorum.[173]

[19.3] Organum vero prout hic sumitur est cantus ex pluribus armonice compositus, unum tantum habens[174] dictamen vel discretionem sillabarum. Dico autem tantum habens unum dictamen. eo quod omnes cantus fundantur super unam discretionem sillabarum.

[19.4] Cantus autem iste dupliciter variatur. Est enim quidam qui supra cantum determinatum puta ecclesiasticum fundatur qui ecclesiis vel locis sanctis decantatur ad dei laudem et [47r] reverentiam summitatis. Et[175] cantus iste appropriato nomine organum appellatur. Alius autem fundatur supra cantum cum eo compositum qui solet in conviviis et festis coram litteratis et divitibus decantari. Et ex hiis nomen trahens appropriato nomine conductus appellatur. Communiter tamen loquentes totum hoc organum dicunt. et sit communis est eis descriptio supradicta.

[19.5] Hoquetus est cantus abscisus ex duobus vel pluribus compositus. Dico autem ex pluribus compositus. quia licet abscisio vel truncatio sit sufficiens inter .2. possunt tamen esse plures. ut cum truncatione consonantia sit perfecta.

169 motetus quid *in marg.* **H3**
170 Possibil[i]a **D1**
171 decorationem] *post corr.* **H2**; corationem **D1**, **H1**

172 quamadmodum **D1**
173 organum quid *in marg.* **H3**
174 tantum habens] habens tantum **D1**
175 Est **D1**

[19.1] But a motet is *cantus* composed from many, having several texts, or multifaceted differentiation of syllables, sounding together in harmony on all sides. I say "composed from many," in that there are 3 *cantus* or 4, "several texts," because any one of these ought to have a differentiation of syllables, apart from the tenor, which has a text in some and not in others. But I say "sounding in harmony on all sides," in that any ought to sound with another according to any of the perfect consonances, namely according to the *diatessaron* or *diapente* or *diapason*, about which we spoke earlier when we were considering principles.

[19.2] This *cantus* ought not to be celebrated in the presence of common people, because they do not notice its subtlety, nor are they delighted in hearing it, but in the presence of the educated and of those who are seeking out subtleties in the arts. And it is customarily sung at their feasts for their enhancement, just as the *cantilena* that is called a *rotundellus* at feasts of the common laity.

[19.3] But *organum*, as accepted here, is *cantus* composed harmonically from many, having only one text or differentiation of syllables. I say "having only one text," because all *cantus* are founded on a single differentiation of syllables.

[19.4] This *cantus* is varied in two ways. For there is one that is founded on a fixed *cantus*, namely the ecclesiastical, which is sung in churches or holy places to the praise of God and the reverence of the Most High. And this *cantus* is called by the appropriated name *organum*. The other is founded on a *cantus* composed with it that is usually sung at banquets and feasts in the presence of the educated and the rich. And taking its name from these, it is called by the appropriated name *conductus*. People speaking commonly, however, call all this *organum*, and thus the description above is common to these.

[19.5] A hocket is an interrupted *cantus* composed from two or more. I say "composed from . . . more" because, while an interruption or truncation may be sufficient between 2, there can be more, nonetheless, so that the consonance with truncation may be perfect.

[19.6] Cantus autem iste colericis et iuvenibus appetibilis est propter sui mobilitatem et velocitatem. Simile enim sibi simile querit et[176] in suo simili delectatur.

[20.1] PArtes autem istorum plures sunt. puta. Tenor. Motetus. Triplum. Quadruplum. Et in hoquetis. Primus. Secundus. Et ultimo eorum duplum.

[20.2] Tenor autem est illa pars supra quam omnes alie fundantur. Quemadmodum partes domus vel edificii super suum fundamentum. Et eas regulat et eis dat quantitatem[177] quemadmodum[178] ossa partibus aliis.

[20.3] Motetus vero est cantus ille qui[179] supra tenorem immediate ordinatur. Et in dyapente ut plurimum incipit. et in eadem proportione qua incipit continuatur vel a[180] dyapason ascendit. Et in hoquetis ab aliquibus dicitur magistrans. ut in hoqueto qui dicitur. Ego mundus.

[20.4] Triplum vero est cantus ille qui supra tenorem in dyapason proportione incipere debet et in eadem proportione, ut plurimum continuari. Dico autem ut plurimum. quia aliquotiens in tenore vel dyapente descendit propter euphoniam. quemadmodum[181] motetus aliquando in dyapason ascendit.

[20.5] Quadruplum vero est cantus qui aliquibus additur propter consonantiam perficiendam. Dico autem aliquibus et cetera. quia in aliquibus sunt tantum .3. et ibi sufficiunt[182] cum perfecta consonantia ex .3. causetur.[183] In aliquibus vero .4us. additur. ut[184] dum unus trium pausat, vel ornate ascendit.[185] vel duo adinvicem se truncant. quartus consonantiam servet.[186]

[20.6] Primus vero in hoquetis est qui primo truncare incipit.

[20.7] Sed secundus qui secundo post primum truncat.

[20.8.] Duplum vero est qui cum tenore minutam facit abscisionem. Et cum eo aliquotiens in dyapente consonat. et aliquando in dyapason proportione. Ad quod multum iuvat bona discretio decantantis.[187]

---

176 et] *om* **D1**
177 dat quantitatem] quanti[ta]tem dat **D1**
178 Quamadmodum **D1**
179 que **D1**
180 a] *om* **D1**
181 quamadmodum **D1**

182 faciunt **D1**
183 causentur **D1**
184 et **D1**
185 ascenderit **D1**
186 servet] *post corr.* **H2**; servat **D1, H1**
187 decantatis **D1**

[19.6] This *cantus* appeals to the hotheaded and the young because of its mobility and speed. For like seeks out like for itself and delights in its own likeness.[109]

[20.1] The parts of these are many, namely tenor, *motetus, triplum, quadruplum*; and in hockets, *primus, secundus*, and finally the *duplum* of these.

[20.2] The tenor is that part on which all the others are founded, just as the parts of a house or a building on their foundation. And it regulates them and gives them quantity, just as bones to other parts.

[20.3] But a *motetus* is that *cantus* which is ordered immediately above the tenor. And it begins on the *diapente*, as many do, and is continued in the same proportion in which it begins or ascends in relation to the *diapason*. And in hockets it is called by some the *magistrans*, as in the hocket called *Ego mundus*.[110]

[20.4] But the *triplum* is that *cantus* which ought to begin above the tenor in the proportion of the *diapason* and to be continued in the same proportion as many do. I say "as many do," because often it descends to the tenor or the *diapente* for euphony, just as the *motetus* sometimes ascends to the *diapason*.

[20.5] But the *quadruplum* is a *cantus* that is added to some in order to perfect the consonance. I say "to some" etc., because in some there are as many as 3 and there they suffice since a perfect consonance is caused from 3. But in some a 4th is added so that while one of the three pauses or ascends ornately, or two mutually truncate themselves, the fourth preserves the consonance.

[20.6] But in hockets the *primus* is what begins to truncate first.

[20.7] But the *secundus* is what truncates second after the *primus*.

[20.8.] But the *duplum* is that which brings about a small interruption with the tenor, and it often sounds together with it in the *diapente* and sometimes in the *diapason* proportion, for which the good judgment of the singer helps a great deal.

[21.1] VOlens autem ista componere, primo debet tenorem ordinare vel componere, et ei modum et mensuram dare. Pars enim principalior debet formari primo. Quoniam ea mediante postea formantur alie: Quemadmodum[188] natura in generatione animalium primo format membra principalia. puta. Cor. Epar. Cerebrum. Et illis mediantibus alia post formantur. Dico autem ordinare. quoniam in motellis et organo tenor ex cantu antiquo est et prius composito. Sed ab artifice [47v] per modum et rectam mensuram amplius determinatur. Et dico componere. quoniam in conductibus tenor totaliter fit et secundum voluntatem artificis modificatur et durat.

[21.2] Tenore autem composito vel ordinato debet supra eum motetum componere vel ordinare. qui ut plurimum cum tenore in dyapente proportione resonat et propter sui armoniam aliquotiens ascendit vel descendit.

[21.3] Sed ulterius debet istis triplum superaddi. Qui cum tenore ut plurimum debet in dyapason proportione resonare. Et propter sui armoniam potest in locis mediis sistere vel usque ad dyapente aliquotiens descendere.

[21.4] Et quamquam ex istis .3. consonantia perficiatur. potest tamen eis aliquotiens decenter addi quadruplum qui cum alii cantus descendent vel ascendent ordinate,[189] vel abscisionem facient, vel pausabunt, consonantiam resonabit.

[21.5] In componendo[190] vero organum, modorum alternationem quam plurimum faciunt. Sed in componendo motellos et alia: modorum unitatem magis servant.

[21.6] Et cum in[191] motellis plura sint dictamina. Si unum sillabis vel dictionibus alium excedat. potes eum per appositionem brevium et semibrevium alteri coequare.[192]

[21.7] Volens autem hoquetum ex duobus puta primo et secundo componere: debet cantum vel cantilenam supra quem[193] fit hoquetus partiri et[194] unicuique partem distribuere. et potest aliquantulum rectus cantus exire cum decenti additione nisi quod eius mensuram observet. Sic enim unus iacet super alium ad modum tegularum[195] et cooperture domus. et sic continua abscisio fiet.

188 Quamadmodum **D1**
189 ordinantem **D1**
190 In componendo] Imponendo **D1**
191 cum in] in cum **D1**

192 coequare] quo equari **D1**
193 quod **D1**
194 vel **D1**
195 regularum **D1**

[21.1] He who wants to compose these ought first to order or compose the tenor and to give it mode and measure. For the more important part ought to be formed first, because through their mediation the others are formed afterwards. Just as in the generation of animals, nature first forms the principal members, namely the heart, liver, brain, and through their mediation the others are formed afterwards. I say "to order," since in *motelli*[111] and *organum*, the tenor is from old and previously composed *cantus*. But it is fixed more fully by the maker through mode and right measure. And I say "to compose," because in *conductus* the tenor is completely made up and is modified and continues according to the will of the artist.

[21.2] Once a tenor is composed or ordered, one ought to compose or order above it the *motetus*, which mostly resounds with the tenor in the *diapente* proportion, and sometimes ascends or descends according to their harmony.

[21.3] But afterwards a *triplum* ought to be added to these. This ought to resound with the tenor in *diapason* proportion as much as possible. And because of its harmony, it can stand in the middle places or sometimes descend as far as the *diapente*.

[21.4] And although a consonance may be perfected from these 3, nevertheless a *quadruplum* can sometimes be fittingly added to them, which will resound a consonance when other *cantus* orderly descend or ascend, or make an interruption or pause.

[21.5] For in composing *organum*, they make an alternation of modes as much as possible. But in composing *motelli* and other things, they rather keep unity of modes.

[21.6] And since in *motelli* there are multiple texts, if one exceeds another in syllables or terms, you can make it equal to the other by apposition of breves and semibreves.

[21.7] One wishing to compose a hocket from two, that is, from a *primus* and a *secundus*, ought to divide up the *cantus* or *cantilena* above which the hocket is made, and to redistribute a part to each. And in a small way a correct *cantus* can emerge with a fitting addition, provided that it observes its measure. For one lies on another in the manner of the tiles and roof of a house, and so a continuous staggering happens.

[21.8] Volens ultimo duplum componere debet minutam abscisionem supra tenorem facere et ei aliquotiens consonare.

[21.9] De mensuratis igitur et eorum partibus et eorum compositione[196] in universali et canonice dicta sufficiant. In quo propositum de musica precise mensurali terminatur.

[22.1] OMnipotens autem pater largifluus a quo mundi creature, esse. vivere. et[197] intelligere receperunt, unum quodque secundum naturam ei debitam ordinavit: Et si secundum sermones morales benefaciens debeat a beneficiato[198] laudem vel remunerationem loco recompensationis recipere: Et iste gloriosus benefactor istorum remuneratione non indigeat. sed per se ipsum sufficiat in se ipso, et eorum bonis operibus et laudibus sit contentus. Ipsum tamen[199] creatorem debent omnia creata recognoscere, et ipsum regratiari et secundum[200] posse suum venerari.

[22.2] Cum itaque inter omnia a deo creata homo post angelum magis recipiat quod est intelligere et ratiocinari, debet ipsi per bonas operationes applaudere, et eum nocte dieque laudare.

[22.3] In isto autem officio angeli sunt potentes propter nobilitatem sue nature. et quoniam organis sensitivis et fatigabilibus non utuntur. Homo vero istam operationem diu continuare non potest. eo **[48r]** quod in materia corporali formam habet et organis[201] corporalibus operatur. Sed et alias[202] operationes oportet eum frequentare. ut est comedere et bibere et dormire et multas alias operationes has sequentes. Et ideo habet homo determinata tempora specialiter in quibus debet magis suum laudare creatorem dum a consuetis operibus requiescit. Cuiusmodi est tempus gloriose nativitatis christi. et tempus sancte kadragesime cum tempore passionis et resurrectionis et ascensionis eiusdem. et festa sanctorum et sanctarum que a legis magistris et latoribus sunt statuta.

[22.4] Et quamquam omnes artes vel scientie et omnis humana eruditio ad hoc tendat quantum potest. tres tamen artes ad hoc propinquius ordinantur. puta gramatica, que scribere cum modo loquendi et proferendi docet. Et ars illa que temporum distinctionem et eorum computationem tradit. quam compotum appellant,[203] que naturali vel astronomie subiugatur. Et cum hiis duabus concurrit musica que de cantu et modo cantandi discernit. Et istas .3. non debet vir ecclesiasticus ignorare.

196 componere **D1**
197 cum **D1**
198 benefaciente **D1**
199 tamen] *post corr.* **H2**; verum **D1, H1**

200 et secundum] *post corr.* **H2**; et unumquodque secundum **D1, H1**
201 et organis] et cum organis **D1**
202 Sed et alias] *post corr.* **H2**; Sed alias **D1, H1**
203 appellat **D1**

[21.8] Finally, one wishing to compose a *duplum* ought to make a small interruption above the tenor and make a consonance with it several times.

[21.9] Therefore, let these words suffice concerning the measured and their parts and their composition in a universal and canonical way. Whereby the theme of precisely measured music is concluded.

[22.1] The almighty, bountiful Father, from whom creatures of the world have received their being, life, and understanding, has ordered each one according to the nature proper to it. Although according to moral discourse, one doing good ought to receive from the beneficiary praise or reward in place of recompense, and this glorious Benefactor does not need reward of these things, but is sufficient through Himself and in Himself and is content with their good works and praise, yet all things created ought to recognize the Creator Himself and to thank Him again and to venerate Him each according to his ability.

[22.2] Since, therefore, among all things created by God, man, after the angel, receives more, namely understanding and reasoning, he ought to acclaim Him through good works and praise Him night and day.

[22.3] In this service the angels are powerful because of the nobility of their nature and since they do not use sensory and weariable organs. But man cannot continue this activity for long, since he has a form in bodily material and works by means of bodily organs. In addition, he has to busy himself with other activities, such as eating, drinking, and sleeping, and the many other activities that follow these. And therefore man has specially appointed times in which he ought to praise his Creator more while he rests from his usual activities. Of such a kind is the season of the glorious Nativity of Christ, and the season of Holy Lent with the season of his Passion, and Resurrection and Ascension, and the feasts of holy men and women which are laid down by the masters and the makers of the law.

[22.4] And although all arts or sciences and all human learning tend towards this as much as it can, three arts, however, are ordained to this more closely, namely grammar, which teaches writing together with the way of speaking and pronouncing; and that art which transmits the distinction of times and their computation, which they call *computus*, which is subject to natural philosophy or astronomy. And music which deals with *cantus* and the way of singing comes together with these two. And a churchman ought not to ignore these 3.

[22.5] De duabus autem primis alibi disserendum[204] est. De tertia vero puta de musica est speculatio presens, quod a principio promissum est. Et de hac prius generaliter sermonem tradidimus prout usui civium necesaria est et prout valet ad bonitatem et conservationem totius civitatis. Nunc vero temptemus specialius de ea dicere, prout viro ecclesiastico necesaria est, et[205] ad creatoris laudem et dei servitium ordinatur.

[23.1] DIvidentes autem servitium ecclesiasticum, totum ad .3. membra generaliter reducunt, puta matutinas. horas. et missam.

[23.2] Matutinas autem appellant illud servitium quod in[206] domibus religionis vel ecclesiis cathedralibus circa mediam noctem fit et dicitur. vel in ecclesiis publicis ante primam in mane. Et partes huius appellant. Invitatorium. venite. hymnus.[207] Antiphona. psalmus. lectio. Responsorium. nocturnale cum suo versiculo. et ultimo Oratio.

[23.3] Horas autem appellant illud servitium quod horis determinatis dicitur, puta in prima. tertia. sexta. nona. vesperis. et complectorio. Cuius particulare sunt hymnus. antiphona. psalmus. et Responsorium. et oratio.

[23.4] Missam autem appellant[208] illud gloriosum servitium in quo maxima et divina misteria sunt completa. In quo etiam bonus christianus et fidelis suo creatori sacrificium reddit per devotam orationem et oblationem. Et in quo maximum sacramentum ecclesie celebratur. Cuius partes sunt Officium vel introitus. Kyrie eleyson. Gloria in excelsis deo. Oratio Epistola. Responsorium. Alleluya. Sequentia. Euvangelium. Credo in deum. Offertorium. Secreta. Prefatio. Sanctus. Canones misse. Agnus. Communio. post communionem.

[23.5] Ad musicum autem non pertinet determinare [48v] de quibusdam partibus hic contentis puta de lectionibus. epistolis. euvangeliis. et orationibus. Hec[209] enim secundum[210] diversos usus diversificantur[211] et regulis accentus et grammaticalibus amplius gubernantur.[212]

[24.1] SEd propter multitudinem aliarum partium musico pertinentium et ob[213] earundem confusionem, necesse fuit musico artem aliquam invenire, mediante qua huius partes uniret, cognosceret, et regularet. Ad quod antiqui plures regulas invenerunt. de hoc plures libros et scripta plurima componentes.

204 discendum **D1**
205 et] *om* **D1**
206 in] *om* **D1**
207 Hymnis **D1**
208 appellat **D1**

209 Hee **D1**
210 secundum] *om* **D1**
211 diversificatur **D1**
212 gubernatur **D1**
213 ab **D1**

[22.5] About the first two, there must be discussion elsewhere. But concerning the third, namely concerning music, there is the present speculation, which has been promised from the outset. And about this we have previously given a general discourse in that it is necessary for the use of citizens, and in that it is helpful for the goodness and the wellbeing of the whole city. But now let us try to speak more particularly about it as far as it is necessary for a churchman and is ordered for the praise of the Creator and the service of God.

[23.1] Those dividing up ecclesiastical service generally reduce the whole to 3 branches, namely Matins, the Hours, and the Mass.

[23.2] They call Matins that service which occurs and is said in religious houses or cathedral churches at around midnight or in public churches before Prime in the morning. And they call its parts the invitatory, the *Venite*, the hymn, the antiphon, the psalm, the reading, the night responsory with its versicle, and finally the prayer.

[23.3] They call the Hours that service which is said at fixed hours, namely at Prime, Terce, Sext, None, Vespers, and Compline. Its components are the hymn, the antiphon, the psalm, and the responsory, and the prayer.

[23.4] They call the Mass that glorious service in which the greatest and the divine mysteries are achieved; in which the good and faithful Christian also renders sacrifice to his Creator through devout prayer and offering; and in which the greatest sacrament of the Church is celebrated. Its parts are the *officium* or introit, the *Kyrie eleison*, the *Gloria in excelsis Deo*, the prayer, the epistle, the responsory, the alleluia, the sequence, the Gospel, the *Credo in Deum*, the offertory, the secret, the preface, the *Sanctus*, the canon of the Mass, the *Agnus*, the communion, [and] the post communion.

[23.5] It does not pertain to the musician to determine anything about those parts contained here, namely about the readings, the epistles, the Gospels, and prayers. For these are diversified according to diverse uses and governed more by rules of accent and grammar.

[24.1] But because of the multitude of other parts relevant to the musician and on account of their confused character, it has been necessary for the musician to discover a certain art by means of which he can bring together, know, and regulate its parts. For this the ancients found many rules, composing many books and very many writings about this. But those following reduced them to fewer. But the moderns use 8 rules which they call tones.

Sequentes vero ad pauciora reduxerunt. Sed moderni .8.[214] regulis utuntur quas tonos appellant. Et ideo antequam de partibus musicalibus per eos regulatis prosequamur: Quid tonus. Quot toni et qualiter[215] adinvicem differunt, est dicendum.

[25.1] DEscribunt autem tonum quidam, dicentes eum esse regulam que de omni cantu in fine iudicat. Sed isti videntur multipliciter peccare. Cum enim dicunt dicitur[216] omni cantu: videntur[217] cantum civilem et mensuratum includere. Cantus autem iste per toni regulas forte non vadit, nec per eas mensuratur: Et adhuc si per eas mensuratur. non dicunt modum per quem nec de eo[218] faciunt mentionem: Amplius autem cum plures toni in[219] fine conveniant puta primus et secundus in .d. gravi: per hoc quod dicunt in fine non articulatam[220] differentiam apponunt, nisi quis per hoc intellexerit[221] principium et medium cum hoc esse: Amplius autem[222] cum dicunt iudicat peccare videntur. Non enim regula iudicat, nisi quis methaforice dicat. sed est illud mediante quo iudicat homo: quemadmodum[223] instrumento mediante mechanicus operatur.

[25.2] Ampliantes autem dictam descriptionem dicentes tonum[224] esse regulam per quam cognoscimus medium et finem cuiuslibet meli, adhuc in aliquo videntur peccantes. puta cum dicunt cuiuslibet. Non enim per tonum cognoscimus cantum vulgalem. puta cantilenam. ductiam. stantipedem. quemadmodum[225] superius dicebatur.

[25.3] Amplius dicentes tonum esse speciem uniuscuiusque dyapason. In aliquo videntur deficere. Cum enim plures sint modi vel species[226] dyapason. et super unumquemque tonum possit dyapason collocari. plures essent toni quam .8. Sed tamen eos ad .8. determinare videntur.[227]

[26.1] TEmptemus igitur aliter describere et dicamus quod tonus est regula per quam quis potest omnem cantum ecclesiasticum cognoscere et de eo iudicare. Inspiciendo ad initium. medium. vel ad finem. Dico autem regula[228] per quam et cetera. quemadmodum[229] in grammatica et in aliis artibus regule

---

214 .4. **D1**
215 toni et qualiter] toni. Qualiter **D1**
216 de **D1**
217 utuntur **D1**
218 de eo] deo **D1**
219 in] *om* **D1**
220 articulata **D1**
221 intellexit **D1**
222 et **D1**

223 quamadmodum **D1**
224 totum **D1**
225 quamadmodum **D1**
226 plures **D1**
227 videtur **D1**
228 autem regula] *post corr.* **H2**; autem hic regula **D1, H1**
229 quamadmodum **D1**

And therefore, before we consider the musical parts regulated through them, we must say what a tone is, how many tones there are, and how they differ from each other.

[25.1] Certain people describe tone by calling it a rule that decides about every *cantus* by its end.[112] But these people seem to err in many ways. For when they say "it is said of every *cantus*," they seem to include civil and measured *cantus*. That *cantus* perhaps does not go by the rules of tone nor is measured through them. And further, if it is measured through them, they do not say through which mode nor do they make mention of it. Moreover, since multiple tones agree at the end, for instance, the first and second on D-grave, through this, where they say "at the end," they do not assign an appropriate *differentia* unless one comprehends the beginning and the middle with it. Further, when they say "that decides," they seem to err. For a rule does not decide, unless someone speaks metaphorically, but rather it is that by means of which man decides, just as an artisan works by means of an instrument.

[25.2] Those who extend the given description, saying that tone is a rule through which we recognize the middle and the end of any tune,[113] still seem to err in something, namely when they say "any." For we do not recognize through tone *cantus* of the people, for instance, the *cantilena, ductia,* [or] *stantipes,* as was said above.

[25.3] Saying further that tone is a species of every single *diapason,* they seem to be deficient in some way. For since there are many modes or species of *diapason,* and a *diapason* can be placed above any tone, there should be more than 8 tones. But yet they seem to fix them at 8.

[26.1] Therefore, let us try to describe this in a different way and let us say that tone is a rule through which one can recognize every ecclesiastical *cantus* and decide about it by paying attention to the beginning, the middle, and to the end.[114] I say here "rule through which" etc., just as in grammar and in other arts, general rules are found for the sake of recognition and easy apprehension of those things included under them. I also say "ecclesiastical *cantus*"

inveniuntur generales propter cognitionem et facilem apprehensionem illo-
rum que sub eis continentur. Dico etiam cantum ecclesiasticum. ut excludan-
tur[230] cantus publicus et precise mensuratus, qui tonis non subiciuntur. Sed
dico respiciendo et cetera. quoniam per hoc toni abinvicem distinguntur.

[26.2] Ad .8. beatitudines quas theologi discernunt inspicientes, tonum in
.8. modos **[49r]** distribuunt. vel forte magis arismetice considerantes, inspiciendo ad rationem et proprietatem octonarii qui cubicorum primus est. Quemadmodum enim corpus cubicum proiectum super unum latus firmiter
iacet. Ita fere omnis cantus ecclesiasticus sub uno istorum .8. modorum con-
tineri videtur. Dico autem fere. quoniam quidam cantus vel legende de novo
fiunt qui ad plenum istis regulis non gubernantur. forte tamen ad eos reduci
possunt.

[26.3] Et differentiam ponentes inter istos .8. modos per denominationem
finem. medium. et initium. eos communi nomine et numerali appellaverunt. puta[231] primus. secundus.[232] tertius. et cetera. Dicentes impares, principales. Autenticos masculinos. pares vero, differentiis contrariis nuncupando.
Et ex hoc nomen cuiuslibet proprium concludebant. unde primus dicitur
autenticus protus .idest. primus auctorizatus. Secundus vero plaga proti. Tertius autenticus deuterus .idest. secundo auctorizatus. Quartus plaga deuteri.
Quintus autenticus tritus .idest. tertius auctorizatus. Sextus plaga triti. Septimus autenticus tetrardus .idest. quartus auctorizatus. Octavus vero plaga
tetrardi.

[26.4] Adhuc .4. principales aliter nominantur. puta dorius. frigius. lidius.
missolidius. Sed alii .4. ypodorius. ypofrigius. ypolidius. ypermissolidius
appellantur.

[26.5] Et cantus qui primi toni sunt .scilicet. qui ad eum pertinent et etiam
secundi dixerunt in .d. gravi terminari. Qui vero .3ii.[233] et .4i.[234] in .E. gravi.
Qui vero .5i.[235] et .6i.[236] in .F. gravi. Sed qui .7i.[237] et .8i.[238] sunt, in .g. gravi
finem habent.

230 concludantur **D1**

231 appellaverunt. puta] appellaverint impares
principales puta **D1**

232 primus. secundus] primus et secundus. **D1**

233 .3ii.] *post corr.* **H2**; .3. **D1, H1**

234 .4i.] *post corr.* **H2**; .4. **D1, H1**

235 .5i.] *post corr.* **H2**; .5. **D1, H1**

236 .6i.] *post corr.* **H2**; .6. **D1, H1**

237 .7i.] *post corr.* **H2**; .7. **D1, H1**

238 .8i.] *post corr.* **H2**; .8. **D1, H1**

so that *cantus* both public and precisely measured, which are not subject to the tones, are excluded. But I say "by attending to" etc., since tones are distinguished from each other through this.

[26.2] Paying attention to the 8 beatitudes that theologians discern, they distribute tone into 8 modes, or perhaps considering more arithmetically, by paying attention to the rationale and property of the octad, which is the first of the cubes. For just as a cubic body, once thrown, lies firmly on one side, so almost every ecclesiastical *cantus* seems to be contained under one of those 8 modes. I say "almost," since certain *cantus* and readings are being newly made, which are not fully governed by these rules; perhaps, nonetheless, they can be reduced to them.

[26.3] And placing a differentiation between these 8 modes through specification—end, middle, and beginning—they have called them by a common name and numeral, namely first, second, third, etc., calling the odd ones principals, authentic masculine, but naming the even ones by opposing differentiation. And from this, they used to derive the proper name of each, whence, the first is called authentic *protus*, that is, the first according to authority;[115] but the second plagal of the *protus*; the third authentic *deuterus*, that is, the second according to authority; the fourth plagal of the *deuterus*; the fifth authentic *tritus*, that is, the third according to authority; the sixth plagal of the *tritus*; the seventh authentic *tetrardus*, that is, the fourth according to authority; but the eighth plagal of the *tetrardus*.

[26.4] The 4 principals are also named in a different way, namely *dorian, phrygian, lydian, mixolydian*. But the other 4 are called *hypodorian, hypophrygian, hypolydian, hypermixolydian*.[116]

[26.5] And they have said that *cantus* which are of the first tone, namely which pertain to it, and also of the second, are terminated on D-grave; but those of the 3rd and 4th on E-grave; but those of the 5th and 6th on F-grave. And those of the 7th and 8th have their end on G-grave.

[26.6] Differunt etiam medio quantum ad[239] ascensum et descensum. Nam auctentici sive principales usque ad suum dyapason ascendunt vel parum ultra et descendunt usque ad suum finem. plagales vero usque ad suum dyapente ascendunt et sub suo fine descendunt usque ad suum dyatessaron. vel dyapente. Quemadmodum enim masculus universaliter excedit femellam in caliditate et virtute: ita principales suos plagales ascensu excedere dignum esse videtur.

[26.7] Et quamquam ut videtur quilibet tonus plures possit habere inceptiones infra terminos sue latitudinis; determinatas tamen unicuique attribuunt. puta primo .5que.[240] scilicet. in .d. et .E. gravibus et .e. f. a. acutis. Secundo vero .4or.[241] scilicet. in .e. gravi. et .d. et[242] .e. et .f. acutis. Tertio .6. scilicet. in .d. e. f. et .g. gravibus. et in[243] .a. et .C. acutis. Quarto vero .5. scilicet. in .c. d. e. f. g. Quinto .4. scilicet. in[244] .f. gravi. et .b. rotundo. et .b. c. quadratis. Sexto vero .3. scilicet. in .d. e. et .f. gravi. Septimo .4. scilicet. in .g. gravi.[245] et .b. c. d. acutis. Octavo .4. scilicet. in .f. et .g. gravibus et .a. et .c. acutis.

[26.8] Istorum autem exempla quis inveniet in aliorum tractatibus figurata. vel per se invenire poterit si gradualem et antiphonarium et alios libros ecclesiasticales revolvat ad **[49v]** diversitates finis ascensus et descensus inspiciendo. Per istos enim .8. modos fere totus istorum[246] cantus regulatur. necnon et totus cantus a beato gregorio institutus.

[26.9] Quid igitur sit tonus et quot tonorum modi et qualiter adinvicem diversificantur, universaliter sit premissum.

[27.1] NUnc vero considerandum de partibus musice ecclesiastice prius enumeratis. Quarum consideratio difficilis nisi viro experto et multum exercitato circa diversos usus ecclesiarum. Quamquam enim plures sint partes in se et diverse, adhuc[247] secundum diversos usus et consuetudines in tantum diversificantur, quod earum diversitas vix posset[248] ad aliquam unitatem reduci. Temptantes tamen eas universaliter notificare prout promisimus unamquamque per ordinem describamus. Qualiter etiam[249] secundum .8.[250] modos diversificantur, ultimo earum compositionem trahendo.[251]

239 ad] *om* **D1**
240 .5que.] *post corr.* **H2**; .5. **D1, H1**
241 .4or.] *post corr.* **H2**; .4. **D1, H1**
242 et] *om* **D1**
243 in] *om* **D1**
244 in] *om* **D1**
245 gravibus **D1**

246 iustorum **D1**
247 ad hunc **D1**
248 possit **D1**
249 etiam] *om* **D1**
250 .4. **D1**
251 tradendo **D1**

[26.6] They also differ in the middle according to ascent and descent. For authentics or principals ascend as far as their *diapason* or a little beyond and descend as far as their end; but plagals ascend as far as their *diapente* and descend below their end as far as their *diatessaron* or *diapente*. For just as the male universally exceeds the female in warmth and strength, so it seems fitting for principals to exceed their plagals in ascent.

[26.7] And although, as it seems, any tone can have many beginnings within the limits of its range, they nevertheless assign fixed [beginnings] to each, for instance, 5 to the first, namely on D- and E-grave and e-, f-, a-acute; but 4 to the second, namely on E-grave and d- and e- and f-acute; 6 to the third, namely on D-, E-, F-, and G-grave and on a- and c-acute; but 5 to the fourth, namely on C, D, E, F, G; 4 to the fifth, namely on F-grave or b-*rotundus* and b-, c-*quadratus*; but 3 to the sixth, namely on D-, E-, and F-grave; 4 to the seventh, namely on G-grave and b-, c-, d-acute; 4 to the eighth, namely on F- and G-grave and a- and c-acute.[117]

[26.8] Anyone who finds figured examples of these in the treatises of others may be able to find them by himself if he peruses the gradual and the antiphonary and other ecclesiastical books by looking at the variations of the end, ascent, and descent. For through these 8 modes almost all *cantus* of these is regulated, and indeed all *cantus* was instituted by blessed Gregory.

[26.9] Let this be universally acknowledged, therefore, for what is tone, and how many modes of tones, and how they may be differentiated from one another.

[27.1] But now the parts of ecclesiastical music previously listed must be considered. Consideration of these is difficult except for a man experienced in and very familiar with the diverse uses of churches. For although there are many parts among them, and diverse ones are also diversified according to diverse uses and customs to such an extent that their diversity can scarcely be reduced to any unity, nevertheless, in trying to consider them universally, as we promised, let us describe each in order; also how they are diversified according to the 8 modes, finally by drawing out their composition.

[27.2] Invitatorium est cantus ex pluribus concordantiis compositus habens ascensum et descensum iuxta aliquem tonum. qui ante venite incipitur. et post[252] totus vel eius pars post quemlibet[253] versum eius resumitur. Dico autem ex pluribus concordantiis compositus ad modum simplicis conductus et sine tenore consideratus.

[27.3] Venite est cantus ex pluribus versibus compositus. cuius cantus diversificatur secundum suum invitatorium et suum tonum. Et ideo post quemlibet[254] eius versum semper invitatorium resumitur vel pars eius.

[27.4] Ista autem secundum diversos tonos diversificantur. Est[255] enim invitatorium primi toni. ut regem regum. cum suo venite. Secundi. ut martinus ecce. vel venite adoremus. Tertii ut regem precursoris. Quarti. ut adoremus regem. vel christus natus est pro[256] nobis. Quinti. ut dominum qui fecit nos. Sexti. ut surrexit. Septimi. ut non sit vobis. Sed octavi. ut regem cui omnia vivunt.

[27.5] Invitatorium autem cum suo venite primo cantatur ad invitandum christi fideles ad dei servitium ut ibi etiam orent pro se et pro omni populo christiano.

[27.6] Hymnus est cantus ornatus plures habens versus. Dico autem ornatus ad modum cantus coronati qui habet concordantias pulcras et ornate ordinatas.[257] Sed ab eo differt eo quod in cantu coronato est numerus determinatus ad .7. vel eo circa. In hymnis vero ad plus et ad minus ut[258] plurimum est[259] inventus.

[27.7] Et cantus iste immediate post Invitatorium et venite in matutinis. et post deus in adiutorium in horis decantatur ut christi fidelibus invitatis. eorum corda et animos excitet, et ad devotionem extollat, ad psalmos et legendas audiendum. et iterum post legendas resumitur ut eos revigilet[260] et revigoret ad psalmos euvangelistas et vigorosius exorandum.

[27.8] Sunt autem psalmi euvangelistas. cuiusmodi est. benedictus. magnificat. et Nunc dimittis.

252 post] *om* **D1**
253 quamlibet **D1**
254 quamlibet **D1**
255 Et **D1**
256 pro] *om* **D1**

257 ordinantas **D1**
258 vel **D1**
259 est] *om* **D1**
260 evigilet **D1**

[27.2] The invitatory is a *cantus* composed from several concords, having ascent and descent according to any tone; it is begun before the *Venite* and then all or part of it is resumed after each verse. I say "composed from several concords" considered in the manner of a simple *conductus* and without a tenor.

[27.3] The *Venite* is a *cantus* composed from several verses, of which the *cantus* is diversified according to its invitatory and its tone. And therefore the invitatory, or part of it, is always resumed after any of its verses.

[27.4] These are diversified according to diverse tones. For there is the invitatory of the first tone, such as *Regem regum*[118] with its *Venite*; of the second, such as *Martinus ecce*,[119] or *Venite adoremus*;[120] of the third, such as *Regem precursoris*;[121] of the fourth, such as *Adoremus regem*,[122] or *Christus natus est pro nobis*;[123] of the fifth, such as *Dominum qui fecit nos*;[124] of the sixth, such as *Surrexit*;[125] of the seventh, such as *Non sit vobis*;[126] but of the eighth, such as *Regem cui omnia vivunt*.[127]

[27.5] The invitatory with its *Venite* is sung first to invite the faithful of Christ to the service of God, so that there they may also pray both for themselves and for all Christian people.

[27.6] The hymn is an ornate *cantus*, having several verses. I say "ornate" in the manner of a *cantus coronatus*, which has beautiful and ornately ordered concords. But it differs from it in that, in *cantus coronatus*, the number is fixed at 7 or thereabouts, but in hymns it is very often found to be more and less.

[27.7] And this *cantus* is sung directly after the invitatory and the *Venite* at Matins, and after *Deus in adiutorium* in the Hours, so that when the faithful of Christ have been invited in, it may rouse their hearts and minds and exhort them to devotion, so as to listen to psalms and readings, and again it is resumed after the readings in order to reawaken and reinvigorate them for the Gospel psalms and for praying more vigorously.

[27.8] There are Gospel psalms, such as *Benedictus, Magnificat*, and *Nunc dimittis*.

[27.9] **[50r]** Istum autem cantum secundum .8. modos vel tonos non diver-
sificant. quamquam forte posset secundum eorum regulas variari. Sed eum
variant per cantum versuum vel diversitatem sillabarum. Dico autem per
cantum versuum et cetera. eo quod in quibusdam est equalitas sillabarum
diversitas tamen in cantu. ut in veni creator. et Conditor alme. In aliis autem
diversitas[261] in sillabis et in cantu. ut in. O quam glorifica. et[262] ut queant
lapsis.

[28.1] REsponsorium nocturnale est cantus ordinatus recte ascendens
vel descendens iuxta regulam alicuius toni. quem immediate sequitur versiculus[263] cum gloria patri. Versiculus[264] vero est cantus leviter ascendens et
descendens. et post eum et similiter post gloria patri resumitur pars responsorii vel totum aliquotiens quemadmodum[265] Invitatorium post venite vel
Responsoria in cantilenis post suas partes. Et semper gloria patri secundum
euphoniam versiculi decantatur.

[28.2] Cuilibet autem tono appropriatur unus versiculus. Si igitur invenian-
tur aliqui ab illis .8. differentibus, regulas tonorum excedunt, et debent iuxta
se habere gloria patri notatum.

[28.3] Sed quilibet tonus plura habet Responsoria: primi toni sunt. ut. Ecce
apparebit. cum suo versiculo. et gloria patri. Secundi. ut letentur celi. Tertii.
ut. Audite verbum. Quarti. ut. Rex noster. Quinti. ut. Hodie nobis. Sexti. ut
Qui venturus. Septimi. ut. bethleem civitas. Sed octavi. ut Participem me fac.
cum suo versiculo. ut. Aspice in me. et suo gloria patri.

[28.4] Cantus autem iste in legendis inseritur. et semper inter .2. lectiones
decantatur.

[29.1] ANtiphona est cantus leviter ascendens et descendens iuxta regulam
alicuius tonorum.

[29.2] Incipitur autem ante psalmum. ut ea audita cantor iuxta eius modum
intonationem psalmi faciat. Differunt enim intonationes in diversis modis a
parte principii. medii.[266] et finis. A parte principii. Nam primus cum sexto
fa. sol. la. semper habeto. tertius octavus ut re. fa. sicque secundus. La. sol.
la. quartus ut. mi. sol. sit tibi quintus. Septimus est mi. fa. sol. sic omnes esse
recordor. Et ista supra .8. dictiones figurant. puta pater.[267] In filio. filius In
patre. Spiritus sanctus ab utroque procedens.

261 autem diversitas] autem est diversitas **D1**
262 et] *om* **D1**
263 versiculis **D1**
264 Versiculis **D1**
265 quamadmodum **D1**
266 medium **D1**
267 patri **D1**

[27.9] They do not diversify this *cantus* according to the 8 modes or the tones, although it can perhaps be varied according to their rules. But they vary through the *cantus* of the verses or the diversity of syllables. I say "through the *cantus* of the verses" etc., in that in some there is an equality of syllables yet a diversity in *cantus,* as in *Veni creator*[128] and *Conditor alme,*[129] in others, diversity in syllables and in *cantus,* as in *O quam glorifica*[130] and *Ut queant lapsis.*[131]

[28.1] The night responsory is a regular *cantus,* directly ascending or descending according to the rule of some tone; the versicle with the *Gloria patri* follows this directly. But the versicle is *cantus* lightly ascending and descending, and after it and similarly after the *Gloria patri,* part or all of the responsory is resumed several times, just like the invitatory after the *Venite* or the responsories in the *cantilenae* after their parts. And the *Gloria patri* is always sung according to the euphony of the versicle.

[28.2] A single versicle belongs to each tone. If therefore any are found outside those 8 different ones, they go beyond the rules of the tones and ought to have the *Gloria patri* indicated next to them.

[28.3] But each tone has several responsories: of the first tone are such as *Ecce apparebit,*[132] with its versicle and *Gloria patri*; of the second, such as *Laetentur caeli;*[133] of the third, such as *Audite verbum;*[134] of the fourth, such as *Rex noster;*[135] of the fifth, such as *Hodie nobis;*[136] of the sixth, such as *Qui venturus;*[137] of the seventh, such as *Bethlehem civitas;*[138] and of the eighth, such as *Participem me fac*[139] with its versicle, such as *Aspice in me,*[140] and its *Gloria patri.*

[28.4] This *cantus* is inserted in the readings and is always sung between the 2 readings.

[29.1] An antiphon is a *cantus* lightly ascending and descending according to the rule of each of the tones.

[29.2] It is begun before the psalm, so that, once heard, the cantor may then make the intonation of the psalm according to its mode. For intonations in diverse modes differ according to the part of the beginning, middle, and end. According to the part of the beginning, for: "the first with the sixth you must always have fa sol la; third, eighth ut re fa and similarly the second. You must have la sol la the fourth, ut mi sol the fifth. The seventh is mi fa sol. Thus I remember everything."[141] And they figure them above 8 terms, such as *Pater, In filio, Filius, In patre, Spiritus, Sanctus, ab utroque, procedens.*[142]

[29.3] A parte vero medii sic differunt et conveniunt. quoniam primus et sextus et septimus fa. mi. re. mi. dant. Secundus quintus. octavus. quisque .fa. sol. fa. Tertius sol. fa. mi. fa. Sed quartus dat ut. re. mi. re.

[29.4] Sed a parte finis multipliciter differunt. et istas differentias appellant seculorum Amen. Differunt enim secundum diversos modos. et adhuc in eodem tono differunt secundum diversos usus ecclesiarum et etiam secundum diversarum antiphonarum inceptiones. Quas diversitates fastidium esset in presenti enarrare.

[29.5] Cantus autem **[50v]** iste post psalmos decantatur. et aliquotiens neupma additur. puta post psalmos euvangelistas.

[29.6] Est autem neupma quasi cauda vel exitus sequens ad antiphonam. quemadmodum[268] in viella post cantum coronatum vel stantipedem exitus quem. modum viellatores appellant.

[29.7] Cantus autem iste secundum .8.[269] tonos diversificatur. Et sunt primi toni ut. Primum querite regnum dei. cum suo neupmate. Qui designatur per .Re. ut. fa. sol. la. sol. la sol.[270] fa. mi. fa. sol. mi. sol. la. sol[271] mi. fa. mi. mi. re. Secundi vero. ut. O sapientia. et eius neupma .mi. fa. mi. re. ut. re. mi. fa. re. mi. fa. mi. re. ut. re. mi. fa. re. Tertii. ut tertia dies est quod hec facta sunt. Neupma .mi. re. sol. lare. mi. fa. sol. fa. mi. fa. mi. re. ut. re. ut utsol. fa. lare. mi. fa. mi. utsol. fa. sol. la. sol. la. sol. fa. mi. Quarti. ut Quarta vigilia venit ad eos. Neupma .mi. fa. sol. sol. fa. mi. fa. sol. fa. fa. re. ut. re. fa. sol. la. sol. sol. fa. mi. Quinti. ut. Quinque prudentes virgines. Neupma .re. fa. sol. la. sol. fa. mi. re. re. mi. fa. sol. sol. fa. mi. re. mi. re. mi. re.[272] re. ut. Sexti. ut. Sexta hora sedit[273] super puteum. Neupma .fa. mi. fa. re. ut. fa. sol. la. sol. la. sol. sol. fa. Septimi. ut. Septem spiritus sunt ante tronum dei. Neupma .ut. re. fa. sol. la. sol. fa. mi. re. mi.[274] fa. sol. fa. mi. re. mi.[275] re. re. ut. Et octavi. ut. octo sunt beatitudines. Cuius neupma describitur per .ut. re. fa. sol. fa. mi. fa. re. utsol. fa. lare. fa. fa. mi. re. mi. re. re. ut. Et quamquam ista sint neupmata ut plurimum: possent tamen forte subtiliora et pulcriora fieri. etiam[276] inspiciendo ad latitudinem cuiuslibet toni.

268 quamadmodum **D1**
269 .4. **D1**
270 sol.] *om* **D1**
271 sol.] *om* **D1**
272 re. mi. re.] *om* **D1**

273 sedit] *om* **D1**
274 mi. re. mi.] mi. re. re. mi. **D1**
275 mi. re. mi.] mi. mi. re. mi **D1**
276 et **D1**

[29.3] But according to the part of the middle, they differ and agree thus, because, "the first and sixth and seventh give fa mi re mi; the second, fifth, eighth each fa sol fa; the third sol fa mi fa; but the fourth gives ut re mi re."[143]

[29.4] But according to the part of the end they differ in many ways, and these *differentiae* they call *Saeculorum Amen*. For they differ according to diverse modes, and further they differ in the same tone according to the diverse uses of churches and also according to the beginnings of diverse antiphons. It would be an odious task to explain these diversities at present.

[29.5] This *cantus* is sung after the psalms, and a *neuma* is often added, as after the Gospel psalms.

[29.6] A *neuma* is like a tail or an ending following an antiphon, just like on the vielle after a *cantus coronatus* or a *stantipes*, the ending which vielle players call mode.[144]

[29.7] This *cantus* is diversified according to the 8 tones.[145] And those of the first tone, are such as *Primum quaerite regnum dei*[146] with its *neumata*, which is designated through: re ut fa sol la sol la sol fa mi fa sol mi sol la sol mi fa mi mi re. But of the second, such as *O sapientia*[147] and its *neuma*: mi fa mi re ut re mi fa re mi fa mi re ut re mi fa re. Of the third, such as *Tertia dies est quod haec facta sunt*;[148] *neuma*: mi re sol la-re mi fa sol fa mi fa mi re ut re ut ut-sol fa la-re mi fa mi ut-sol fa sol la sol la sol fa mi. Of the fourth, such as *Quarta vigilia venit ad eos*;[149] *neuma*: mi fa sol sol fa mi fa sol fa fa re ut re fa sol la sol sol fa mi. Of the fifth, such as *Quinque prudentes virgines*;[150] *neuma*: re fa sol la sol fa mi re re mi fa sol sol fa mi re mi re mi re re ut. Of the sixth, such as *Sexta hora sedit super puteum*;[151] *neuma*: fa mi fa re ut fa sol la sol la sol sol fa. Of the seventh, such as *Septem spiritus sunt ante thronum dei*;[152] *neuma*: ut re fa sol la sol fa mi re mi fa sol fa mi re mi re re ut. And of the eighth, such as *Octo sunt beatitudines*;[153] the *neuma* of which is described through: ut re fa sol fa mi fa re ut-sol fa la-re fa fa mi re mi re re ut. And although these are *neumata* usually, they can, however, perhaps also be made yet more subtle and more beautiful by inspecting the range of any tone.[154]

[30.1] INtroitus misse vel officium est cantus recte ascendens et descendens secundum aliquem tonorum et post eum intonatur versus alicuius psalmi cum eo in sententia concordans cum gloria patri. et Iterum post hoc resumitur quemadmodum[277] antiphona post psalmos.

[30.2] Cantus autem iste in principio misse cantatur. et ostenditur[278] in cuius honore missa debeat celebrari. puta in reverentia trinitatis vel spiritus sancti. vel beate et gloriose virginis. vel aliorum .scilicet. apostolorum. martyrum. confessorum. atque virginum.

[30.3] Diversificatur autem cantus iste secundum .8. tonos quemadmodum[279] et alii. Primi enim toni sunt. ut. gaudeamus. et eius versiculus .scilicet. Eructavit. cum gloria patri. secundum eandem intonationem. Secundi. ut Salve sancta parens. Tertii. ut Ego autem. Quarti. resurrexi.[280] Quinti. domine refugium. Sexti. Respice in me. Septimi. puer natus. Octavi. Ad te levavi animam meam. versiculus vias tuas. cum gloria patri. Eodem modo et cum aliis versibus intonatur.[281]

[31.1] **[51r]** KYrie eleyson est cantus ex pluribus concordantiis compositus ascendendo et descendendo. Dico autem ex pluribus concordantiis compositus. ad modum simplicis[282] cantilene.

[31.2] Cantus autem iste in principio misse immediate post introitum cantatur. Est enim laus divina multum generalis. generale vero ante specialia debet introduci.[283]

[31.3] Cantus etiam[284] iste ter in se reciprocatur in reverentia trinitatis.

[31.4] Et[285] profertur in ydiomate greco. aut quia latini a grecis principia omnium artium optinere dicuntur.[286] aut quia sermones greci ponderosiores sunt aliis. aut magis proprie designantes. aut propter aliud misterium quod non tenemur[287] exprimere.[288]

[32.1] HUnc autem cantum sequitur. gloria in excelsis deo. qui est cantus ex pluribus concordantiis ascendendo et descendendo sicut alius[289] quasi ex versibus compositus. Dico autem quasi ex versibus quia ibi sunt quasi versiculi. puta. Qui sedes ad dexteram. Et Qui tollis peccata mundi. et sic de aliis.

277 quamadmodum **D1**
278 ostendit **D1**
279 quamadmodum **D1**
280 Quarti. resurrexi] Quarti ut resurrexit **D1**
281 versibus intonatur] *post corr.* **H2**; versibus suis versibus intonatur **D1, H1**
282 simplici **D1**

283 Est enim laus divina multum generalis. generale vero ante specialia debet introduci.] *om* **D1**
284 autem **D1**
285 Est **D1**
286 indentur **D1**
287 tenetur **D1**
288 exprimere] exprimere in presenti. **D1**
289 aliud **D1**

[30.1] The introit of the Mass, or the *officium*, is a *cantus* directly ascending and descending according to any of the tones; and after it the verse of some psalm concordant with it in meaning is intoned with the *Gloria patri*; and after this, it is resumed again just like the antiphon after the psalms.

[30.2] This *cantus* is sung at the beginning of the Mass, and it is shown in whose honor the Mass is celebrated, for instance, in reverence of the Trinity or of the Holy Spirit, or of the Blessed and Glorious Virgin, or of others, namely of apostles, martyrs, confessors, and virgins.

[30.3] This *cantus* is diversified according to the 8 tones, just like the others. Now, of the first tone, there are such as *Gaudeamus*[155] and its versicle, namely *Eructavit*[156] with *Gloria patri* following the same intonation; of the second, such as *Salve sancta parens*;[157] of the third, such as *Ego autem*;[158] of the fourth, *Resurrexi*;[159] of the fifth, *Domine refugium*;[160] of the sixth, *Respice in me*;[161] of the seventh, *Puer natus*;[162] of the eighth, *Ad te levavi animam meam.*[163] The versicle *Vias tuas*[164] with *Gloria patri* is intoned in the same mode and with other verses.

[31.1] The *Kyrie eleison* is a *cantus* composed from several concords ascending and descending. I say "composed from several concords" in the way of a simple *cantilena*.

[31.2] This *cantus* is sung at the beginning of the Mass directly after the introit. For divine praise is very general; but a general thing ought to be introduced before particulars.

[31.3] This *cantus* also recurs three times in itself in reverence of the Trinity.

[31.4] And it is pronounced in the Greek language, either because the Latins are said to obtain the principles of all the arts from the Greeks, or because Greek words are more weighty than others or signify more closely, or because of some other mystery that we are unable to express.

[32.1] The *Gloria in excelsis deo* follows this *cantus*, which is a *cantus* composed from several concords ascending and descending, just as another as if from verses. I say "as if from verses" because there they are like little verses, such as *Qui sedes ad dexteram* and *Qui tollis peccata mundi* and likewise for others.

[32.2] In cantu autem isto laudatur specialiter creator puta cum dicitur. Laudamus te. benedicimus te. et cetera.

[32.3] Et missa multotiens invenitur sine isto cantu. quod est tempore tristitie vel meroris ut cum celebratur²⁹⁰ pro defunctis fidelibus vel in sancta kadragesima. et aliis ieiuniis. Sed sine kyrie eleyson numquam invenitur.

[32.4] Isti autem cantus cantantur²⁹¹ tractim et ex longis et perfectis ad modum cantus coronati. ut corda audientium ad devote orandum promoveantur. et ad devote audiendum orationem quam immediate dicit sacerdos vel ad hoc ordinatus.

[32.5] Isti etiam cantus non diversificantur secundum .8. modos. sed solum secundum diversa festa et diversos usus ecclesiarum.

[33.1] REsponsorium misse est cantus ascendens et descendens quemadmodum²⁹² Responsorium. nocturnale habens versiculum sicut illud. Differt tamen ab eo quoniam illud habet tantummodo in quolibet tono unum versiculum determinatum. hoc vero plures versiculos sub eodem tono habet quemadmodum²⁹³ et responsoria.

[34.1] HUnc²⁹⁴ autem cantum sequitur alleluya. qui est cantus letitie ascendens et descendens secundum regulas tonorum. Dico autem cantum letitie. primo enim incipitur alleluya. quod in generali letitiam christianis sub ydiomate greco representat. Et post hoc in versu specificatur magis ut cum dicitur.²⁹⁵ Alleluya. Letabitur iustus. In fine autem versus resumitur alleluya. Et alleluya additur cauda sicut²⁹⁶ neupma in antiphonis.

[34.2] Et multotiens loco caude cantatur sequentia. puta cum missa celebratur cum maiori sollempnitate.

[35.1] ESt autem sequentia cantus²⁹⁷ ex pluribus versiculis compositus. Sicut. Letabundus. vel Benedicta es celorum. Cantus autem iste per tonos regulatur sicut alii. Et duo versiculi sese sequentes in²⁹⁸ [51v] eadem concordantia ut plurimum decantantur.

[35.2] Isti autem .3. cantus puta. Responsorium. alleluya. et sequentia cantantur²⁹⁹ immediate post epistolam. et ante euvangelium in misterio et reverentia trinitatis.

---

290 cum celebratur] Concelebratur **D1**
291 cantatur **D1**
292 quamadmodum **D1**
293 quamadmodum **D1**
294 Hiis **D1**

295 cum dicitur] condicitur **D1**
296 cauda sicut] cauda que sicut **D1**
297 cantus] *om* **D1**
298 cum **D1**
299 cantatur **D1**

[32.2] In this *cantus*, the Creator is especially praised, such as when *Laudamus te, benedicimus te* etc. is said.

[32.3] And the Mass is often found without this *cantus*, which occurs in a season of sadness or of sorrow, as when it is celebrated for the faithful departed, or in Holy Lent and other fasts. But it is never found without the *Kyrie eleison*.

[32.4] These *cantus* are sung in a drawn-out way and with longs and perfects in the manner of a *cantus coronatus*, so that the hearts of listeners are moved to praying devoutly, and to devoutly hearing the prayer, which the priest, or someone ordained for this, says directly.

[32.5] Also, these *cantus* are not diversified according to the 8 modes, but only according to the diverse feasts and diverse uses of churches.

[33.1] The responsory of the Mass is a *cantus* ascending and descending in the same way as the night Responsory, having a versicle just like it. [The responsory of the Mass] differs from it, however, in that the former has in any one tone only one versicle specified, whereas the latter has many versicles under the same tone, just like responsories.

[34.1] The alleluia, which is a *cantus* of joy ascending and descending according to the rules of the tones, follows this *cantus*. I say "a *cantus* of joy," for initially it begins with "alleluia," which in general recalls joy for Christians in the Greek language.[165] And subsequently this is specified further in the verse, as when *Alleluia Laetabitur iustus*[166] is said. At the end of the verse the alleluia is resumed, and to the alleluia is added a tail, just like a *neuma* in antiphons.

[34.2] And often a sequence is sung in place of a tail, for example, when a Mass is celebrated with greater solemnity.

[35.1] The sequence is a *cantus* composed from many versicles, just as *Laetabundus*[167] or *Benedicta es caelorum*.[168] This *cantus* is regulated through the tones, just like others. And two versicles, one following the other, are usually sung in the same concord.

[35.2] These 3 *cantus*, namely the responsory, alleluia, and sequence, are sung directly after the epistle and before the Gospel for the mystery and reverence of the Trinity.

[35.3] Responsorium autem et alleluya decantantur ad modum stantipedis vel cantus coronati. ut[300] devotionem et humilitatem in cordibus auditorum imponat.

[35.4] Sed sequentia cantatur ad modum ductie ut ea ducat et letificet. ut recte[301] recipiant verba novi testamenti. puta sacrum euvangelium quod statim postea decantatur.

[35.5] Et missa aliquotiens est sine alleluya et sequentia puta tempore luctus vel penitentie. Et loco istorum cantatur tractus. qui est cantus ex versibus agregatus. Cuiusmodi est. De profundis vel. Sicut cervus.

[36.1] CRedo in deum est cantus leviter ascendens vel[302] descendens ad modum ductie parum differens in partibus. Dico autem parum differens et cetera. eo quod habet plures partes in cantu consimiles.

[36.2] Cantus autem iste dicitur symbolum apostolorum. Et cantatur immediate post euvangelium. Eo[303] forte quod cum euvangelio videtur generaliter in sententia concordare. Ibi enim generaliter omnes articuli fidei christiane exprimuntur.

[37.1] HUnc autem cantum sequitur offertorium. Quod est cantus ex pluribus concordantiis compositus ad modum simplicis conductus et ascendit et descendit recte, et etiam incipit et mediatur et finitur secundum regulas tonorum, et secundum .8. modos plenarie variatur. Et cantatur ad modum ductie. vel cantus coronati. ut corda fidelium excitet ad devote offerendum. Tunc enim sacerdos oblationem deo patri offert et levat[304] calicem dicens. Suscipe sancta trinitas et cetera. Tunc etiam christiani debent deo sacrificium offerre per manum sacerdotis.

[38.1] PRefatio est cantus levem habens concordantiam, ad modum quasi ductie ex pluribus versibus compositus in eadem concordantia exeuntibus. Et in diversis sollempnitatibus eius versus diversificantur. Alia .enim. est prefatio[305] christi nativitatis[306] et eius resurrectionis. et sic de aliis.

[38.2] Cantus autem iste immediate cantatur post secretam orationem a sacerdote. et ante sanctus. ut alios fideles devotos et preparatos faciat ad eum .scilicet. sanctus sollempniter decantandum. Ecclesia enim hec terrestris et militans signum est et ymago illius celestis triumphantis. In qua sunt angeli et archangeli sine fine dicentes.

---

300 et **D1**

301 lete **D1**

302 et **D1**

303 Et **D1**

304 elevat **D1**

305 Alia .enim. est prefatio] Alia est per .enim. perfecto **D1**

306 christi nativitatis] christianitatis **D1**

[35.3] The responsory and alleluia are sung in the manner of a *stantipes* or a *cantus coronatus*, so that it impresses devotion and humility on the hearts of the hearers.

[35.4] But the sequence is sung in the manner of a *ductia*, so that it may lead and give joy, so that they may rightly receive the words of the New Testament, namely the Holy Gospel, which is sung immediately after.

[35.5] And the Mass is sometimes without an alleluia and a sequence, as in a season of mourning or repentance. And in their place a tract is sung, which is a *cantus* compiled from verses, such as *De profundis*[169] or *Sicut cervus*.[170]

[36.1] The *Credo in deum* is a *cantus* lightly ascending or descending in the manner of a *ductia*, differing a little in the parts. I say "differing a little" etc., since it has many parts exactly similar in the *cantus*.

[36.2] This *cantus* is called the Apostles' Creed,[171] and it is sung directly after the Gospel, perhaps because it seems generally to agree in meaning with the Gospel. For in general there all the articles of Christian faith are expressed.

[37.1] The offertory follows this *cantus*, which is a *cantus* composed from many concords in the manner of a simple *conductus*, and it ascends and descends directly; and it also begins and progresses and ends according to the rules of the tones, and it is varied fully according to the 8 modes. And it is sung in the manner of a *ductia* or of a *cantus coronatus*, so that it may encourage the hearts of the faithful to devout offering. For then the priest offers sacrifice to God the Father and raises the chalice saying, "*Suscipe sancta trinitas*" etc. Then Christians should also offer sacrifice to God through the hand of the priest.

[38.1] The preface is a *cantus* having a light concord, as if in the manner of a *ductia*, composed from many verses ending in the same concord. And its verses are diversified in diverse religious festivals, for there is one preface for Christ's Nativity, another for His Resurrection, and so on for others.

[38.2] This *cantus* is sung directly after the secret prayer by the priest, and before the *Sanctus*, so that it may make the other faithful devoted and prepared for it, namely the solemn singing of the *Sanctus*. For this earthly and militant Church is a sign and an image of that heavenly triumph in which the angels and archangels are declaring without end:

[39.1] SAnctus. sanctus. et cetera.

[39.2] Est autem sanctus cantus qui dicitur hymnus glorie dei. Et cantatur[307] ornate et tractim. ut christianos moveat ad ferventem karitatem et dilectionem dei—Tunc enim sacerdos facit elevationem corporis christi.

[39.3] Diversificatur autem **[52r]** cantus iste secundum diversa festa et diversas sollempnitates.

[40.1] PAter noster est cantus habens duas partes ad modum puncti ductie vel stantipedis. Et incipit secunda pars cum dicitur. Panem nostrum. Et clauditur ultimo cum dicitur. Et ne nos.

[40.2] Cantus autem iste dominicalis oratio dicitur eo quod a domino facta. Et cantatur post elevationem corporis christi.

[41.1] Agnus dei est cantus .3. versus habens quorum duo eundem cantum habent. et tertius differentem et ultimo clauditur cum dicitur. Dona[308] nobis pacem—Et similiter cum celebratur pro defunctis, cum dicitur. Dona eis requiem sempiternam. Diversificatur etiam[309] quemadmodum[310] sanctus. Hic etiam cantus signum est pacis et concordie. Cum enim cantatur sacerdos frangit panem. Et tunc recipitur verus agnus .scilicet. christus. qui pacem reformavit vere inter deum patrem et naturam fragilem et humanam.

[42.1] COmmunio est cantus ex pluribus concordantiis quasi officium vel offertorium compositus. quemadmodum[311] alii secundum .8. modos diversificatus.[312]

[42.2] Cantatur autem cantus iste cum sacerdos communicavit corpus christi. Et quasi ad modum puncti clausi ductie vel stantipedis missam claudit. Tunc enim boni christiani et fideles debent stare in vera contemplatione et in memoria retinere ea que in aliis misse partibus anterius dicta erant.

[43.1] IN componendo partes predictas debet artifex dictamen vel materiam ab alio puta theologo vel legista recipere. Et post hec formam ei debitam debet musicus applicare. Sic enim se adinvicem se iuvant artes mecanice, ut in sutoria et corii[313] preparativa sensui fit apertum.

307 cantus **D1**
308 Da **D1**
309 etiam] *om* **D1**
310 quamadmodum **D1**

311 quamadmodum **D1**
312 diversificatur **D1**
313 corio **D1**

[39.1] *Sanctus, sanctus* etc.

[39.2] The *Sanctus* is a *cantus* that is called a hymn to the glory of God. And it is sung ornately and in a drawn-out way, so that it may move Christians to fervent charity and the love of God. For then the priest performs the elevation of the Body of Christ.

[39.3] This *cantus* is diversified according to diverse feasts and diverse solemnities.

[40.1] The *Pater noster* is a *cantus* having two parts in the manner of a *punctus* of a *ductia* or *stantipes*. And the second part begins when *Panem nostrum* is said, and closes at the end when *Et ne nos* is said.

[40.2] This *cantus* is called the Lord's Prayer, since it was made by the Lord, and it is sung after the elevation of the body of Christ.

[41.1] The *Agnus dei* is a *cantus* having 3 verses, of which two have the same *cantus* and the third a different one, and it is finally closed when the *Dona nobis pacem* is said; and likewise, when there is a celebration for the dead, when *Dona eis requiem sempiternam* is said. For it is diversified just like the *Sanctus*. This *cantus* is also a sign of peace and concord. For when it is sung, the priest breaks the bread. And thus is received the True Lamb, namely Christ, who truly restored peace between God the Father and weak human nature.

[42.1] The communion is a *cantus* composed from many concords, like the *officium* or the offertory, diversified just like the others according to the 8 modes.

[42.2] This *cantus* is sung when the priest has imparted the Body of Christ. And it closes the Mass, as if in the manner of a closed *punctus* of a *ductia* or *stantipes*. For then good and faithful Christians ought to stand in true contemplation and retain in memory those things that were said before in the earlier parts of the Mass.

[43.1] In composing the abovementioned parts, the artist ought to receive text or material from another, for instance, a theologian or a jurist. And after this, the musician ought to apply the requisite form to them. In this way the mechanical arts help each other, just as is made clear to sense in shoemaking and the preparation of hide.

[43.2] Quidam autem cantus non fiunt neque renovantur, puta illi qui non diversificantur secundum .8. modos. Cuiusmodi est kyrie eleyson. Et gloria in excelsis. Sed fiunt eis alique additiones que vocantur[314] farse.[315] Est autem farsa[316] additio interposita, cum cantu et sententia litterali aliquantulum concordans: Et alie partes que plenarie diversificantur secundum .8. modos cuiusmodi est antiphona. offertorium et cetera. fiunt per regulas tonorum. inspiciendo ad initium medium et finem et ad ascensionem et descensionem alicui tonorum appropriatam. Tonus enim est regula vel exemplar que debet componentem regulare quemadmodum[317] veritas prima regulat speculativum in perfectam inquisitione veritatis.

[43.3] Que quidem igitur sint partes musice ecclesiastice et qualiter diversificantur secundum tonos et qualiter componantur generaliter est tractatum. In quo terminatur intentio de musica ecclesiastica que ordinatur ad laudem creatoris omnipotentis. Qui vivit et regnat in trinitate cum deo patre et filio et spiritu sancto. Et ipse sit[318] gloriosus sit benedictus in sempiterna secula seculorum. Amen.

Explicit tractatus musice.[319]

314 vocant **D1**

315 false **D1**

316 falsa **D1**

317 quamadmodum **D1**

318 sit] *om* **D1**

319 Explicit tractatus musice] *om* **D1**; explicit theoria magistri iohannis de grocheio. **D1**; regens **D3**; ?Parisius; Scriptori flamen sacrum. tribuat decus amen. **D1**

[43.2] Certain *cantus* are neither made nor are they renewed, namely those that are not diversified according to the 8 modes. Of this type are the *Kyrie eleison* and the *Gloria in excelsis*. But certain additions are made to them that are called *farse*.[172] A *farse* is an inserted addition agreeing somewhat with the *cantus* and the literal meaning. And other parts, which are fully diversified according to the 8 modes, such as the antiphon, the offertory, etc., are made through the rules of the tones by inspecting the beginning, middle, and end and the ascent and descent appropriate to each of the tones. For tone is a rule or exemplar that ought to regulate the composer just as prime truth regulates the inquirer towards the perfect search for truth.

[43.3] What therefore are the parts of ecclesiastical music, and how they are diversified according to the tones and how they are composed, has been dealt with in general. With this, the intention concerning ecclesiastical music, which is ordered to the praise of the Almighty Creator, who lives and reigns in the Trinity with God the Father and the Son and the Holy Spirit, is concluded. And may He be glorious and be blessed eternally for ever and ever. Amen.

Here ends the treatise on music.

NOTES

1. Cf. Aristotle, *Physica* 3.1.200b12, trans. James of Venice, p. 96: "Quoniam autem natura quidem est principium motus et status et mutationis, scientia autem nobis de natura est, oportet non ignorare quid sit motus; necessarium enim est ignorato ipso ignorari et naturam." Also compare Isidore of Seville, *Etymologiae* 3.17.1: "Itaque sine Musica nulla disciplina potest esse perfecta, nihil enim sine illa."

2. A proper sensible is something that can be sensed by one of the five senses only. Cf. Aristotle, *De anima* 2.6.418a15, trans. James of Venice: "Sensibilium autem secundum se propria proprie sunt sensibilia, et ad que substantia apta nata est uniuscuiusque sensus."

3. Cf. Aristotle, *Physica* 1.1–2.184a15, trans. James of Venice, pp. 7–8: "Sunt autem nobis primum manifesta et certa que confusa magis, posterius autem ex his fiunt nota elementa et principia dividentibus hec."

4. Cf. Aristotle, *Physica* 1.1, trans. Michael Scot, fol. 14r: "et erit intentio quiditatis talis dispositionis, id est qualitatis: et intentio eius talis mensuræ, id est quantitatis eadem intentio."

5. The mechanical arts are mentioned by Johannes Scottus Eriugena (ninth century) in his *Annotationes in Marcianum* 79.12, p. 74. "Dos a virgine a si dixisset: Postquam Mercurius dederit septem liberales artes, tunc virgo dabit septem mechanicas." On the mechanical arts in Paris during the thirteenth century, see Whitney, "Paradise Restored," pp. 134–45.

6. Cf. Isidore of Seville, *Etymologiae* 3.15.1: "Et dicta Musica per derivationem a Musis. Musae autem appellatae apo tou masai, id est a quaerendo, quod per eas, sicut antiqui voluerunt, vis carminum et vovis modulatio quaereretur." On medieval conflations of the Muses, water, and the discovery of music, see Swerdlow, "Musica Dicitur a Moys, Quod Est Aqua."

7. Cf. Petrus Comestor, *Historia scholastica* 28, col. 1079: "*Nomen fratris ejus Tubal, pater canentium in cithara, et organo* [Genesis 4.21]. Non instrumentorum quidem, quæ longe post inventa fuerunt, sed inventor fuit musicæ, id est consonantiarum, ut labor pastoralis quasi in delicias verteretur: Et quia audierat Adam prophetasse de duobus judiciis, ne periret ars inventa, scripsit eam in duabus columnis, in qualibet totam." On the reception of Petrus Comestor (d. ca. 1178) in Paris during the thirteenth century, see Daly, "Peter Comestor: Master of Histories."

8. Boethius, *De institutione musica* 1.10, pp. 196–98: "Quemadmodum Pythagoras proportiones consonantiarum investigaverit."

9. Boethius, *De institutione musica* 1.1, p. 180: "Hinc etiam internosci potest, quod non frustra a Platone dictum sit, mundi animam musica convenientia fuisse coniunctam." Cf. Plato, *Timaeus* 36E, p. 29: "Et corpus quidem caeli siue mundi uisibile factum, ipsa uero inuisibilis, rationis tamen et item modulaminis compos cunctis intellegibilibus praestantior a praestantissimo auctore facta."

10. Boethius, *De institutione musica* 1.10, pp. 197–98: "Cum interea divino quodam nutu praeteriens fabrorum officinas pulsos malleos exaudit ex diversis sonis unam quodam modo concinentiam personare . . . "

11. Aristotle, *Physica* 2.1.192b15, trans. James of Venice, p. 43: "quod est natura principium alicuius et causa movendi et quiescendi in quo est primum per se et non secundum accidens."

12. The infinite continuation of consonances result from the perpetual addition of one or more consonances above existing consonances. See for example, Hascher-Burger Anon., *Tractatulus de musica*, p. 4: "et rursus ex addita diapente super diapason diapason cum diapente nova consonantia est producta, ita possunt infinitae aliae symphoniae per additionem diapente et diapason super alias consimiliter procreari."

13. See for example, Lambert, *Tractatus de musica*, CS 1:258–59: "Diatesseron est quedam consonantia . . . Diapente est quedam consonantia . . . Diapason autem est quedam consonantia . . . "

14. Cf. Boethius, *De institutione musica* 1.10, pp. 196–98: "Quemadmodum Pythagoras proportiones consonantiarum investigaverit."

15. Cf. Boethius, *De institutione musica* 2.18, pp. 249–50: "De consonantiarum merito vel modo secundum Nicomachum."

16. Cf. Plato, *Timaeus* 32B, ed. Waszink, p. 25: "idcirco mundi opifex inter ignem terramque aera et aquam inseruit libratis isdem elementis salubri modo . . . "

17. Cf. Plato, *Timaeus* 32A, p. 24: "Cum enim ex tribus uel numeris uel molibus uel ulla alia potentia medietas imo perinde quadrat ut summitas medio . . . " For this consider any two cubes (or cubic numbers), for example, 8 = 2 times 2 times 2 and 27 = 3 times 3 times 3. Between them are the numbers 12 and 18 which lie in equal proportions between them, that is to say, the proportions between adjacent numbers in the list 8, 12, 18, 27 are always the same, in this case 2:3. There are always two such numbers between any two cubes. See John N. Crossley and Carol Williams, "Studying *Musica* in Thirteenth-Century Paris: The Expectations of Johannes de Grocheio," in *Communities of Learning: Networks and the Shaping of Intellectual Identity in Europe 1100–1500*, ed. Mews and Crossley, pp. 137–50. For an explanation of this passage, see Lebedev, "Zu einigen *loci obscuri*," pp. 93–95.

18. Boethius, *De institutione musica* 1.16, pp. 201–3: "De consonantiis proportionum et tono et semitonio."

19. Cf. Aristotle, *Metaphysica* 1.5.985b24, trans. William of Moerbeke, p. 23: "In hiis autem et ante hos uocati Pytagorici mathematica tangentes primi ea produxerunt, et in eis nutriti horum principia omnium esse putauerunt."

20. Cf. Aristotle, *Metaphysica* 14.3.1090b, trans. William of Moerbeke, p. 311: "Quin immo et si sunt, sensibilium autem erunt omnia; in hiis enim ratio dixit. Propter quid igitur separabilia erunt? Adhuc autem inquiret utique aliquis, non ualde promptus existens, de numero quidem omni et mathematicis nichil conferri inuicem priora posterioribus."

21. The five species of proportion are described in Boethius, *De institutione musica* 1.4, pp. 191–92: "De speciebus inaequalitatis."

22. A superparticular ratio is one of the form 1 + 1/n : 1, for example, 1 1/2 : 1 or 1 1/3 : 1. That is to say, a whole and one part. These ratios are individually named as sesquialterate, and sesquitertial, etc. A superpartiens ratio is one of the form 1 + m/n : 1, where m < n, for example, 1 2/3 : 1 or 1 4/5 : 1. That is to say, a whole and more than one part. A multisuperpartiens ratio is one of the form k + m/n : 1, where k > 1 and m < n. That is to say, more than one whole and several parts. Examples are 2 3/4 : 1 or 3 3/5 : 1.

23. Boethius, *De institutione musica* 1.5, pp. 192–93: "Ex his igitur inaequalitatis generibus postrema duo . . . "

24. Cf. Aristotle, *Physica* 2.2.194a28, trans. James of Venice, p. 53: "Natura autem finis est et cuius causa fit . . . "

25. Cf. Aristotle, *Physica* 2.2.193b31, trans. James of Venice, pp. 50–51: "De his quidem igitur negotiatur mathematicus, sed non in quantum phisici corporis terminus est unusquisque . . . "

26. Psalm 150:3 (Latin Vulgate).

27. John of Damascus, *De fide orthodoxa* 26.2.12, p. 113: "Quia vero haec ita se habebant, ex visibili et invisibili natura condit hominem, propriis manibus, secundum suam imaginem et similitudinem . . . "

28. Cf. Johannes de Garlandia, *De mensurabili musica* 9.14, p. 70: "Et sciendum, quod supradictae concordantiae possunt sumi in infinitum." See also Franco of Cologne, *Ars cantus mensurabilis* 11.18, p. 68: "Et nota quod tam concordantiae quam discordantiae possunt sumi in infinitum . . . "

29. See for example, Johannes de Garlandia, *Musica plana, reportatio* 3.32, p. 40: "et sunt eius partes 13, silicet [*sic*] unisonus, diapason, diapente, diatesseron, tonus, semitonius, ditonus, semiditonus, semitonium cum diapente, tonus cum diapente, semiditonus cum diapente, ditonus cum diapente, tritonus."

30. Cf. Plato, *Timaeus* 30B, p. 23: "Hac igitur reputatione intellectu in anima, porro anima in corpore locata, totum animantis mundi ambitum cum ueneranda illustratione composuit. Ex quo apparet sensibilem mundum animal intellegens esse diuinae prouidentiae sanctione." Aristotle, *Physica* 8.2.252b26, trans. James of Venice, p. 285: "Si namque in parvo mundo fit, et in magno: et si in mundo fit, et in infinito, si quidem contingit moveri infinitum et quiescere tutum."

31. Cf. Bede, *De tabernaculo* 3.1176, p. 123: "Vnde et a physiologis graece homo microcosmos, id est minor mundus, uocatur." See also Bede, *De temporum ratione* 35.21, p. 392: "Sed et homo ipse, qui a sapientibus microcosmos, id est munor mundus appellatur . . . " On thirteenth-century scholastic conceptions of the *minor mundus*, see Finckh, *Minor mundus homo*, pp. 82–87.

32. Grocheio incorrectly interprets the semiditone, which comprises two tones *minus* a semitone, as two tones *plus* a semitone, which is equivalent to the *diatessaron*.

33. Cf. Johannes de Garlandia, *Musica plana, reportatio* 3.34, p. 40: "Unde notandum est quod unisonus in sonis est equalitas, in numeris ut unitas ad unitatem."

34. The anonymous *Theorica Planetarum* describes various uses of the *aux*; see for example, *Theorica Planetarum* 1.1–6, pp. 15–16: "Pars ecentrici qui maxime remouetur a centro mundi dicitur aux uel longitudo longior, sed pars que maxime accedit ad ipsum dicitur oppositum augis . . . Aux solis in 2a [i.e., secunda] significatione dicitur arcus zodiaci cadens inter caput arietis et linea . . . "

35. Cf. [Pseudo] Odo, *Dialogus de musica* 8, GS 1:257: "Tonus vel modus est regula, quae de omni cantu in fine diiudicat. Nam nisi scieris finem, non poteris cognoscere ubi incipi, vel quantum elevari vel deponi debet cantus." Lebedev ("Zu einigen *loci obscuri*," p. 106) has suggested that Grocheio's knowledge of the *Dialogus* definition of *tonus* is unusual for the period, but this definition is widely cited in music theory of the thirteenth century.

36. Cf. Johannes de Garlandia, *Musica plana, reportatio* 3.101, p. 47: "Tonus dicitur sesquioctavum ut 9 ad 8."

37. Cf. Boethius, *De institutione musica* 1.16, p. 202: "Rursus tonus in aequa dividi non potest . . . "

38. Cf. Johannes de Garlandia, *Musica plana, reportatio* 3.103, p. 47: "Semitonium dicitur superpartiens 13 [et] 243, ut 256 ad 243."

39. Cf. Johannes de Garlandia, *Musica plana, reportatio* 3.46 and 102, pp. 43 and 47: "Ditonus quasi duos tonos in se continens . . . Ditonus dicitur superpartiens decimas septimas ut 81 ad 64."

40. Cf. Johannes de Garlandia, *De mensurabili musica* 9.8, p. 68: "Imperfecta [concordantia] . . . sunt due species, scilicet ditonus et semiditonus."

41. Cf. Johannes de Garlandia, *Musica plana, reportatio* 3.48, p. 43: "Diatesseron consistit in proporcione sesquitercia sicut 4 ad 3 et continet in se duos tonos et semitonium minus." Grocheio is incorrect here: the semiditone contains a tone plus a semitone.

42. Cf. Johannes de Garlandia, *Musica plana, reportatio* 3.52, p. 44: "Diapente consonantia consistit in proporcione sesqualtera sicut 3 ad 2 et continet in se tres tonos et semitonium minus."

43. Cf. Johannes de Garlandia, *Musica plana, reportatio* 3.62, p. 45: "Diapason consistit in proportione dupla sicut duo ad unum, et continet in se quinque tonos et duo semitonia minora . . . "

44. Cf. Johannes de Garlandia, *Musica plana, reportatio* 3.97, p. 47: "Diapason . . . dicitur a dia quod est de et pan quod est totum quasi continens omnes species alias in se."

45. Cf. Johannes de Garlandia, *Musica plana, reportatio* 3.9, p. 39: "Unde musica est scientia de numero relato sonoro."

46. See for example, Isidore, *Etymologiae* 3.15.1: "Musica est peritia modulationis sono cantuque consistens." [Pseudo] Odo, *Dialogus de musica* 1, GS 1:252: "D[iscipulus]. Quid est Musica? M[agister]. Veraciter canendi scientia, et facilis ad canendi perfectionem via."

47. See for example, Aristotle, *De partibus animalium* 2.3.650a, trans. William of Moerbeke: "Quoniam autem necesse omne quod crescit accipere alimentum, alimentum autem omnibus ex humido et sicco, et horum digestio fit et permutatio per virtutem calidi, et animalia omnia et plante, et utique si non propter aliam causam, sed propter hanc necessarium habere principium calidi naturale, et hoc quemadmodum operationes alimenti plurium sunt partium." On the *calidum naturale*, see McVaugh, "'Humidum radicale' in Thirteenth-Century Medicine."

48. On the practical intellect, see Aristotle, *De anima* 3.10.433a15, trans. James of Venice: "Et appetitus propter aliquid omnis est: non enim appetitus hic practici intellectus est."

49. Boethius, *De institutione musica* 1.2, p. 187: "Et prima quidem mundana est, secunda vero humana, tertia, quae in quibusdam constituta est instrumentis . . . "

50. Johannes de Garlandia, *Musica plana, reportatio* 3.10, p. 39: "Item musica alia mundana alia humana et alia instrumentalis."

51. Natural instruments contribute to the production of sound in the voice. See for example, Lambert, *Tractatus de musica*, CS 1:253: "Naturale vero est ut pulmo, guttur, lingua, dentes, palatum et cetera membra spiritualia."

52. Cf. Aristotle, *De caelo* 2.9.290b30, trans. William of Moerbeke: "Manifestum autem ex hiis quoniam et dicere fieri latorum armoniam, tamquam consonantibus factis sonis, leviter quidem dictum est et superflue a dicentibus, non etiam sic habet veritas."

53. Aristotle is not mentioned in the *Theorica planetarum*.

54. Cf. Plato, *Timaeus* 36E, p. 29: "ast illa complectens caeli ultima circumfusaque eidem exteriore complexu operiensque ambitu suo ipsaque in semet conuertens diuinam originem auspicata est indefessae sapientisque et sine intermissione uitae. Et corpus quidem caeli siue mundi uisibile factum, ipsa uero inuisibilis, rationis tamen et item modulaminis compos cunctis intellegibilibus praestantior a praestantissimo auctore facta." The term *complexio* describes the blending of elements in the human body; see Jacquart, "De *casis* à *complexio*."

55. Cf. Johannes de Garlandia, *Musica Plana, reportatio* 3.17, pp. 39–40: "Concordantia ergo monachordi procedit per tria genera silicet [*sic*] per diatonicum, cromaticum et enormanicum."

56. Cf. Boethius, *De institutione musica* 1.21, p. 213: "in his omnibus secundum diatonum cantilenae procedit vox per semitonium, tonum et tonum in uno tetrachordo . . . "

57. Cf. Boethius, *De institutione musica* 1.21, p. 213: "Chroma autem . . . cantatur per semitonium, semitonium et tria semitonia." Note that there is a disjunct between Boethius and Grocheio.

58. Cf. Boethius, *De institutione musica* 1.21, p. 213: "Enarmonium vero quod est, magis coaptatum est, quod cantatur in omnibus tetrachordis per diesin et diesin et ditonum . . . " Note that there is a disjunct between Boethius and Grocheio.

59. Jacques de Liège (fl. 1300–1330) reported that Guido related enharmonic *cantus* to angels, the chromatic to planets, and the diatonic to "us" although no mention of these relationships survives in the corpus of Guido of Arezzo; Jacobus Leodiensis, *Speculum musicae* 2.55, 2:132: "Unde Guido cantum enharmonicacum ad angelos dicit pertinere, chromaticum ad planetas, diatonicum vero ad nos, quia ille est quo utimur." On the relationship between angels, planets, and the enharmonic, chromatic, and diatonic genera of *cantilena* see Handschin, "Ein mittelalterlicher Beitrag zur Lehre von der Sphärenharmonie."

60. Cf. Boethius, *De institutione musica* 1.20, pp. 205–12: "De additionibus chordarum earumque nominibus."

61. The combination of a note with its possible hexachordal indications comprises a *dictio* of the medieval gamut, itself named after the initial *dictio* formed from "gamma" (G, i.e., low G) and its only possible hexachordal indication, "ut." The *dictiones* of the gamut are given in figure 2.

62. A perfect number is one for which the addition of all its divisors forms that number; see for example, Boethius, *De institutione arithmetica* 1.20, pp. 51–54: "De generatione numeri perfecti."

Dictiones	Quarre	B-olle	Natura	B-quarre	B-olle	Natura	B-quarre	Toni	"Litterae diversa nominatione distinxerunt"
d-la-sol (dd)	sol	la						dd	Superacutus
c-sol-fa (cc)	fa	sol						cc	
b-fa♮-b-mi (bb)	mi	fa						bb	
a-la-mi-re (aa)	re	mi	la					aa	
g-sol-re-ut	ut	re	sol					g	Acutus
f-fa-ut		ut	fa					f	
e-la-mi			mi	la				e	
d-la-sol-re			re	sol	la			d	
c-sol-fa-ut			ut	fa	sol			c	
b-fa♭-b-mi				mi	fa			b	
a-la-mi-re				re	mi	la		a	
G-sol-re-ut				ut	re	sol		G	Gravis
F-fa-ut					ut	fa		F	
E-la-mi						mi	la	E	
D-sol-re						re	sol	D	
C-fa-ut						ut	fa	C	
B-mi							mi	B	
A-re							re	A	
Γ-ut							ut	Γ	
	Sillabae							"Voces per triplicem differentiam distinxerunt"	

Figure 2. How consonances and concords are differentiated

63. B-*quarre*, *natura*, and b-*molle* describe the three types of hexachord of the monochord. The *molle* hexachord takes the note F as "ut" and includes a tone between mi and fa notated using a "round" b (b-*rotundus*); the *natura* hexachord takes the note C as "ut" and does not include the note b; and the *quarre* hexachord takes the note G as "ut" and includes a semitone between mi and fa notated using a "square" b (b-*quadratus*). The hexachords of the gamut are given in figure 2.

64. Cf. Aristotle, *De generatione animalium* 1.1–2.715a1, 716a2, trans. William of Moerbeke: "Quoniam autem de aliis partibus dictum est hiis que in animalibus, et communiter et per unumquodque genus de proporiis sigillatim, quomodo propter talem causam unumquodque . . . De aliorum autem animalium generatione dicendum secundum adiectum sermonem per unumquodque ipsorum, a dictis connectentes."

65. The Benedictine Abbey of the Trinity in Lessay (*Exaquiense*), within the diocese of Coutances in Normandy, was founded in 1056; see Cottineau, *Répertoire topo-bibliographique des abbayes et prieurés*, vol. 1, col. 1592. Grocheio's *sermo* to a monk called Clement in Lessay does not survive; see Palémon Glorieux, *La faculté des arts et ses maîtres au XIIIe siècle*, p. 216.

66. The *cantus coronatus* is mentioned by Guy of Saint-Denis, who draws on Grocheio's description; see Guido von Saint-Denis, *Tractatus de tonis* 2, 2:58: "quemadmodum in viella videmus quod post stantipedem seu cantum coronatum." It is also described in the fifteenth-century *De origine et effectu musicae* 16; see Reaney, "Anonymous treatise *De origine et effectu musicae*," p. 117: "De cantu coronato. Cantus coronatus cantus fractus dicitur quia ad nullum gradum alligatur, sed potest ascendere et descendere in consonantiis perfectis et imperfectis indifferenter. Et cantus naturalis coronari potest, scilicet faburdon." Coussemaker's Anonymous 2 (thirteenth century) describes a *cantilena coronatis*; see Moberg, "Om flerstämmig musik i Sverige under medeltiden," p. 73: "Causa pulchritudinis cantus per se, ut patet in cantilenis coronatis et alibi multis exemplis."

67. *Ausi com l'unicorne*: Chanson R2075 attributed to King Thibaut of Navarre (d. 1253); transcription included in Tischler, *Trouvère Lyrics*, vol. 13, no. 1184:1.

68. *Quant il rousignol*: Chanson R1559 attributed in some sources to Raoul de Ferrières (fl. early thirteenth century) and to Chastelain de Couci (ca. 1165–1203) in others; transcription included in Tischler, *Trouvère Lyrics*, vol. 8, no. 658.

69. *Chanter m'estuet, quer ne m'en puis tenir*: Chanson R1476 attributed to Thibaud of Navarre; transcription included in Tischler, *Trouvère Lyrics*, vol. 9, no. 840.

70. *Au repairier que je fis de prouvence*: Anon. Chanson R624; transcription included in Tischler, *Trouvère Lyrics*, vol. 1, no. 11–2.

71. Seneca, *Ad Lucilium Epistularum Moralium* 4.31, p. 96: "inquis 'labor frivolus et supervacuus et quem humiles causae evocaverunt, non est malus?' non magis quam ille, qui pulchris rebus inpenditur, quoniam animi est ipsa tolerantia, quae se ad dura et aspera hortatur ac dicit: 'quid cessas? non est viri timere sudorem.'"

72. On the relationship between the *rotundellus* and the *rondellus*, see in particular Falck, "*Rondellus*, Canon, and Related Types before 1300," pp. 40–42.

73. *Toute sole passerai le vert boscage*: Anon. Rondeaux GR95; transcription included in Tischler, *Trouvère Lyrics*, vol. 14, no. R39.

74. *A l'entrant d'amors* is not extant.

75. *Certes mie ne cuidoie* is not extant.

76. *Chi encor querez amoretes* is not extant.

77. For the identification of *entata* as a Latinization of *enté* ("grafted"), see Page, "Johannes de Grocheio on Secular Music," p. 27 n. 41. On the term itself, see Ardis Butterfield, "*Enté*: A Survey and Reassessment of the Term in Thirteenth- and Fourteenth-Century Music and Poetry."

78. *Je m'endormi el sentier* is not extant.

79. *Girardo de viana* ("Girart de Vienne"): *Chanson de geste* attributed to Bertrand de Bar-Sur-Aube (fl. 1190–1217); see "Chansons de geste—Girart de Viane."

80. Cf. Isidore, *Etymologiae* 3.21.1: "Secunda est divisio organica in his, quae spiritu reflante completa in sonum vocis animantur, ut sunt tubae, calami, fistulae, organa, pandoria, et his similia instrumenta."

81. Cf. Isidore, *Etymologiae* 3.22.1: "Tertia est divisio rythmica, pertinens ad nervos et pulsum, cui dantur species cithararum diversarum, tympanum quoque, cymbalum, sistrum, acetabula aenea et argentea, vel alia quae metallico rigore percussa reddunt cum suavitate tinnitum et cetera huiuscemodi."

82. Cf. Aristotle, *De anima* 2.8.419b4, trans. James of Venice: "Percussio enim est faciens. Unde et inpossibile est, cum sit unum, fieri sonum."

83. With the exception of the *quitarra sarracenica*, the instruments named by Grocheio are described in Page, *Voices and Instruments*. The only other thirteenth-century theorist known to have mentioned the guitar is Johannes Aegidius de Zamora in his *Ars musica*, p. 108: "Canon et medius canon, et guitarra, et rabe, fuerunt postremo inuenta." Nicolas de Pressorio (d. 1302), a master of theology and canon in Paris, referred in a sermon to the "tambourines and guitars" of the students in the city; see "[Nicolas du Pressoir]," p. 458.: "Les jeunes clercs de notre temps, modo clerici, ne marchent pas ainsi la tête couverte, si ce n'est couverte d'une coiffe de femme . . . ils ne pleurent pas, mais ils ont en main le tambourin et la guitare, ils prennent leurs ébats au son des instruments, et vivent leurs jours dans l'enivrement des plaisirs, pour tomber finalement dans l'enfer."

84. On the intellective soul, see Aristotle, *De anima* 3.4.429a24, trans. James of Venice: "Vocatus itaque anime intellectus (dico autem intellectum quo opinatur et intelligit anima) nichil est actu eorum que sunt, ante intelligere."

85. Cf. Montpellier, Faculté de Médecine, MS 196, fol. 277v: "Entre Copin, et Bourgois, Hanicot et Charlot et Pierron, Sont a Paris Demourant, mout loial compaignon . . . , " transcribed in Tischler, *Montpellier Codex*, 3:70–72.

86. Cf. Montpellier, Faculté de Médecine, MS 196, which includes three motet tenors identified as "chose Tassin": fol. 298v: *Amours dont je sui epris*, fol. 331v: *De chanter me vient talens*, and fol. 336v: *Entre Jehan et Philippet*. Transcribed in Tischler, *Montpellier Codex*, 3:95–97, 137–39, and 141–43.

87. Cf. Johannes de Garlandia, *De mensurabili musica* 9.2–5, p. 67: "Consonantiarum quaedam dicuntur concordantiae, quaedam discordantiae . . . Concordantiarum triplex est modus, quia quaedam sunt perfectae, quaedam imperfectae, quaedam mediae."

88. Cf. Johannes de Garlandia, *De mensurabili musica* 11 and 13, pp. 74–89: "Sequitur de discantu . . . Organum dicitur multipliciter . . ."; Franco of Cologne, *Ars cantus mensurabilis* 11 and 14, pp. 64–75 and 80–82: "De discantu et eius speciebus . . . De organo." See also Fuller, "Discant and the Theory of Fifthing."

89. Cf. Aristotle, *Metaphysica* 10.1.1052b20, trans. William of Moerbeke, p. 196: "Metrum etenim est quo quantitas cognoscitur . . . Quare omnis quantitas cognoscitur in quantum quantitas uno, et quo primo cognoscitur, hoc ipsum unum; quapropter unum numeri principium secundum quod numerus."

90. Cf. Aristotle, *Physica* 7.1.242a17, trans. James of Venice, pp. 257–58: "Quoniam autem omne quod movetur ab aliquo movetur . . . Neque in infinitum adibit, sed stabit alicubi et erit aliquod quod primum causa erit motus."

91. Cf. Aristotle, *Metaphysica* 10.1.1052b18, trans. William of Moerbeke, p. 196: "Maxime uero in eo quod est metrum esse primum uniuscuiusque generis et maxime proprie quantitatis; hinc enim ad alia venit." See also *Metaphysica* 2.2.994a12, trans. William of

Moerbeke, p. 44: "Mediorum enim, extra que est aliquid ultimum et primum, necesse est esse quod prius est causam ipsorum post se."

92. Cf. Aristotle, *Physica* 4.12.221a1, trans. James of Venice, p. 180: "Quoniam autem est tempus metrum motus et eius quod movetur . . . "

93. Cf. Franco of Cologne, *Ars cantus mensurabilis* 1.5, p. 25: "Tempus est mensura tam vocis prolatae quam eius contrarii, scilicet vocis amissae, quae pausa communiter appellatur."

94. Cf. Galen, *De temperamentis* (*De complexionibus*) 9, p. 566: "Laudantque homines quandam Polycleti statuam, canonem [canwn, compare *regula*] appellatam, inde adeo id nomen fortitam, quod partium inter se omnium commoderationem ad unguem habeat."

95. Cf. Aristotle, *Physica* 6.1.231b10, trans. James of Venice, p. 217: "Manifestum autem est et quod omne continuum divisibile et in semper divisibilia est; si enim in indivisibilia divideretur continuum, esset indivisibile indivisibili contactum; unum enim ultimum, et tanguntur, continuorum est."

96. See for example, Isidore, *Etymologiae* 11.1.22: "Auditus appellatus, quod voces auriat; hoc est aere verberato suscipiat sonos."

97. Johannes de Garlandia, *De mensurabili musica* 4.2–10, pp. 52–56: "Unde prima regula primi modi dicitur esse tres ligatae ad invicem in principio et in posterum cum duabus et duabus ligatis etc. . . . "

98. Lambert, *Tractatus de musica*, CS 1:269: "seipsamque in novem partes diminuendo duplicatur partiens, cujus forma quadrangularis efficitur, comam semper in ejus latere dextro fixam per quam natura longitudinis habere meretur, que patet in presenti . . . "

99. Franco of Cologne, *Ars cantus mensurabilis* 3.1–4, pp. 26–27: "Modus est cognitio soni longis brevibusque temporibus mensurati . . . Nos autem quinque tantum ponimus, quia ad hos quinque omnes alii reducuntur."

100. "Four basic syllogisms" are described, for example, in Aristotle, *Analytica prior* 1.1–7.24a1–29b25, trans. Boethius.

101. Cf. Johannes de Garlandia, *De mensurabili musica* 8.3, p. 66: "Pausationum vel tractuum quaedam dicitur recta brevis, quaedam longa, quaedam finis punctorum . . . " See also Franco of Cologne, *Ars cantus mensurabilis* 9.2–3, p. 54: "Pausationum sex sunt species: longa perfecta, longa imperfecta, sub qua comprehenditur altera brevis, eo quod mensuram eandem comprehendant brevis recta, semibrevis maior, semibrevis minor, et finis punctorum."

102. Cf. Franco of Cologne, *Ars cantus mensurabilis* 4.6–12, pp. 29–30: "Longa perfecta prima dicitur et principalis . . . Longa vero imperfecta sub figuratione perfectae duo tantum tempora significat."

103. Cf. Franco of Cologne, *Ars cantus mensurabilis* 4.14, p. 30: "Brevis autem, licet in rectam et alteram brevem dividatur . . . "

104. Cf. Johannes de Garlandia, *De mensurabili musica* 2.20, p. 46: "Semibrevis est, quae formatur ad modum rectae brevis, sed quatuor anguli transpositi ad differentiam rectae brevis."

105. Cf. Johannes de Garlandia, *De mensurabili musica* 2.4, p. 44: "quoniam ille, quae sunt sine littera, debent, prout possunt, amplius ad invicem ligari." See also Franco of Cologne, *Ars cantus mensurabilis* 10.1, p. 59: "Item sciendum quod figura ligabilis non ligata vitiosa est sed magis non ligabilis ligata."

106. Cf. Johannes de Garlandia, *De mensurabili musica* 3.1–4, p. 50: "Sequitur de regulis figurarum ad invicem ligatarum cum proprietate vel sine proprietate etc. . . . Omnis figura sine proprietate et perfecta posita valet per oppositum cum proprietate." See also Franco of

Cologne, *Ars cantus mensurabilis* 7.2–7, p. 44: "Item ligaturarum alia cum proprietate, alia sine, alia cum opposita proprietate; et hoc a parte principii ligaturae."

107. *Tegni* was one of the titles under which Galen's short compendium was known; others include *Ars parva*, *Microtechne*, and *Ars medica*. On the Latin transmission of Galen in the thirteenth century, see Baader, "Galen in mittelalterlichen Abendland."

108. Franco of Cologne, *Ars cantus mensurabilis* 4, pp. 29–31: "De figuris sive signis cantus mensurabilis."

109. Cf. Boethius, *De institutione musica* 1.1, p. 180: "sed amorem delectationemque, ut dictum est, similitudo conciliat."

110. *Ego mundus* is not extant.

111. Cf. Johannes de Garlandia, *De mensurabili musica* 2.3, p. 44: "Et sciendum, quod huiusmodi figurae aliquando ponuntur sine littera, aliquando cum littera; sine littera ut in caudis vel conductis, cum littera ut in motellis."; Lambert, *Tractatus de musica*, CS 1:269: "sed hujusmodi figure aliquando ponuntur cum littera, aliquando sine. Cum littera vero, ut in motellis et similibus . . . " On the use and prevalence of the term *motellus*, see Hofmann, "Zur Entstehungs- und Frühgeschichte des Terminus Motette."

112. Cf. [Pseudo] Odo, *Dialogus de musica* 8, GS 1:257: "Tonus vel modus est regula, quae de omni cantu in fine diiudicat."

113. Cf. Hieronymus de Moravia, *Tractatus de musica* 20, p. 154: "Est autem vulgaris tonus totum modulationis corpus unius cujusque cantus . . . Qui etiam tropus dicitur . . . Aliter adhuc tropus est, per quem cognoscimus principium, medium et finem cujuslibet meli."

114. Cf. Hieronymus de Moravia, *Tractatus de musica* 20, p. 156: "Tonus, inquiunt, prout hic sumitur, est regula, quae de omni cantu dijudicat secundum principium, medium et finem."

115. On the term *auctoritas*, see for example Hieronymus de Moravia, *Tractatus de musica* 20, p. 156: "Nam authenticum Graece auctoritas dicitur Latine."

116. The term *hypermixolydian* probably derives from Boethius, *De institutione musica* 4.17, p. 347: "Cur autem octavus modus, qui est hypermixolydius, adiectus sit, hinc patet."

117. A similar summary of *principia* is found, for example, in Johannes de Garlandia, *Musica plana, introductio* 225–61, pp. 91–96: "Primus tonus habet principia quinque, scilicet .c. .d. .f. .g. graue et .a. acutum . . . "

118. *Regem regum* [*dominum . . . adoremus quia ipse*]: mode 1 invitatory for the feast of Saint Denis, bishop of Paris.

119. *Martinus ecce*: mode 2 invitatory for the feast of Martin, bishop of Tours.

120. *Venite adoremus*: not extant as a mode 2 invitatory (*Venite adoremus et procidamus* = mode 2 introit).

121. *Regem precursoris*: mode 3 invitatory for the feast of John the Baptist.

122. *Adoremus regem* [*apostolorum*]: mode 4 invitatory for the feast of John the Evangelist; *Adoremus regem* [*magnum dominum qui*]: mode 4 invitatory for the Invention of Stephen, protomartyr.

123. *Christus natus est pro nobis*: not extant as a mode 4 invitatory (*Christus natus est nobis* = mode 4 invitatory for Christmas Day).

124. *Dominum qui fecit nos*: mode 5 invitatory for Sundays in summer.

125. *Surrexit* [*dominus vere*]: mode 6 invitatory for Easter Monday.

126. *Non sit vobis* [*vanum*]: mode 7 invitatory for the first Sunday of Lent.

127. *Regem cui omnia vivunt*: not extant as a mode 8 invitatory.

128. *Veni creator [spiritus]*: hymn for Pentecost Sunday.

129. *Conditor alme [siderum]*: hymn for the first Sunday of Advent.

130. *O quam glorifica [luce coruscas]*: Marian hymn.

131. *Ut queant lapsis [resonare fibris]*: hymn for the feast of John the Baptist.

132. *Ecce apparebit [dominus super nubem]*: mode 1 night responsory for the third Sunday of Advent.

133. *Laetentur caeli* [. . . *jubilate*]: mode 2 night responsory for the first Sunday of Advent.

134. *Audite verbum [domini gentes]*: mode 3 night responsory for the first Sunday of Advent.

135. *Rex noster [adveniet]*: mode 4 night responsory for the second Sunday of Advent.

136. *Hodie nobis [caelorum rex]*: mode 5 night responsory for Christmas Day.

137. *Qui venturus [est veniet]*: mode 6 night responsory for the third Sunday of Advent.

138. *Bethlehem civitas [dei]*: mode 7 night responsory for the third Sunday of Advent.

139. *Participem me fac*: mode 8 night responsory for the Monday of the first week of Lent.

140. *Aspice in me [et miserere . . . secundum Participem me fac]*: responsory verse for *Participem me fac.*

141. The mnemonic verse *Primum cum sexto* dates from at least the twelfth century and is included, for example, in Lambert, *Tractatus de musica*, CS 1:262. For a list of manuscripts that preserve *Primum cum sexto*, see Lebedev, "Zu einigen *loci obscuri*," p. 100. The hexachordal incipits summarized in *Primum cum sexto* are applied to the eight psalm tones in figure 3.

142. The mnemonic *Pater in filio* dates from the eleventh century. For a list of tonaries that include this mnemonic, see Huglo, *Les Tonaires: Inventaire, Analyse, Comparaison*, pp. 391–92. *Pater in filio* is reconstructed in figure 4 from Grocheio's citation of *Primum cum sexto*. See also Lebedev, "Zu einigen *loci obscuri*," pp. 100–101.

143. The mnemonic *Septimus et sextus* survives in sources from the thirteenth century, among which is Lambert, *Tractatus de musica*, CS 1:262. The medians given in *Septimus et sextus* are applied to the psalm tones in figure 3.

144. Cf. Lambert, *Tractatus de musica*, CS 1:269: "ita quod omnis cantus qualitercunque fuerit diversificatus ad extremitatem, etiam in modum vielle congrue per illam possit declarari."

145. With the exception of tone 2, the examples of antiphons cited by Grocheio are not office antiphons but Latin intonation formulas, the biblical texts of which begin with the number of the mode that the intonation formula demonstrates. On these formulas, see Bailey, *Intonation Formulas of Western Chant.*

146. *Primum quaerite regnum dei*: mode 1 Latin intonation formula.

147. *O sapientia [quae ex ore]*: mode 2 antiphon, one of the six, great "O" antiphons sung with the Magnificat at Vespers.

148. *Tertia dies est quod haec facta sunt*: mode 3 Latin intonation formula.

149. *Quarta vigilia venit ad eos*: mode 4 Latin intonation formula.

150. *Quinque prudentes virgins*: mode 5 Latin intonation formula.

151. *Sexta hora sedit super puteum*: mode 6 Latin intonation formula.

152. *Septem spiritus sunt ante thronum dei*: mode 7 Latin intonation formula.

153. *Octo sunt beatitudines*: mode 8 Latin intonation formula.

154. Refer to figure 5, which includes a reconstruction of Grocheio's antiphons and *neumata* (Antiphon settings from Lambert, *Tractatus de musica* in Siena, Bibliotheca comunale, L.V.30, fols. 21r–23v)

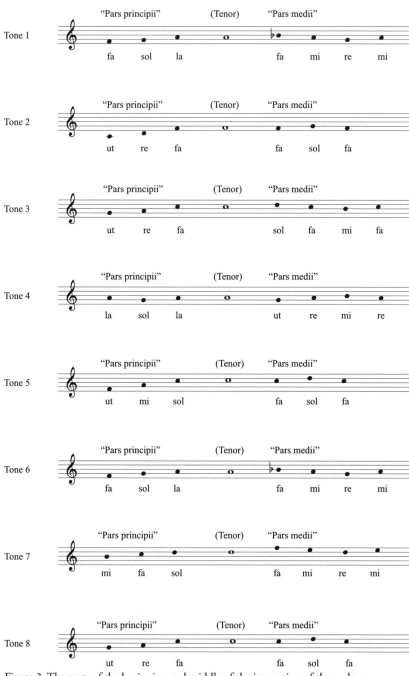

Figure 3. The parts of the beginning and middle of the intonation of the psalms

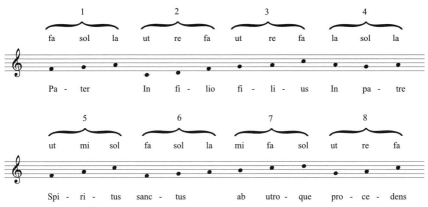

Figure 4. *Pater in filio*

155. *Gaudeamus [omnes in domino]*: mode 1 introit for saints' feast days.

156. *Eructavit [cor meum]*: verse from Psalm 44 sung with *Gaudeamus omnes in domino*.

157. *Salve sancta parens*: mode 2 introit for Marian feast days.

158. *Ego autem [sicut oliva]*: mode 3 introit for saints' feast days.

159. *Resurrexi [et adhuc tecum sum]*: mode 4 introit for Eastertide.

160. *Domine refugium [factus es]*: mode 5 introit for the Wednesday after the first Sunday of Lent.

161. *Respice in me [et miserere mei]*: mode 6 introit for the third Sunday after the Octave of Pentecost.

162. *Puer natus [est nobis]*: mode 7 introit for feasts of the Savior.

163. *Ad te levavi animam meam*: mode 8 introit for the first Sunday of Advent.

164. *Vias tuas [domine deomonstra]* introit verse for *Ad te levavi*.

165. Grocheio is of course incorrect; the word "alleluia" is from the Hebrew.

166. *Alleluia Laetabitur iustus [in Domino]*: alleluia verse for feasts days for martyrs.

167. *Laetabundus [exultet]*: sequence for Christmas.

168. *Benedicta es caelorum*: sequence for the Purification.

169. *De profundis [clamavi ad te]*: mode 8 tract for the Mass of the Dead and Septuagesima Sunday.

170. *Sicut cervus [desiderat]*: mode 8 tract for the Eve of Pentecost.

171. *Credo in deum* ("Credo in Deum Patrem omnipotentem Creatorem caeli et terrae") is recited before the hours. *Credo in unum deum* ("Credo in unum Deum, Patrem omnipotentem, factorem caeli et terrae, visibilium omnium et invisibilium"), or the Nicene Creed, is sung in the Mass. Grocheio identifies the *Credo in deum* as part of the Mass.

172. On farsed chants, see Hiley, *Western Plainchant*, pp. 233–38.

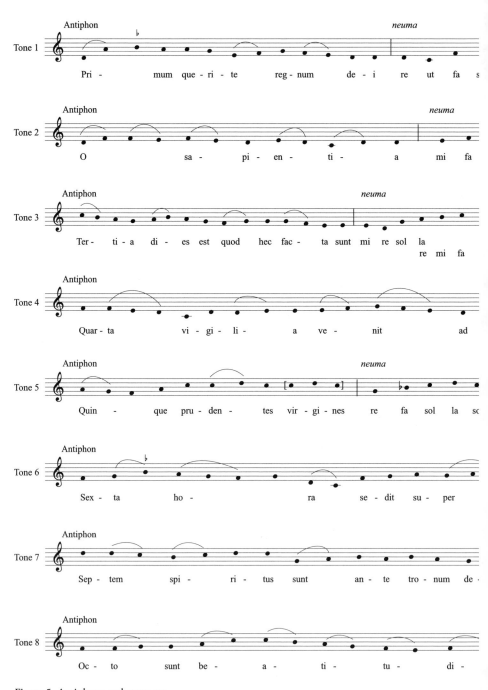

Figure 5. Antiphons and *neumata*

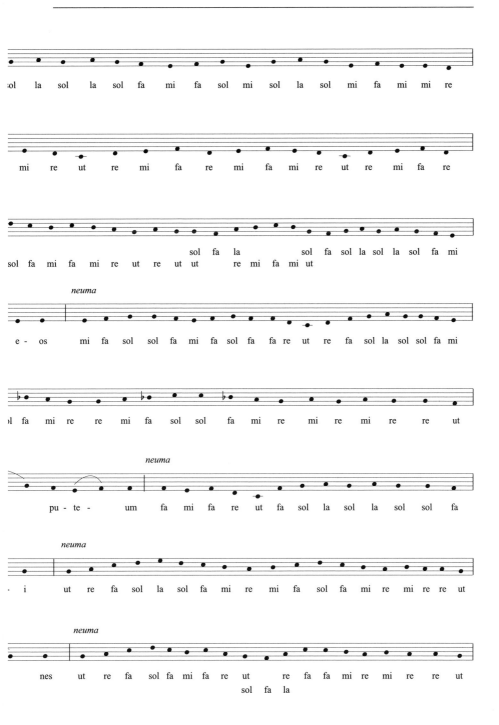

Lexicon

Word forms are based on those given in the Latin text.

A lentrant damors: *A l'entrant d'amors* (a *stantipes*) [9.7]

abreviatio: contracting (of a string) [7.7]; ***abreviatio cordarum***: shortening of strings [12.2]

abscisio: interruption (of melody) [19.5] [20.8] [21.4]; ***continua abscisio***: continuous staggering (of tiles) [21.7]; ***minuta abscisio***: small interruption (of melody) [21.8]

accentus: (rules of) accent [23.5]

accidentalis: accidental (of occurrence) [1.4]

acquiesco: accede [0.1]

acuendus: tightening (of a string) [7.7]

acuitas: height (of pitch) [4.11] [4.12] [7.3]

acutus: acute (of register) [7.7] [26.7]

Ad te levavi animam meam: *Ad te levavi animam meam* (an introit) [30.3]

additamentum: supplement (in *cantilena*) [10.1] [10.6]

additio: addition (process of) [4.18], addition (to a musical item) [43.2]; ***decens additio***: fitting addition (to a musical item) [21.7]; ***additio interposita***: inserted addition (to a musical item) [43.2]

adoremus regem: *Adoremus regem* (an invitatory) [27.4]

adversitas: adversity [9.3] [9.5]; ***adversitates hominum innate***: innate trials of humanity [9.1]

aer: air [8.1]

cum affectu: affectionately [0.1]

afflatus: blowing [12.1]

agnus: *Agnus dei* [23.4] [41.1]; ***verus agnus***: True Lamb [41.1]

agregatio concordantiarum: assemblage of concords (= a *punctus*) [13.2]

alamire: a-la-mi-re (example of a *dictio*) [7.7]

alleluya: alleluia (of the Mass) [23.4] [34.1] [35.2] [35.3] [35.5], alleluia (expression of joy) [34.1]

Alleluya Letabitur iustus: *Alleluia Laetabitur iustus* (an alleluia verse) [34.1]

alternatio: alternation (of modes of measure) [21.5]

alterno: swap around [1.3]

amicitia: friendship [0.1] [9.4]

amicus: friend [0.1]

amor hereos: lovesickness [9.8]

anathomisatio: describing (of) parts [8.1]

angelus: angel [5.8] [22.2] [22.3] [38.2]; ***cantus angelorum***: *cantus* of the angels [5.9]

angulus: angle [18.5]

anima: soul [5.2] [12.1]; ***anima humana***: human soul [3.4]; ***anima brutorum***: soul of brutes [3.4]; ***anima intellectiva***: intellective soul [12.2]

animal: animal [2.9] [8.1]

de animalibus: *De animalibus* (Aristotle) [8.1]

animatus: animated [8.1]

animus: spirit [9.4], mind [27.7]; ***animi iuvenum***: spirits of young men [9.7]; ***animi puellarum***: spirits of girls [9.7]; ***animus hominis***: spirit of man [12.2] [12.5]; ***animus facientis***: spirit of the performer [12.6]; ***animus advertentis***: spirit of the observer [12.6]; ***animi divitum***: minds of the rich [12.6]

antiphona: antiphon [23.2] [23.3] [29.1] [29.4] [29.6] [30.1] [34.1] [43.2]

antiphonarium: antiphonary [26.8]

antiquus: the ancients [3.3] [5.6] [15.2]

[18.2] [24.1], the aged [9.3]; *antiqui patres*: ancient fathers [9.3]; *antiqui viri*: men of old [9.3]; *antiqui consideratores*: ancient thinkers [16.2]

apertus: open (part of a *punctus*) [13.2]

apostoli: apostles [30.2]

appositio: apposition [21.6]

apprehensio: apprehension [26.1]

apprehensivus: apprehensive [0.2]

aqua: water [1.1] [8.1]

archangeli: archangels [38.2]

are: A-re (example of a *dictio*) [7.7]

arismetice: arithmetically [26.2]

arismeticus: the Arithmetician [17.1]; *nichomacus arismeticus*: Nicomachus the arithmetician [2.5]; *arismetici*: arithmeticians [7.7]

aristoteles: Aristotle [0.3] [2.10] [4.9] [5.6] [8.1]; *discipuli aristotelis*: disciples of Aristotle [2.6]; *aristotelis sententia*: opinion of Aristotle [2.8]

armonia: harmony [1.3] [2.7] [4.9] [5.5] [10.3] [13.2] [21.2] [21.3]; *mirabilis armonia*: wonderful harmony [1.3]; *una perfecta armonia*: one perfect harmony [2.2]; *in sonis trina armonia perfecta*: perfect threefold harmony in sounds [3.2]; *armonia prima*: first harmony [3.3]

de armonia musicalis: on musical harmony (= *De institutione musica* of Boethius) [1.2]

armonialiter: in harmony [19.1]

armonice: harmonically [2.2] [5.3] [19.3]

de armonice proprietates: of harmonic properties (= *De institutione musica* of Boethius) [2.5]

armonicus: harmonic (of sound) [5.3]

ars: an art [0.2] [0.5] [5.2] [5.3] [7.10] [12.5] [19.2] [22.4] [24.1] [26.1]; *ars musice*: art of music [*incipit*]; *ars humana*: human art [0.5] [4.9]; *ars divina*: divine art [0.5]; *forma artis*: form of the art [1.4]; *principia artis*: principles of art [2.1] [31.4]; *ars ad cantandum deputatam*: art applied to

singing [5.1]; *operatio artis*: operation of the art [5.10]; *artis regule*: rules of art [5.10]; *ars liberalis*: liberal art [6.1]; *ars scribendi*: art of writing [7.2]; *ars describendis*: art of writing down [15.4]; *ars signandi*: art of notating [15.4]; *bonitas artis*: goodness of the art [18.6]; *ars medicine*: art of medicine [18.7]; *ars magistri franconis*: Art of Master Franco (of Cologne) (= *Ars cantus mensurabilis*) [18.7]; *ars mecanica*: mechanical art [43.1]

articuli fidei christiane: articles of Christian faith [36.2]

artifex: artist [2.1] [14.1] [21.1] [43.1]; *bonus artifex*: good artist [12.3]; *voluntas artificis*: will of the artist [21.1]

artificialis: artificial (of instruments) [5.5]; *instrumenta artificialia*: artificial instruments [9.1]; *sonus artificialis*: artificial sound [12.1]; *artificialis forma*: artificial form [14.1]

artificialiter: by artifice [18.5]

artificiatus: artificial thing [1.4]

ascendendus: ascending [13.2] [31.1] [32.1]

Aspice in me: *Aspice in me* (a night responsory versicle) [28.3]

astronomia: astronomy [22.4]

Au repairier que je fis de prouvence: *Au repairier que je fis de prouvence* (a *cantus versualis*) [9.5]

auctenticus: authentic (of plainchant mode) [26.6]; *autenticus masculinus*: authentic masculine (of plainchant mode) [26.3]; *autenticus protus*: authentic *protus* (= mode 1) [26.3]; *autenticus deuterus*: authentic *deuterus* (= mode 3) [26.3]; *autenticus tritus*: authentic *tritus* (= mode 5) [26.3]; *autenticus tetrardus*: authentic *tetrardus* (= mode 7) [26.3]

auctorizatus: according to authority (of plainchant mode) [26.3]

audacia: boldness [9.4]

audiendus: listen to [27.7], hearing [32.4]

audiens: hearing [1.3]; *audientes*: listeners [32.4]

Audite verbum: *Audite verbum* (a night responsory) [28.3]

auditor: hearer [35.3]; *novi auditores*: new listeners [7.10]

auditus: having heard [9.3], heard [29.2], hearing [16.4] [19.2]; *organum auditus*: organ of hearing [2.7] [7.7]

auris: ear [4.14]

Ausi com lunicorne: *Ausi com l'unicorne* (a *cantus coronatus*) [9.4]

aux: apogee (in planetary motion) [4.12]

aves: birds [2.9]

b quadratus: b-*quadratus* (= b-natural) [26.7]

b rotundus: b-*rotundus* (= b-flat) [26.7]

balare: dancing [12.5]

beatitudines: beatitudes [26.2]

beata et gloriosa virgo: the Blessed and Glorious Virgin [30.2]

beatus gregorius: Blessed Gregory [26.8]

beatus stephanus: Blessed Stephen [9.3]

bemi: B-mi (example of a *dictio*) [7.7]

bemolle/bmolle: b-*molle* (= hexachord with b-flat) [7.7]

Benedicta es celorum: *Benedicta es caelorum* (a sequence) [35.1]

benedictus: *Benedictus* (a Gospel psalm = canticle) [27.8], blessed [43.3]

benefaciens: one doing good [22.1]

benefactor: benefactor [22.1]

beneficiatus: beneficiary [22.1]

bequarre/bquarre: b-*quarre* (= hexachord with b-natural) [7.7]

bethleem civitas: *Bethlehem civitas* (a night responsory) [28.3]

bfabmi: b-fa-b-mi (example of a *dictio*) [7.7] [7.8]

boetius: Boethius [1.2] [1.3] [2.8] [5.5]; *boetius vir latinus*: Boethius the Latin man [2.5]

bonitas: goodness [3.2] [22.5]; excellence [9.4] [9.5]; *bonitas artis*: goodness of the art [18.6]

bonus: good [7.8]; *bonum regimen*: good government [9.4]; *bonus artifex*: good maker [12.3]; *bona discretio*: good judgment [20.8]; *bona opera*: good works [22.1]; *bone operationes*: good works [22.2]; *bonus christianus et fidelis*: good and faithful Christian [23.4] [42.2]

breviora: brevity [18.6]

brevis: breve [18.4] [18.5] [21.6]; *sub brevibus*: in brief [0.1]; *recta brevis*: proper breve [18.4]; *altera brevis*: altered breve [18.4]

bruta: brutes (brute animals) [3.4]

calamitas: disaster [9.3]

calami: reed pipes [12.1]

caliditas: warmth [26.6]

calidum naturale: natural heat [5.2]

calix: chalice [37.1]

campane: bells [12.1]

canes: dogs [2.9]

canones misse: canon of the Mass [23.4]

canones universales: universal rules [18.7]

canonicus: canonical (conforming to rule) [21.9]; *musica canonica*: canonic music [6.2]

cantandus: singing [5.1], [5.3] [16.5]; *modus cantandi*: way of singing [22.4]

cantilena: *cantilena* [5.8] [9.2] [9.5] [9.6] [9.7] [9.8] [9.9] [10.5] [10.7] [12.3] [19.2] [21.7] [25.2] [28.1]; *cantilena entata*: *cantilena entata* ("grafted *cantilena*") [9.9]; *simplex cantilena*: simple *cantilena* [31.1]

canto: sing [1.2] [5.3] [5.9] [9.6] [18.7] [27.5] [30.2] [31.2] [32.4] [34.2] [35.2] [35.4] [35.5] [36.2] [37.1] [38.2] [39.2] [40.2] [41.1] [42.2]

cantor: cantor [29.2]

cantus: *cantus* [4.12] [4.13] [5.8] [7.2] [7.3] [7.5] [7.7] [7.9] [9.2] [9.4] [9.5] [9.6] [9.7] [9.9] [10.2] [10.4] [10.7] [11.1] [12.3] [15.1] [15.2] [16.3] [16.5] [17.10] [17.11] [18.1] [18.3] [18.6] [18.7] [18.8] [19.1] [19.2] [19.3] [19.4] [19.6] [20.3] [20.4] [20.5] [21.4] [21.7]

[22.4] [25.1] [26.1] [26.2] [26.5] [26.8]
[27.2] [27.3] [27.7] [27.9] [28.1] [28.4]
[29.1] [29.5] [29.7] [30.1] [30.2] [30.3]
[31.1] [31.2] [31.3] [32.1] [32.2] [32.3]
[32.4] [32.5] [33.1] [34.1] [35.1] [35.2]
[35.5] [36.1] [36.2] [37.1] [38.1] [38.2]
[39.2] [39.3] [40.1] [40.2] [41.1] [42.1]
[42.2] [43.2], song (of birds) [2.9];
principia cantus: principles of *cantus*
[1.2]; *melodia in cantu*: melody in *cantus* [4.13]; *cantus angelorum*: *cantus* of
the angels [5.9]; *cantus insertus*: *cantus
insertus* ("inserted *cantus*") [9.9]; *cantus
precise mensuratus*: precisely measured
cantus [15.2] [26.1]; *cantus abscisus*:
cantus abscisus (= hocket) [15.3], interrupted *cantus* (in hocket) [19.5]; *cantus
mensuratus*: measured *cantus* [18.5]
[25.1]; *cantus determinatus*: fixed
cantus (= *cantus firmus*) [19.4]; *cantus
antiqus*: old *cantus* [21.1]; *rectus cantus*:
correct *cantus* [21.7]; *cantus civilis*: civil
cantus [25.1]; *cantus vulgalis*: *cantus* of
the people [25.2]; *cantus ecclesiasticus*:
ecclesiastical *cantus* [26.1] [26.2]; *cantus
publicus*: public *cantus* [26.1]; *cantus
ornatus*: ornate *cantus* [27.6]; *cantus
ordinatus*: regular *cantus* [28.1]; *cantus
letitie*: *cantus* of joy [34.1]

cantus coronatus: *cantus coronatus* [9.2]
[9.4] [9.6] [10.3] [10.4] [11.1] [12.3]
[12.4] [27.6] [29.6] [32.4] [35.3] [37.1]

cantus gestualis: *cantus gestualis* [9.2] [9.3]
[10.2] [11.1]

cantus versiculatus: *cantus versiculatus*
[9.2] [11.1]

cantus versualis: *cantus versualis* [9.5]

cantus versicularis: *cantus versicularis*
[10.4]

cathedralis: cathedral [23.2]

cauda: (melodic) tail [29.6] [34.1] [34.2]

causa: reason [2.1], cause [4.9] [16.1];
consonantie causa: cause of consonance
[2.7]; *causa occulta*: occult cause [2.8];
causa non nominata: not-named cause
[2.8]

celestis: heavenly [38.2]; *corpus celestis*:
heavenly body [5.5], celestial body [5.6]

celum: heaven [4.8]

centrum terre: center of the earth [0.4]

cerebrum: brain [21.1]

certes mie ne cuidoie: *Certes mie ne cuidoie*
(a *stantipes*) [9.7]

cfaut: C-fa-ut (example of a *dictio*) [7.7]

Chanter mesteut quer ne men puis tenir:
Chanter m'estuet, quer ne m'en puis tenir (a
cantus versualis) [9.5]

Chi encor querez amoretes: *Chi encor
querez amoretes* (a *ductia*) [9.8]

choree: *caroles* (circle dances) [9.8] [12.5]

christus: Christ [41.1]; *christi fideles*:
faithful of Christ [27.5] [27.7]; *nativitas
christi*: Christ's Nativity [38.1]

christiani: Christians [34.1] [37.1] [39.2];
bonus christianus et fidelis: good and
faithful Christian [23.4] [42.2]; *populus
christianus*: Christian people [27.5]

christus natus est pro nobis: *Christus natus
est pro nobis* (an invitatory) [27.4]

cythara: cithara [12.2]; *corde cithare*:
strings of the cithara [7.5]

cives: citizens [6.1]; *cives laborantes*:
working citizens [9.3]

civilis: civil [6.2] [25.1]

civitas: city [6.1] [9.3] [22.5]

claudo: close [9.9] [10.2] [40.1] [41.1]
[42.2], enclose [13.2]

clausus: closed (part of a *punctus*) [13.2]

clemens exaquiense monacus: Clement,
monk of Lessay [9.1]

coequo: make equal [16.5] [21.6], make
commensurable [18.1]

cogitatio prava: depraved thought [9.7]
[12.6]

cognitio: knowledge [0.2] [2.10], recognition [26.1]; *completa cognitio*: complete
knowledge [0.2]; *cognitio humana*:
human knowledge [0.3]; *cognitio sensitiva*: sensory knowledge [0.3]; *cognitio
intellectiva*: intellectual knowledge [0.3];
naturalis cognitio: natural awareness
[3.4]; *principiorum cognitio*: knowledge

of principles [5.3]; *cognitio universalis*:
universal knowledge [8.1]; *cognitio perfecta*: perfect knowledge [8.1]; *cognitio
compositionis*: knowledge of composition [8.1]; *partium cognitio*: knowledge
of parts [8.1]; *cognitio de animalibus*:
knowledge of animals [8.1]; *cognitio
veritatis*: knowledge of the truth [18.7]
cognoscendus: knowing [8.1]
colericus: hotheaded [19.6]
combinationes: combinations [7.7]
combino: combine [7.7]
communia: commonalities [0.3]
communico: impart [42.2]
communio: communion [23.4] [42.1];
    post communionem: post communion
    [23.4]
communis: common [7.1] [15.4] [19.4];
    commune nomen: common name [16.2]
    [26.3]; *communa mensura*: common
    measure [16.5]
communiter: commonly [12.3] [13.2]
    [19.4], in general [13.1]
complectorio: Compline [23.3]
compleo: complete [2.10]
completus: achieved [23.4]; *completa cog-
    nitio*: complete knowledge [0.2]; *tonus
    completus*: complete tone [7.7]
complexio: constitution [5.7]; *tempera-
    mentum complexionis*: moderation
    of the constitution [5.5]; *complexio
    humana*: human constitution [5.7]
componendus: composing [21.5] [43.1];
    modus componendi: way of composing
    [10.7] [11.1]
componens: composer [43.2]
compono: compose [43.3]
compositio: composition [14.2] [15.1]
    [21.9] [27.1]; *instrumentorum composi-
    tio*: composition of instruments [12.2]
compositor: composer [10.2] [10.4]
compositus: composed [1.4] [7.2] [7.7]
    [15.1] [15.2] [19.1] [19.3] [19.4] [19.5]
    [21.1] [21.2] [27.2] [27.3] [31.1] [32.1]
    [35.1] [37.1] [38.1] [42.1], com-
    pound [2.8]; *concordantia composita*:

compound concord [4.18] [7.5] [7.7];
    musica composita: composed music
    [6.2] [14.3]; *consonantia composita*:
    compound consonance [7.5] [7.7]
compotus: computus [22.4]
computatio: computation [22.4]
conclusio: conclusion [2.1]
concordans: agreeing [43.2], concordant
    [30.1]
concordantia: concord [2.2] [2.3] [4.5]
    [4.9] [4.12] [4.13] [4.14] [4.15] [4.16]
    [4.17] [4.19] [7.5] [7.7] [9.5] [10.3]
    [27.2] [27.6] [31.1] [32.1] [35.1]
    [37.1] [38.1] [42.1]; *concordantie
    infinite*: concords (are) infinite [4.6];
    in sonis concordantie 7: 7 concords in
    sounds [4.8]; *concordantia composita*:
    compound concord [4.18] [7.5] [7.7];
    concordantia simplex: simple concord
    [4.18] [7.5] [7.7]; *concordantie mono-
    cordi*: concords of the monochord [5.8];
    concordantie diverse: diverse concords
    [7.2] [7.4]; *numerus concordantiarum*:
    number of concords [7.7] [13.4]; *bona
    concordantia*: good concord [7.8]; *con-
    cordantiarum discretio*: distinction of
    concords [12.6]; *agregatio concordan-
    tiarum*: assemblage of concords [13.2]
concordia: concord [41.1]
concordo: agree [36.2], be concordant [10.6]
Conditor alme: *Conditor alme* (a hymn)
    [27.9]
conductus: *conductus* [5.10] [19.4] [21.1];
    simplex conductus: simple *conductus*
    [9.4] [27.2] [37.1]
confessi: confessors [30.2]
confuse: imprecisely [8.1]
confusio: confused character [24.1]
conservatio: well-being [22.5]
considerandus: considered [27.1]
consideratio: consideration [27.1]
consonantia: consonance [1.3] [2.2] [2.3]
    [2.5] [2.7] [2.8] [2.9] [3.5] [4.5] [4.14]
    [4.19] [7.5] [7.7] [7.8] [10.2] [15.1]
    [20.5] [21.4]; *consonantia dyatessaron*:
    consonance of the *diatessaron* [1.3];

consonantia dyapente: consonance of the *diapente* [1.3]; *consonantie infinite*: consonances (are) infinite [2.4]; *tres consonantie*: the three consonances [2.5] [2.9]; *numerus consonantiarum*: number of consonances [2.7] [2.10] [4.14]; *consonantie causa*: cause of consonance [2.7]; *consonantia naturalis*: natural consonance [2.10]; *consonantia perfectissima*: most perfect consonance [3.3]; *consonantia dyapason*: *diapason* consonance [4.1]; *consonantia simplex*: simple consonance [7.5] [7.7]; *consonantia composita*: compound consonance [7.5] [7.7]; *bona consonantia*: good consonance [7.8]; *consonantia dictaminis*: consonance of text [9.7] [10.2]; *consonantia perfecta*: perfect consonance [13.3] [15.1] [15.2] [19.1] [20.5]; *consonantia imperfecta*: imperfect consonance [15.1]; *cum truncatione consonantia*: consonance with truncation (in hocket) [19.5]

consono: be consonant [10.6], sound together [19.1]

consuetudo: custom [27.1]

continuans: continuing [7.7]

continuatio: continuation [7.7]

continuatus: continued [4.12]

continuum: continuum [16.4]

continuus: continuous [2.2] [4.11]

convictus: community life [6.1]

convivium: banquet [19.4]; *magnus convivium*: great celebration [9.6]

cooperaturus: roof (of a house) [21.7]

cor: heart [21.1] [27.7]; *corda puellarum et iuvenum*: hearts of girls and young men [9.8]; *corda audientium*: hearts of the listeners [32.4]; *corda auditorum*: hearts of the hearers [35.3]; *corda fidelium*: hearts of the faithful [37.1]

corda: a string [4.1] [7.3] [7.7] [12.1] [12.2] [13.4]; *corde cithare*: strings of the cithara [7.5]; *abreviatio et elengatio cordarum*: shortening and lengthening of strings [12.2]

cordosus: stringed (instruments) [12.2]

cornu: horns [2.9]

coronatus: *coronatus* (mode of *cantus*) [9.2] [9.5]; *cantus coronatus*: *cantus coronatus* [9.2] [9.4] [9.6] [10.3] [10.4] [11.1] [12.3] [12.4] [27.6] [29.6] [32.4] [35.3] [37.1]

corono: crown [9.4]

corporalis: bodily [22.3]

corpus: body [16.5]; *corpus solis*: body of the sun [0.4]; *corpus celestis*: heavenly body [5.5], celestial body [5.6]; *corpus humanus*: human body [5.5]; *corpus simplex*: simple body [8.1]; *corpus cubicum*: cubic body [26.2]; *corpus christi*: Body of Christ [39.2] [40.2] [42.2]

corrigo: correct [0.2]

corrumpo: corrupt [0.5] [1.3] [2.7]

corruptio: decay [4.9]

creator: the Creator [0.2] [3.4] [22.1] [22.3] [23.4] [32.2]; *omnium sublimis creator*: the sublime Creator of all things [3.2]; *laudandum creator*: praise of the Creator [6.2]; *creator omnipotens*: the Almighty Creator [43.3]

creatum: thing created [22.1]

creature: creatures (of the world) [22.1]

creatus: created [3.4]

Credo in deum: *Credo in deum* (Apostles' Creed) [23.4] [36.1]

cromaticum: chromatic (genus of tetrachord) [5.8]

cubicum corpus: cubic body [26.2]

cubicus: cube (= cubic number) [2.5] [26.2]

cum opposita proprietate: with opposite propriety [18.6]

cum proprietate: with propriety [18.6]

cymbala: cymbals [12.1]

david: David (prophet) [3.2]

De profundis: *De profundis* (a tract) [35.5]

decantandus: singing [38.2]

decantans: singer [20.8]

decanto: sing [9.4] [9.6] [9.8] [19.2] [19.4] [27.7] [28.1] [28.4] [29.5] [35.1] [35.3] [35.4] [38.2]

decoratio: enhancement [9.6] [19.2]
demonstratio: demonstration [1.2]
denominatio: specification [26.3]
depressio: depression (in *cantus*) [4.12]
describendus: description [7.2] [7.4], writing down [15.4] [18.8]
descriptio: writing down [7.8], description [8.1] [9.9] [11.1] [19.4] [25.2]
descendendus: descending [13.2] [31.1] [32.1]
designandus: designating [18.8]
determinans: determined [12.6]
determinatio: specification [18.3]
determinatus: fixed [10.2] [10.3] [10.4] [10.6] [18.1] [27.6], specified [33.1]; *numerus determinatus*: fixed number [4.7]; *determinata tempora*: appointed times [22.3]; *hora determinata*: fixed hour [23.3]; *determinata* (*inceptio*): fixed (beginning) [26.7]
Deus in adiutorium: *Deus in adiutorium* [27.7]
deus pater: God the Father [37.1] [41.1] [43.3]
deuterus: *deuterus* (second modal group encompassing mode 3 ("authentic *deuterus*") and mode 4 ("plagal of the *deuterus*")) [26.3]
devote: devoutly [32.4]
devotio: devotion [27.7] [35.3]
devotus: devoted [38.2]; *devota oratio*: devout prayer [23.4]; *devotus offerendus*: devout offering [37.1]
dicendus: saying [4.9], discussed [12.4]
dictamen: text [9.4] [9.5] [10.6] [11.1] [12.5] [18.6] [19.1] [19.3] [21.6] [43.1]; *consonantia dictaminis*: consonance of text [9.7] [10.2]
dictio: [7.2] term (including combination of a letter and solmization syllable) / [7.7] [7.10] [18.5] [21.6] [29.2]
dictum: view [4.7], saying [4.8], claim [5.6], discussion [12.4], word [21.9]; *dicta poetarum*: sayings of the poets [4.8]
dies: day [0.5] [22.2]; *7 dies*: 7 days (of the week) [4.8]; *dies nostri*: our days [6.1]

differens: different [13.2], different one [28.2]
differentia: differentiation [7.4] [26.3], *differentia* (psalm cadence) [29.4]; *triplex differentia*: threefold differentiation [7.7], threefold way (of differentiating) [9.2]; *diversa differentia*: diverse differentiation [18.6]; *articulata differentia*: appropriate *differentia* (psalm cadence) [25.1]; *differentia contraria*: opposing differentiation [26.3]
difficilis res: difficult piece (of music) [13.4]
diffinitio: definition [8.1]
dimensio: dimension [16.5]
discantus: discant [15.1]
discipuli: disciples (of Aristotle) [2.6]
discordans: discordant [10.2]
discretio: distinction [16.4]; *soni discretio*: discernment of sound [12.2]; *concordantiarum discretio*: distinction of concords [12.6]; *discretio sillabarum*: separation of syllables [18.6], differentiation of syllables [19.1] [19.3]; *bona discretio*: good judgment [20.8]
distantia: distance [0.4]
distinctio: distinction [12.6] [22.4]
distinguendus: distinguishing [8.1]
diversi: different people [17.1]
diversifico: diversify [23.5] [27.1] [27.3] [27.4] [27.9] [29.7] [30.3] [32.5] [38.1] [39.3] [41.1] [42.1] [43.2] [43.3], differentiate [26.9]
diversimodi: diverse ways [18.7]
diversitas: diversity [0.5] [4.9] [9.7] [12.2] [18.7] [27.1] [27.9] [29.4], variation [26.8]; *scriptorum diversitas*: diversity of writings [0.5]; *opinionum diversitas*: diversity of opinions [0.5]; *signa diversitatis*: diversifying signs (in notation) [7.7]; *diversitas sillabarum*: diversity of syllables [27.9]
diversus: diverse [6.1] [27.1], different [10.7]; *diversi soni*: diverse sounds [5.10]; *diversi usus*: diverse uses [6.1] [23.5] [27.1] [29.4] [32.5]; *diversa*

ydiomata: diverse idioms [6.1]; *diverse lingue*: diverse tongues [6.1]; *civitates vel regiones diverse*: diverse cities or regions [6.1]; *diversus cantus*: diverse *cantus* [7.2], *cantus* different (to another) [9.6]; *diverse concordantie*: diverse concords [7.2] [7.4]; *diversa figuratio*: diverse figuring [7.7]; *diversa nominatio*: diverse naming [7.7]; *figura diversa*: diverse figure [7.7]; *diversi modi*: different modes [17.1], diverse modes [29.2] [29.4]; *diversi toni*: diverse tones [17.6] [27.4]; *diverse differentie*: diverse differentiations [18.6]; *diversi tractus*: diverse treatises [18.7]; *diverse antiphone*: diverse antiphons [29.4]; *diversa festa*: diverse feasts [32.5] [39.3]; *diverse sollempnitates*: diverse religious festivals [38.1], diverse solemnities [39.3]

dives: the rich [12.3] [12.6] [19.4]

divinus: divine (of nature or art) [0.5]; *divinus spiritus*: divine inspiration [1.3]; *laus divina*: divine praise [3.2] [31.2]; *lex divina*: divine law [4.9]; *inspiratio divina*: divine inspiration [5.9]; *divinum misterium*: divine mystery [23.4]

divisibilis: divisible [16.4]

divisio: division [5.9] [5.10] [12.1] [12.2]; *divisio particularia*: particular division [5.9]; *recta divisio*: correct division [6.1]; *divisio musice*: division of music [7.11]

divisus: divided (of a whole) [6.1]

doceo: teach [3.3] [22.4]

doctrina musicalis: musical teaching [0.1]

domine refugium: *Domine refugium* (an introit) [30.3]

dominum qui fecit nos: *Dominum qui fecit nos* (an invitatory) [27.4]

dominus: Lord [40.2]

domus: house [20.2]; *cooperturus domus*: roof of a house [21.7]; *domi religionis*: religious houses [23.2]

Dona eis requiem sempiternam: *Dona eis requiem sempiternam* (in the *Agnus dei* for the dead) [41.1]

Dona nobis pacem: *Dona nobis pacem* (in the *Agnus dei*) [41.1]

dona spiritus: gifts of the spirit [4.8]

dorius: dorian (= mode 1) [26.4]

dsolre: D-sol-re (example of a *dictio*) [7.7]

duco: draw (towards something) [9.8], lead [35.4]

ductia: *ductia* [7.8] [9.2] [9.8] [10.6] [12.3] [12.4] [12.5] [12.6] [13.1] [13.3] [14.1] [14.2] [25.2] [35.4] [36.1] [37.1] [38.1] [42.2]; *ductia pierron*: ductia Pierron [13.3]; *punctus ductie*: punctus of a *ductia* [40.1]

ductus: led [1.3] [3.3] [13.4]

dupla proportio: duple proportion [1.3] [4.1] [4.17]

duplum: *duplum* (= part above a tenor) [20.1] [20.8] [21.8]; *duplum organum*: organum duplum [15.1]

durus: harsh (of sound) [4.14]

dyapason: diapason (= octave) [1.3] [1.4] [2.8] [3.3] [4.1] [4.10] [4.17] [19.1] [20.3] [20.4] [25.3] [26.6]; *dyapason consonantia*: diapason consonance [4.1]; *duplex dyapason*: double *diapason* [7.7]; *dyapason proportio*: proportion of the *diapason* [20.4], *diapason* proportion [20.8] [21.3] ; *species dyapason*: species of *diapason* [25.3]; *modus dyapason*: mode of *diapason* [25.3]

dyapente: diapente (= fifth) [1.3] [1.4] [2.8] [3.3] [4.2] [4.10] [4.16] [4.17] [4.18] [7.7] [19.1] [20.3] [20.4] [20.8] [21.3] [26.6]; *consonantia dyapente*: consonance of the *diapente* [1.3]; *dyapente proportio*: *diapente* proportion [21.2]

dyatessaron: diatessaron (= fourth) [1.3] [1.4] [2.8] [3.3] [4.3] [4.10] [4.15] [4.17] [19.1] [26.6]; *consonantia dyatessaron*: consonance of the *diatessaron* [1.3]

dyatonicum: diatonic (genus of tetrachord) [5.8]

dyesis/dyesys: diesis (= minor semitone) [1.4] [4.13] [5.8] *dytonus/ditonus*: ditone [1.4] [4.10] [4.14] [4.18]

Ecce apparebit: *Ecce apparebit* (a night responsory) [28.3]
ecclesia: church [19.4] [27.1] [29.4] [32.5], the Church [23.4] [38.2]; *cathedrales ecclesie*: cathedral churches [23.2]; *ecclesie publice*: public churches [23.2]
ecclesiasticalis: ecclesiastical (of books) [26.8]
ecclesiastici: churchmen [4.12]
ecclesiasticus: ecclesiastical (of music/*cantus*) [5.10] [6.2] [19.4]; *vir ecclesiasticus*: churchman [22.4] [22.5]; *servitium ecclesiasticum*: ecclesiastical service [23.1]; *cantus ecclesiasticus*: ecclesiastical *cantus* [26.1] [26.2]; *musica ecclesiastica*: ecclesiastical music [27.1] [43.3]
econtrario: reverse [17.3] [17.5] [17.9]
econtrarius: conversely [4.12]
edificium: building [0.5] [20.2]
efficiens: agent [1.4] [2.10]
Ego autem: *Ego autem* (an introit) [30.3]
Ego mundus: *Ego mundus* (a hocket) [20.3]
elevatio: elevation (in *cantus*) [4.12]; *elevatio corporis christi*: elevation of the Body of Christ [39.2] [40.2]
elementa: elements [2.5]; *mixtio elementorum*: mixing of elements [5.5]
elongatio: stretching (of a string) [7.7]; *elongatio cordarum*: lengthening of strings [12.2]
enarmonicum: enharmonic (genus of tetrachord) [5.8]
epar: liver [21.1]
epistola: epistle [23.4] [23.5] [35.2]
equalis: equal [4.11] [16.4] [18.2] [18.5]
equalitas sillabarum: equality of syllables [27.9]
equi: horses [2.9]
Eructavit: *Eructavit* (an introit) [30.3]
eruditio: learning [22.4]
Et ne nos: *Et ne nos* (from the *Pater noster*) [40.1]

euphonia: euphony [20.4] [28.1]
euvangelium: Gospel [23.4] [23.5] [35.2] [36.2]; *psalmus euvangelista*: Gospel psalm [27.7] [27.8]; *euvangelium sacrum*: Holy Gospel [35.4]
examinans: examining [1.3]
exaquiense: Lessay [9.1]
exempla: examples [26.8]
exemplar: exemplar [43.2]
exitus: (melodic) ending [29.6]
exorandus: praying [27.7]
experientia: experience [3.3] [4.7] [4.10] [4.18] [5.9] [15.1]
expertus: experienced (in) [27.1]
explico: explain [0.1], articulate [5.2]

fa: fa (solmization syllable) [7.7] [29.2] [29.3] [29.7]; *faut*: fa-ut (hexachordal mutation) [7.7]
fabrorum officia: workshops of blacksmiths [1.3]
fabulose: in fables [1.1]
faciens: performer [12.5] [12.6]
facultas: nature (quality of something) [0.3]
falsa musica: false music [7.8]
fantasia: conjecture [17.8]
farsa: farse [43.2]
fastidium: scorn [18.7], odious thing [29.4]
femella: female [26.6]
festum: feast [9.6] [12.2] [12.3] [19.2] [19.4], feast (ecclesiastical) [22.3] [32.5] [39.3]
fides: faith [9.3]; *articuli fidei christiane*: articles of Christian faith [36.2]
fideles: faithful [38.2]; *christi fideles*: faithful of Christ [27.5] [27.7]; *defunctus fidelis*: faithful departed [32.3]; *corda fidelium*: hearts of the faithful [37.1]
fidelitas: loyalty [0.1]
figura: (notational) figure [12.5] [17.2] [17.4] [17.6] [17.7] [18.5] [18.7], (numerical) figure [18.5]; *figura diversa*: diverse figure [7.7]; *figure similes et disiuncta*: figures similar and distinct

(= figures of the same shape but of different durational value) [17.4]; *figura consimilis*: similar figure [17.7]; *figura similis*: similar figure [17.8]; *figura indeterminata*: indeterminate figure [18.3]; *figura quadrata*: square figure [18.3]; *ligatio figurarum*: binding of figures (= ligatures) [18.6]; *figura ligata*: ligated figure (= ligature) [18.6]; *pluralitas figurarum*: plurality of figures [18.6]

figurandus: figuring [16.5]

figurans: figuring [7.7]

figuratio diversa: diverse figuring [7.7]

figuratus: figured [26.8]

figuro: figure [7.10] [29.2]

filia: daughter [3.3]

finio: end [37.1], finish [9.9]

finis: end [2.10] [4.12] [9.9] [13.2] [18.6] [25.1] [25.2] [26.1] [26.3] [26.5] [26.6] [26.8] [29.2] [29.4] [34.1] [43.2]; *sine fine*: without end [38.2]

finis punctorum: *finis punctorum* (type of pause) [18.2]

finitus: finite (in number) [4.7]

fistule: pipes [12.1]; *sonus fistularum*: sound of pipes [2.9]

forma: form [1.4] [2.10] [5.1] [5.3] [11.1] [22.3]; *forma artis*: form of the art [1.4]; *forma naturalis*: natural form [2.6] [12.2] [14.1]; *forma musicalis*: musical form [9.1] [11.2] [12.2] [12.3]; *forma artificialis*: artificial form [14.1]; *forma debita*: requisite form [43.1]

fortitudo: bravery [9.4]

franco: Franco (of Cologne) [17.10] [18.7]

frigius: *phrygian* (= mode 3) [26.4]

fundamentum: foundation [2.6] [20.2]

galienus: Galen [18.7]

gallice: in the French [9.4] [9.5] [9.6] [9.7] [9.8] [9.9]

gamaut: Gamma-ut (example of a *dictio*) [7.7]

gaudeamus: *Gaudeamus* (an introit) [30.3]

generalis: general [31.2], general thing [31.2]; *in generali*: in general [34.1]

generaliter: generally [11.1] [12.3] [15.3] [23.1] [36.2], general [22.5], in general [36.2] [43.3]

generatio: generation (process of) [4.9] [8.1]; *generatio animalium*: generation of animals [21.1]

generatus: generated [12.1]

genus: genus [7.7] [16.1], kind [5.5] [5.8] [6.2]

gestualis: gestulais (mode of *cantus*) [9.2]; *cantus gestualis*: *cantus gestualis* [9.2] [9.3] [10.2] [11.1]

gestum: epic [10.2]; *gesta heroum*: deeds of heroes [9.3]

de Girardo de viana: *About Girardo de Viana* (a *cantus gestualis*) [10.2]

gloria: glory [0.2] [39.2]; *in sonis nomen glorie*: name of glory in sounds [3.2]

gloria in excelsis: *Gloria in excelsis* [23.4] [32.1] [43.2]

gloria patri: *Gloria patri* [28.1] [28.2] [28.3] [30.1] [30.3]

gloriosus: glorious [43.3]; *trinitas gloriosa*: glorious Trinity [3.3]; *gloriosus benefactor*: glorious benefactor [22.1]; *gloriosa nativitas christi*: glorious Nativity of Christ [22.3]; *gloriosum servitium*: glorious service [23.4]; *gloriosa virgo*: the Glorious Virgin [30.2]

graduale: the gradual [26.8]

gramatica/grammatica: grammar [22.4] [26.1]

gramaticus/grammaticus: grammarian [7.2] [18.5]

grammaticalis: (rules of) grammar [23.5]

gratia: grace [0.6]

gravandus: slackening (of a string) [7.7]

gravis: grave (of register) [7.7] [25.1] [26.5] [26.7]

gravitas: depth [4.11] [4.12] [7.3]

greci: Greeks [31.4]

grecus: Greek [31.4]; *ydioma greca*: Greek language [31.4] [34.1]

gregorius: Gregory the Great [5.10]; *beatus gregorius*: Blessed Gregory [26.8]

Gsolreut: G-sol-re-ut (example of a *dictio*) [7.7]

Gut: Γ-ut (example of a *dictio*) [7.7]

hastiludium: spear game [12.2]

heroes: heroes [9.3]

Hodie nobis: *Hodie nobis* (a night responsory) [28.3]

homo: man [0.5] [2.9] [3.1] [4.9] [22.2] [22.3] [25.1]; ***homines***: people [1.2]; ***homines parisius***: people in Paris [6.1] [6.2]

hoquetus: hocket [15.3] [19.5] [20.1] [20.3] [20.6] [21.7]

hore: Hours (of the Divine Office) [23.1] [23.3] [27.7]; ***hora determinata***: fixed hour [23.3]

humanus: (*musica*) *humana* [5.5], human [41.1]; ***cognitio humana***: human knowledge [0.3]; ***ars humana***: human art [0.5] [4.9]; ***anima humana***: human soul [3.4]; ***leges et operationes humane***: human laws and operations [4.9]; ***corpus humanus***: human body [5.5]; ***complexio humana***: human complexion [5.7]; ***vox humana***: human voice [9.1] [9.2] [11.2] [12.5] [18.2]; ***humana eruditio***: human learning [22.4]

humilitas: humility [35.3]

hymnus: hymn [23.2] [23.3] [27.6]; ***hymnus glorie dei***: hymn to the glory of God (= the *Sanctus*) [39.2]

hystoria regis karoli: *History of King Charlemagne* (a *cantus gestualis*) [9.3]

de hystoriis: *De historiis* (Aristotle) [8.1]

ictus: *ictus* [12.5]; ***ictus malleorum***: hammer blows [1.3]

ignis: fire [8.1]

ignorans: ignorant [5.6]

ignoro: not know [1.2], be ignorant [5.9], ignore [22.4]

illiteratus: unlettered [12.5]; ***sonus illiteratus***: unlettered sound [12.5] [12.6]

immediatus: without mediation [3.4]

immensurabilis: unmeasured (of music) [5.10]

imperfectio: imperfection [3.4]

imperfectus: imperfect [4.14] [18.5]

improportionalis: not in proportion [1.3]

in actu: actual [1.4]

inceptio: beginning [26.7] [29.4]

incipiens: beginning [7.7]

incipio: begin [*incipit*] [9.6] [9.9] [10.5] [20.3] [20.4] [20.6] [27.2] [29.2] [34.1] [37.1] [40.1]

inclinatio naturalis: natural inclination [2.9] [3.3] [13.4]

incompositus: in disorder [5.8]

increatus: uncreated (of truth) [0.5]

indeterminatus: indeterminate (of notational figures) [18.3]

industria naturalis: natural effort [15.1]

inequalis: unequal [18.5]

inequalitas: (species of) inequality [2.8]

infinitum: infinity [16.4]; infinite (of consonances) [2.4], infinite (of concords) [4.6]

initium: beginning [26.1] [26.3] [43.2]

innatus: innate [1.2] [3.4] [9.1]

inspiciendus: paying attention [26.1] [26.2], looking [26.8], inspecting [29.7] [43.2]

inspiratio divina: divine inspiration [5.9]

instrumentum: instrument [5.2] [25.1]; ***primum instrumentum***: first instrument [5.2]; ***principale instrumentum***: principal instrument [5.2]; ***soni instrumentorum***: sounds of instruments [5.5]; ***instrumenta naturalia***: natural instruments [5.5] [17.8]; ***instrumenta artificialia***: artificial instruments [5.5] [9.1]; ***instrumenta***: (musical) instruments [12.1] [12.2]; ***instrumentorum compositio***: composition of instruments [12.2]; ***instrumentorum divisio***: division of instruments [12.2]; ***instrumenta cum cordis***: instruments with strings [12.2]; ***instrumenta cordosa***: stringed instruments [12.2]

instrumentalis: instrumental [11.2],

instrumental (division of music) [5.9]; ***instrumentalis musica***: *musica instrumentalis* [5.5], instrumental music [5.8]

intellectus: intellect [16.1]; ***intellectus practicus***: practical intellect [5.2] [5.3]

intentio: intention [0.2] [0.4] [0.6] [6.1]

intimo: explain [0.2]

intonatio: intonation (formula) [29.2] [30.3]; ***intonatio psalmi***: intonation of the psalm [29.2]

intono: intone [30.3]

introitus: introit [23.4] [30.1] [31.2]

inveniendus: finding [0.4], discovering [1.5]

inventio: discovery [0.5] [1.5]; ***inventio litterarum***: invention of letters [7.2]

inventor: (first) discoverer (= Pythagoras) [2.5]

inventus: found [27.6]

ad invitandum: invite [27.5]

invitatorium: invitatory [23.2] [27.2] [27.3] [27.4] [27.5] [27.7] [28.1]

invitatus: invited [27.7]

Iohanne damasceno: John of Damascus [3.4]

Iohannes de garlandia/guerlandia/guearlandia: Johannes de Garlandia [4.7] [4.14] [5.5] [17.7]

iuncture manuum: joints of the hands [7.10]

iuvamentum: support [0.1]

iuvenes: young men [0.1] [9.6] [9.7] [9.8], the young [9.5] [19.6]

Je mendormi el sentier: *Je m'endormi el sentier* (a *cantus insertus/cantilena entata*) [9.9]

kadragesima: Lent [22.3] [32.3]

karitas: charity [39.2], love [9.4]

karolus: Charlemagne [9.3]

kyrie eleyson: *Kyrie eleison* [23.4] [31.1] [32.3] [43.2]

la: la (solmization syllable) [7.7] [29.2]

[29.7]; ***lare***: la-re (hexachordal mutation) [29.7]

labor: labor [9.5]

laborans: working (citizens) [9.3]

lambertus: Lambert [17.8]

lapides: stones [8.1]

latini: the Latins [31.4]; ***vir latinus***: the Latin man (= Boethius) [2.5]

latitudo: (melodic) range [26.7] [29.7]

latores: makers of the law [22.3]

latus: side (of a cube) [26.2]

Laudamus te benedicimus te: *Laudamus te benedicimus te* (from the *Gloria in excelsis deo*) [32.2]

laudandus: praise [6.2]

laudo: praise [3.2] [22.2] [22.3] [32.2]

laus: praise [0.2] [0.5] [19.4] [22.1] [22.5] [43.3]; ***laus divina***: divine praise [3.2] [31.2]

lectio: reading [23.2] [23.5] [28.4]

legenda: readings [26.2] [27.7] [28.4]

legistus: lawyer [43.1]

Letabundus: *Laetabundus* (a sequence) [35.1]

letentur celi: *Laetentur caeli* (a night responsory) [28.3]

leges: laws [4.9]; ***lex divina***: divine law [4.9]

liber: book [24.1]; ***liber de armonia musicali***: book on musical harmony (= *De institutione musica* of Boethius) [1.2]; ***liber qui thimeo intitulatur***: book entitled the *Timaeus* (Plato) [2.5]; ***liber de proprietatibus armonicis***: book of harmonic properties (= *De institutione musica* of Boethius) [2.5]; ***liber de theoria planetarum***: book *On the Theory of the Planets* (anon.) [5.6]; ***liber qui de animalibus intitulatur***: book which is called *De animalibus* (Aristotle) [8.1]; ***liber qui de hystoriis dicitur***: book which is called *De historiis* (Aristotle) [8.1]; ***liber qui de partibus appellatur***: book which is called *De partibus* (Aristotle) [8.1]; ***liber galieni qui dicitur tegni***: book of Galen which is called *Tegni*

[18.7]; *libri ecclesiasticales*: ecclesiastical books [26.8]

liberalis: liberal (art) [6.1]

liberalitas: liberality [9.4]

lidius: *lydian* (= mode 5) [26.4]

ligatio figurarum: binding of figures (= ligatures) [18.6]

ligatus: ligated (figure) [18.6]

linea: line [7.3] [7.5] [7.7] [13.2] [18.1] [18.2] [18.3] [18.6]; *linea extensa*: extended line [16.5]

lingua: tongue (language) [3.2]; *diverse lingue*: diverse tongues [6.1]

lira: lyre [12.2]

littera: letter (of the alphabet) [7.7] [7.10] [12.5] [18.5]; *inventio litterarum*: invention of letters [7.2]

litterati: the educated [19.2] [19.4]

logicus: logic [5.6]

longa: a long [9.4] [18.3] [18.5] [32.4]; *longus tempus*: long time [0.1]; *longus tractus*: drawn-out longs [9.6]; *longa perfecta*: perfect long [18.3]; *longa imperfecta*: imperfect long [18.3]

loquendus: speaking [22.4]

ludi: games [12.3]

magistri: masters [9.4]; *magister pytagoras*: Master Pythagoras [2.5]; *magister Iohannes de garlandia/guerlandia/guearlandia*: Master Johannes de Garlandia [4.7] [4.14] [5.5] [17.7]; *magister franco*: Master Franco (of Cologne) [17.10] [18.7]; *legis magistri*: masters of the law [22.3]

magistrans: *magistrans* (in hocket) [20.3]

magnanimitas: magnanimity [9.4]

magnificat: *Magnificat* (a Gospel psalm = canticle) [27.8]

malleus: hammer [1.3]; *ictus malleorum*: hammer blows [1.3]

manus: hand [1.3]; *manus sacerdotis*: hand of the priest [37.1]; *iuncture manuum*: joints of the hands [7.10]

martinus ecce: *Martinus ecce* (an invitatory) [27.4]

martyres: martyrs [30.2]

martyria sanctorum: martyrdom of saints [9.3]

masculus: male [26.6]

mater: mother [3.3]

matematica: mathematics [2.5] [2.10]

materia: material [1.4] [5.1] [11.1] [43.1]; *subiecte materia*: subject matter [0.3]; *materia propria*: proper material [5.3]; *delectabilis materia et ardua*: delightful and lofty material [9.4]; *copia materie*: abundance of material [10.2] [10.4]; *tota sententia materie*: whole statement of the material [10.3]; *materia naturalis*: natural material [14.1]; *materia corporalis*: bodily material [22.3]

matutinus: Matins [23.1] [23.2] [27.7]

mecanicus/mechanicus: mechanical art [0.5] [6.1], artisan [25.1]

medio: progress [37.1]

mediocres: ordinary people [9.3]

medium: middle [25.1] [25.2] [26.1] [26.3] [26.6] [43.2]

melioro: improve [0.2] [0.5]

melodia in cantu: melody in *cantus* [4.13]

melos: tune [25.2]

membrum: branch (of music) [5.9] [6.1] [6.2] [7.1] [7.11] [9.1] [23.1]; *membra dividentia*: dividing branches [6.1]; *membra generalia*: general branches (of music) [6.2]; *membra principalia*: principal members (of a body) [21.1]

memoria: memory [42.2]

mensura: measure [16.2] [16.3] [16.4] [16.5] [17.1] [17.10] [17.11] [18.8] [21.1] [21.7]; *uniformis mensura*: uniform measure [15.2]; *mensura motus*: measure of motion [16.1]; *communa mensura*: common measure [16.5]; *recta mensura*: right measure [21.1]

mensurabilis: measured (of music) [5.10]

mensurandus: being measured [15.4], measuring [17.11] [18.8]

mensurans: measured [12.5], that (which) measures [16.1]

mensuratus: measured [5.10] [18.1], the

measured [18.8] [21.9]; *musica mensurata*: measured music [6.2]; *cantus mensuratus*: measured *cantus* [18.5] [25.1]

mensuro: measure [4.8] [4.13] [5.10] [12.5] [15.4] [16.3] [16.5]

metalla: metals [8.1]

methaforice: metaphorically [25.1]

methaphora: metaphor [3.3]

mi: mi (solmization syllable) [7.7] [29.2] [29.3] [29.7]; *mifa*: mi-fa (solmization syllables) [7.7]

microcosmus: microcosm [4.9]

mineralia: minerals [8.1]

minor mundus: lesser world [4.9]

miserie: miseries [9.3]

missa: Mass [23.1] [23.4] [30.1] [30.2] [31.2] [32.3] [33.1] [34.2] [35.5] [42.2]

missolidius: mixolydian (= mode 7) [26.4]

misterium: mystery [31.4] [35.2]; *divinum misterium*: divine mystery [23.4]

mixti: mixtures [8.1]

mixtio: mixing [4.14]; *mixtio elementorum*: mixing of elements [5.5]

mobilitas: mobility [19.6]

moderni: the moderns [7.8] [15.2] [15.3] [16.5] [17.10] [18.2] [18.7] [24.1]

modice regule: modest rules [15.1]

modus: way [0.2] [1.2] [4.12] [5.2] [5.10] [7.7] [15.2] [18.2] [31.1], means [7.6], mode (of measure) [17.2] [17.8] [17.10] [21.1], type [9.1] [9.2], (plainchant) mode [25.1] [26.2] [26.3] [26.8] [27.1] [27.9] [29.2] [30.3] [32.5] [37.1] [42.1] [43.2], mode (= a melodic ending) [29.6]; *modus procedendi*: way of proceeding [0.3], manner of proceeding [0.6]; *modus inveniendi*: method of finding [0.4], manner of discovering [1.5]; *modus subtiliori*: more subtle way [4.8] [7.7]; *modus describendi*: method of description [7.2], means of description [7.4], way of writing down [18.8]; *modus diversitatis*: way of diversification [7.7]; *modi cantus*: types of *cantus* [9.5]; *ad modum circuli*: like a circle [9.6]; *modus cantilenarum*: type of *cantilena* [9.9]; *ad modum cantilenarum*: in the way of *cantilena* [9.9]; *modus componendi*: way of composing [10.7] [11.1]; *modus mensurandi*: way of being measured [15.4], way of measuring [17.11] [18.8]; *diversus modus*: different mode [17.1], diverse mode [29.2] [29.4]; *modus designandi*: way of designating [18.8]; *modorum alternatio*: alternation of modes (of measure) [21.5]; *modorum unitas*: unity of modes (of measure) [21.5]; *ad modum tegularum*: in the manner of the tiles [21.7]; *modus loquendi*: way of speaking [22.4]; *modus proferendi*: way of pronouncing [22.4]; *modus cantandi*: way of singing [22.4]; *modus dyapason*: mode of *dyapason* [25.3]; *tonorum modi*: modes of tones [26.9]; *ad modum simplicis conductus*: in the manner of a simple *conductus* [27.2] [37.1]; *ad modum cantus coronati*: in the manner of a *cantus coronatus* [27.6] [32.4] [35.3] [37.1]; *ad modum stantipedis*: in the manner of a *stantipes* [35.3] [40.1]; *ad modum ductie*: in the manner of a *ductia* [35.4] [36.1] [37.1] [38.1]; *ad modum puncti ductie*: in the manner of a *punctus* of a *ductia* [40.1]; *ad modum puncti clausi*: in the manner of a closed *punctus* [42.2]

monacus: monk (= Clement of Lessay) [9.1]

monocordum: monochord [5.8] [7.7]

mores: behavior [8.1]; *mores hominum*: behavior of men [0.2]

motellus: *motellus* (= motet) [21.1] [21.5] [21.6]

motetus: motet [5.10] [15.3] [19.1], *motetus* (= part above a tenor) [20.1] [20.3] [20.4] [21.2]

motus: movement [0.2] [12.5], motion [2.2] [4.12] [5.5]; *motus facientis*: movement of the performer [12.5]; *mensura motus*: measure of motion [16.1]

movendus: movement [5.6]; *ad ornate movendum*: to move decorously [12.5] *movens*: moving thing [0.2], that (which) moves [16.1]

multiplex: multiplex [2.8]; *multiplex superparticularis*: multiplex superparticular [2.8]; *multiplex superpartiens*: multiplex superpartient [2.8]

multitudo: multitude [24.1]

mundus: world [4.9]; *minor mundus*: lesser world [4.9]; *mundi creature*: creatures of the world [22.1]

muse: the Muses [1.1]

musica: music [0.2] [1.1] [1.2] [1.4] [4.19] [5.1] [5.3] [5.4] [5.5] [5.6] [5.10] [5.11] [6.1] [6.2] [22.4] [22.5]; *principia musice*: principles of music [0.4] [1.2] [1.5] [2.2] [4.5]; *tota musica*: all music [4.19]; *musica mundana/mondana*: *musica mundana* [5.5]; *musica humana*: *musica humana* [5.5]; *musica instrumentalis*: *musica instrumentalis* [5.5], instrumental music [5.8]; *musica nullo modo mensurata*: music not measured in any way [5.10]; *operatio musice*: operation of music [5.10]; *musica simplex*: simple music [6.2] [14.2]; *musica civilis*: civil music [6.2]; *musica vulgalis*: music of the people [6.2] [14.2]; *musica composita*: composed music [6.2] [14.3]; *musica regularis*: regulated music [6.2] [14.3]; *musica canonica*: canonic music [6.2]; *musica mensurata*: measured music [6.2]; *falsa musica*: false music [7.8]; *divisio musice*: division of music [7.11]; *musica precise mensurali*: precisely measured music [21.9]; *musica ecclesiastica*: ecclesiastical music [27.1] [43.3]

musicalis: musical [24.1]; *doctrina musicalis*: musical teaching [0.1]; *principia musicales*: musical principles [4.19]; *forma musicalis*: musical form [9.1] [11.2] [12.2] [12.3]

de musicalis armonia: on musical harmony (= *De institutione musica* of Boethius) [1.2]

musicus: musician [1.4] [2.1] [5.9] [7.2] [18.5] [23.5] [24.1] [43.1]

mutatio: (hexachordal) mutation [7.7]; *vocum mutatio*: mutation of syllables [7.7]

nativitas christi: Nativity of Christ [22.3], Christ's Nativity [38.1]

natura: nature [5.6] [11.1] [21.1] [22.1], natural (= hexachord with no b) [7.7], nature (quality) [22.3]; *natura divina*: divine nature [0.5]; *tota natura*: full nature [6.1]; *natura fragilis et humana*: weak human nature [41.1]

naturalis: natural thing [1.4] [2.5], natural [2.10], natural philosophy [2.10] [22.4]; *forma naturalis*: natural form [2.6] [12.2] [14.1]; *naturalis inclinatio*: natural inclination [2.9] [3.3] [13.4]; *naturalis cognitio*: natural awareness [3.4]; *calidum naturale*: natural heat [5.2]; *instrumenta naturalia*: natural instruments [5.5] [17.8]; *res naturales*: natural things [8.1]; *materia naturalis*: natural material [14.1]

naturaliter: naturally [1.2]

necessarium vite: necessities of life [0.1]

necessarius: necessary [0.2] [4.18] [6.1] [7.2] [22.5]

negotium: work [2.6]

neupma: *neuma* (melismatic appendage to an antiphon) [29.5] [29.6] [29.7] [34.1]

nichomacus arismeticus: Nicomachus the arithmetician [2.5]

nobilis: noble (of character) [1.2], nobles [9.4]

nobilitas: nobility (of character) [22.3]

nomen: name [1.1] [3.2] [4.17] [19.4]; *in sonis nomen glorie*: name of glory in sounds [3.2]; *commune nomen*: common name [16.2] [26.3]; *appropriatus nomen*: appropriated name [19.4]; *nomen proprium*: proper name [26.3]

nominatio: naming [7.7]

non ita precise mensuratus: not so precisely measured [5.10]

non sit vobis: *Non sit vobis* (an invitatory) [27.4]

nona: None (little hour of the Divine Office) [23.3]

normannia: Normandy [9.6]

nota: note (in notation) [7.7], *nota* (= musical sign with 4 *puncta*) [13.3]

notatus: indicated [28.2]

notitia: knowledge [8.1]

notificatio: awareness [8.1]

notule: little marks (of notation) [7.3]

novi auditores: new listeners [7.10]

novum testamentum: New Testament [35.4]

numeralis: numeral [26.3]

numerans: numbering [18.5]

numeratus: numbered [5.3] [5.6]

numerus: number [2.5] [2.6] [2.7] [3.3] [4.11] [5.3] [7.5] [10.6] [13.3] [13.4] [17.1] [27.6]; *numerus elementorum*: number of the elements [2.5]; *numerus consonantiarum*: number of consonances [2.7] [2.10] [4.14]; *numerus determinatus*: fixed number [4.7]; *numerus relatus ad sonos*: number related to sounds [5.1]; *numerus concordantiarum*: number of concords [7.7] [13.4]; *numerus senarius*: hexad number [7.7]; *numerus versuum*: number of verses [10.2] [10.3] [10.4]; *maior numerus*: greater number [12.2]; *numerus minor*: lesser number [12.2]; *numerus punctorum*: number of *puncta* [13.3] [13.4]; *numerus infinitus*: unbounded number [18.5]

Nunc dimittis: *Nunc dimittis* (a Gospel psalm = canticle) [27.8]

nuncupandus: naming [26.3]

O quam glorifica: *O quam glorifica* (a hymn) [27.9]

O sapientia: *O sapientia* (an antiphon) [29.7]

obiectum: object [0.2]

oblatio: offering [23.4]; sacrifice [37.1]

occidens: the West [9.6]

occultus: occult [2.8]

octavus: eighth (plainchant mode) [26.3], eighth (plainchant tone) [26.7] [27.4]

[28.3] [29.7] [30.3], eighth (psalm tone) [29.2] [29.3]

octo sunt beatitudines: *Octo sunt beatitudines* (an antiphon = intonation formula) [29.7]

octonarius: octad [26.2]

offerendus: offering [37.1]

offertorium: offertory [23.4] [37.1] [42.1] [43.2]

officio: service [22.3]

officium: *officium* (= introit) [23.4] [30.1] [42.1]

officia: workshops (of blacksmiths) [1.3]

operandus: operation [5.3]

operatio: activity [0.5] [22.3], operation [5.1] [5.2] [5.3]; *operatio humana*: human operation [4.9]; *operatio musice*: operation of music [5.10]; *operatio artis*: operation of the art [5.10]; *bone operationes*: good works [22.2]

opero: operate [5.3], produce [0.5], work [16.1] [22.3] [25.1]

opinio: opinion [4.9]; *opinionum diversitas*: diversity of opinion [0.5]; *opinionum pluralitas*: plurality of opinions [0.5]

oppositus: opposite [18.5]

opus: a work [0.2] [2.10], work [0.5] [9.3], achievement [9.3]; *presens opus*: the present work [0.2]; *consuetum opus*: usual labor [9.3], usual activity [22.3]; *bona opera*: good works [22.1]

orandus: praying [32.4]

oratio: prayer [23.2] [23.3] [23.4] [23.5] [32.4]; *devota oratio*: devout prayer [23.4]; *secreta oratio*: secret prayer [38.2]; *dominicalis oratio*: Lord's Prayer [40.2]

orbes: orbs [5.6]

ordinans: ordered [27.6]

ordinate: ordered [3.3]

ordinatus: ordained [32.4], ordered [13.2] [21.2]

ordino: ordain [0.2] [9.1] [22.4], order [6.2] [20.3] [21.1] [21.2] [22.1] [22.5] [43.3], arrange [7.7]

ordo: order [2.1] [27.1]
organum: *organum* [15.3] [19.3] [19.4] [21.1] [21.5], organ (musical instrument) [12.1]; *organum auditus*: organ of hearing [2.7] [7.7]; *organa sensitiva et fatigabilia*: sensory and weariable organs [22.3]; *organum corporale*: bodily organ [22.3]
origo: source [4.8]
oro: pray [27.5]
ossa: bones [20.2]
otium: idleness [9.5]

Panem nostrum: *Panem nostrum* (from the *Pater noster*) [40.1]
parisius: in Paris [18.7] [6.1] [6.2]
pars: a part [20.2] [27.2] [27.3] [28.1]; *partes*: parts (of a whole) [4.19] [6.1] [8.1] [9.6] [9.7] [10.1] [10.7] [13.1] [13.2] [14.2] [15.1] [17.8] [17.9] [18.2] [18.5] [18.8] [20.1] [20.2] [21.1] [21.7] [21.9] [23.2] [23.4] [23.5] [24.1] [27.1] [28.1] [36.1] [40.1] [42.2] [43.1] [43.2] [43.3]; *pars temporis*: part of time [2.2] *pars motus*: part of motion [2.2]; *pars principii*: the part of the beginning [18.6] [29.2]; *pars finis*: the part of the end [18.6] [29.2] [29.4]; *partes musicales*: musical parts [24.1]; *pars medii*: the part of the middle [29.2] [29.3] *de partibus*: *De partibus* (Aristotle) [8.1]
Participem me fac: *Participem me fac* (a night responsory) [28.3]
particularia: details [18.7]
passio: passion [9.8], Passion (of Christ) [22.3]
pater. In filio. filius In patre. Spiritus sanctus ab utroque procedens: *Pater, In filio, Filius, In patre, Spiritus, Sanctus, ab utroque, procedens* (mnemonic for psalm tone incipits) [29.2]
Pater noster: *Pater noster* (Our Father) [40.1]
patres: (ancient) fathers [9.3]
pausa: pause [16.3] [18.2]; *pausa universalis*: universal pause [18.2]

pauso: pause [18.2] [20.5] [21.4]
percutiendus: beating [12.1]
percussio: beating [12.1] [12.6]; *decens percussio*: appropriate beat [12.5]; *recta percussio*: correct beat [12.5], correct beating [14.1]
percutientes: those striking [1.3]
perfectio: perfection [4.13] [16.5], perfection (= three *tempora*) [16.5] [17.4] [17.7] [17.8] [17.9] [18.2]; *in sonis perfectio*: perfection in sounds [3.1] [3.4]; *perfecti*: perfects [9.4] [32.4]; *perfecta perfectio*: perfect perfection [18.5]
perfectus: perfect (number) [7.7] [17.1], perfect [19.5] [43.2]; *una perfecta armonia*: one perfect harmony [2.2]; *in sonis trina armonia perfecta*: perfect threefold harmony in sounds [3.2]; *cognitio perfecta*: perfect knowledge [8.1]; *consonantia perfecta*: perfect consonance [13.3] [15.1] [15.2] [19.1] [20.5]; *longa perfecta*: perfect long [18.3]; *perfecta perfectio*: perfect perfection [18.5]
philosophus: the Philosopher (= Aristotle) [16.1]
physica: *Physics* (Aristotle) [0.3] [2.10]
pierron: Pierron (a *ductia*) [13.3]
plagalis: plagal (of plainchant mode) [26.6]; *plaga proti*: plagal of the *protus* (= mode 2) [26.3]; *plaga deuteri*: plagal of the *deuterus* (= mode 4) [26.3]; *plaga triti*: plagal of the *tritus* (= mode 6) [26.3]; *plaga tetrardi*: plagal of the *tetrardus* (= mode 8) [26.3]
plana: plain (music) [5.10]
planeta: planet [4.8] [5.8] [5.9]
plato: Plato [1.2] [4.9]; *plato studiosus*: studious Plato [2.5]
pluralitas: plurality [4.8] [17.10]; *pluralitas opinionum*: plurality of opinions [0.5]; *pluralitas figurarum*: plurality of figures [18.6]
poetae: poets [4.8]
ponendus: placing [7.7]
positio: position [2.4] [2.6]; *prepositio*:

placing before [18.5]; *postpositio*: placing after [18.5]

possibilis: possible [4.9] [7.7]

possibilitas: hypothesis [5.6]

potens: powerful [22.3]

potentia apprehensiva: apprehensive ability [0.2]

practica: practice [0.5]

practicus: practical (of the intellect) [5.2]

preces: requests [0.1]

prefatio: preface [23.4] [38.1]

prelia: struggles [9.3]

prima: Prime (little hour of the Divine Office) [23.2] [23.3]

primum: first thing [16.1]

primum mobile: *primum mobile* [16.1]

Primum querite regnum dei: *Primum quaerite regnum dei* (an antiphon = intonation formula) [29.7]

primus: first (mode of measure) [17.8], basic one [17.10], *primus* (in hocket) [20.1] [20.6] [20.7] [21.7], first (plainchant tone) [25.1] [26.7], first (plainchant mode) [26.3], first (psalm tone) [29.2] [29.3]; *primus inventor*: first discoverer (= Pythagoras) [2.5]; *prime qualitates*: prime qualities [2.6]; *prima scientiarum principia*: first principles of the sciences [2.6]; *prima armonia*: first harmony [3.3]; *primum instrumentum*: first instrument [5.2]; *prima mensura*: first measure [16.1], prime measure [16.1]; *primus movens*: prime mover [16.1]; *primus motus*: first motion [16.1]; *primus modus*: first mode (of measure) [17.2]; *primus auctorizatus*: first according to authority (of plainchant mode) [26.3]; *primus tonus*: first (plainchant) tone [26.5] [27.4] [28.3] [29.7] [30.3]; *prima veritas*: prime truth [43.2]

prima philosophia: First Philosophy (= *Metaphisica* of Aristotle) [16.1]

principalis: principal (of plainchant mode) [26.3] [26.4] [26.6]; *instrumentum principale*: principal instrument [5.2]

principatus: primacy [12.2]

principes terre: princes of the earth [9.4]

principium: principle [0.3] [0.4] [1.4] [2.1] [4.8] [4.9] [4.18] [5.3] [6.1] [19.1], the very beginning [1.2], the beginning [3.2], beginning [13.2] [18.6] [25.1] [29.2] [30.2] [31.2], outset [22.5]; *principia musice*: principles of music [0.4] [1.2] [1.5] [2.2] [4.5]; *principia cantus*: principles of *cantus* [1.2]; *principia artis*: principles of art [2.1] [31.4]; *prima principia scientiarum*: first principles of the sciences [2.6]; *principia musicales*: musical principles [4.19]

probabilis: demonstrable [3.1]; *rationes probabiles*: demonstrable reasons [4.8]

probabilitas: demonstration [4.6]

procedendus: proceeding [0.3] [0.6]

procedens: proceeding [3.3] [7.7], *procedens* [29.2]

proferendus: pronouncing [22.4]

prohemialiter: by way of introduction [0.6]

prohemium: preface [0.3]

prologus: prologue [*incipit*]

propheta: prophet [1.1] [5.9]

proportio: proportion [2.6] [2.7] [2.8] [4.12] [4.15] [20.3] [20.4]; *proportiones malleorum*: proportions of the hammers [1.3]; *dupla proportio*: duple proportion [1.3] [4.1] [4.17]; *sexquialtera proportio*: sesquialter proportion [1.3] [4.2] [4.16]; *sexquitertia proportio*: sesquitertian proportion [1.3] [4.3] [4.15]; *sexquioctava proportio*: sesquioctave proportion [1.3] [4.12]; *species proportionis*: species of proportion [2.8]; *subdupla proportio*: subduple proportion [7.7]; *dyapason proportio*: *diapason* proportion [20.8] [21.3]; *dyapente proportio*: *diapente* proportion [21.2]

proportionalis: suiting [11.1]; *media proportionalis*: intermediate proportion [2.5]

propositum: matter at hand [7.11], subject [14.2], theme [21.9]

proprietas: property [4.4] [4.13] [8.1]

[26.2]; *cum proprietate*: with propriety [18.6]; *cum opposita proprietate*: with opposite propriety [18.6]

de proprietatibus armonicis: of harmonic properties (= *De institutione musica* of Boethius) [2.5]

proprie: properly [5.3] [5.7], closely [31.4]

proprius: proper [26.3]; *sensibilia propria*: proper sensibles [0.2]; *materia propria*: proper material [5.3]

prothomartyr: Protomartyr (= Saint Stephen) [9.3]

protus: *protus* (first modal group encompassing mode one ("authentic *protus*") and mode two ("plagal of the *protus*")) [26.3]

psalmus: psalm [23.2] [23.3] [27.7] [29.2] [29.5] [30.1]; *psalmus euvangelista*: Gospel psalm [27.7] [27.8] [29.5]

psalterium: psaltery [12.2]

puelle: girls [9.6] [9.7] [9.8]

puer natus: *Puer natus* (an introit) [30.3]

pueri: boys [7.10]

puncta: *puncta* (of a *cantus coronatus/ductial/stantipes*) [10.3] [12.6] [13.1] [13.3] [13.4] [14.1]

punctus: *punctus* (of a *ductial/stantipes*) [13.2] [40.1]; *punctus clausus*: closed *punctus* [42.2]

pytagoras/pictagoras/pythagoras: Pythagoras [1.2] [1.4] [2.5] [7.7]

pytagorici: Pythagoreans [3.3] [5.6]

quadratus: square [18.4]; *figura quadrata*: square figure [18.3]; *b quadratus*: b-*quadratus* (= b-natural) [26.7]

quadruplum: *quadruplum* (= part above a *triplum*) [20.1] [20.5] [21.4]

qualitas: quality [0.4]; *prima qualitas*: prime quality [2.6]

Quant li roussignol: *Quant li rousignol* (a *cantus coronatus*) [9.4]

quantitas: quantity [0.4] [18.1] [20.2]

Quarta vigilia venit ad eos: *Quarta vigilia venit ad eos* (an antiphon = intonation formula) [29.7]

quartus: fourth (mode of measure) [17.5], fourth (plainchant mode) [26.3], fourth (plainchant tone) [26.7] [27.4] [28.3] [29.7] [30.3], fourth (psalm tone) [29.2] [29.3]; *quartus auctorizatus*: fourth according to authority (of plainchant mode) [26.3]

Qui sedes ad dexteram: *Qui sedes ad dexteram* (from the *Gloria in excelsis deo*) [32.1]

Qui tollis peccata mundi: *Qui tollis peccata mundi* (from the *Gloria in excelsis deo*) [32.1]

Qui venturus: *Qui venturus* (a night responsory) [28.3]

quiditas: quiddity (whatness) [0.4]

Quinque prudentes virgines: *Quinque prudentes virgines* (an antiphon = intonation formula) [29.7]

quintus: fifthing (technique of) [15.1], fifth (mode of measure) [17.6], fifth (plainchant mode) [26.3], fifth (plainchant tone) [26.7] [27.4] [28.3] [29.7] [30.3], fifth (psalm tone) [29.2] [29.3]

quitarra sarracenica: Saracen guitar [12.2]

ratio: rationale [2.4] [13.4] [26.2], reasoning [2.5] [7.7] [17.1], reason [10.3], quality [16.4]; *rationes probabiles*: demonstrable reasons [4.8]

rationabilis: reasonable [4.9]

rationabiliter: in a reasoned way [2.5]

re: re (solmization syllable) [7.7] [29.2] [29.3] [29.7]; *resol*: re-sol (hexachordal mutation) [7.7]; *reut*: re-ut (hexachordal mutation) [7.7]

reductio: reduction [17.10]

refractorium: refrain [10.1]

refractus: refrain [9.6] [9.7]

regem cui omnia vivunt: *Regem cui omnia vivunt* (an invitatory) [27.4]

regem precursoris: *Regem precursoris* (an invitatory) [27.4]

regem regum: *Regem regum* (an invitatory) [27.4]

regimen: government [9.4]

regiones diverse: diverse regions [6.1]

regula: rule [5.2] [15.1] [18.6] [24.1] [25.1] [25.2] [26.1] [26.2] [27.9] [28.1] [29.1] [43.2]; *artis regule*: rules of art [5.10]; *modice regule*: modest rules [15.1]; *regula policleti*: Rule of Polykleitos [16.3]; *uniformis regula*: uniform rule [18.1]; *regule accentus*: rules of accent [23.5]; *regule grammaticalis*: rules of grammar [23.5]; *regule generales*: general rules [26.1]; *regule tonorum*: rules of the tones [28.2] [34.1] [37.1] [43.2]

regulatus: regulated [15.2]; *musica regularis*: regulated music [6.2] [14.3]

regulo: rule [5.3], regulate [20.2] [24.1] [26.8] [35.1] [43.2]

res: piece (of music) [13.4], thing [16.1]; *res naturales*: natural things [8.1]; *difficilis res*: difficult piece (of music) [13.4]

Respice in me: *Respice in me* (an introit) [30.3]

respiciendus: attending [26.1]

responsorium: response [9.6] [10.1] [10.5] [10.6]; responsory [23.3] [23.4] [28.1] [28.3] [33.1] [35.2] [35.3]; *responsorium nocturnale*: night responsory [23.2] [28.1] [33.1]

resumptus: repetition [4.8]

resurrexi: *Resurrexi* (an introit) [30.3]

reverentia: reverence [19.4] [30.2] [31.3] [35.2]

revolutio: rotation [16.3]

rex: king [9.4]; *rex karolus*: King Charlemagne [9.3]; *reges terre*: kings of the earth [9.4]

Rex noster: *Rex noster* (a night responsory) [28.3]

rogo: ask [0.1]

rotundellus: *rotundellus* [9.6] [10.6] [19.2]

rotundus: *rotundus* [9.2], round [9.6]; *b rotundus*: b-*rotundus* (= b-flat) [26.7]

sacerdos: priest [32.4] [37.1] [38.2] [39.2] [41.1] [42.2]

sacramentum ecclesie: sacrament of the Church [23.4]

sacrificium: sacrifice [23.4] [37.1]

Salve sancta parens: *Salve sancta parens* (an introit) [30.3]

sancta: holy woman [22.3]

sanctus: saint [9.3], holy man [22.3], *sanctus* (in *cantus* texts) [29.2] [30.3] [37.1], the *Sanctus* [23.4] [38.2] [39.1] [39.2] [41.1]; *viri sancti*: holy men [1.1]; *loci sancti*: holy places [19.4]; *sancta kadragesima*: Holy Lent [22.3] [32.3]; *spiritus sanctus*: Holy Spirit [30.2] [43.3]

sciendus: knowing [0.4]

scientia: knowledge [0.5], science [2.6] [5.3] [22.4]

scribendus: writing [7.2]

scriptum: writing [0.5] [7.9] [24.1], written [16.1]

scriptura: writing [7.2]

secreta: secret [23.4]; *secreta oratio*: secret prayer [38.2]

seculorum Amen: *Saeculorum Amen* (= *differentia* or psalm cadence) [29.4], (for ever and) ever Amen [43.3]

secundus: second (mode of measure) [17.3], *secundus* (in hocket) [20.1] [20.7] [21.7], second (plainchant tone) [25.1] [26.7] [27.4] [28.3] [29.7] [30.3], second (plainchant mode) [26.3], second (psalm tone) [29.2] [29.3]; *secundus physica*: second [book] of the *Physics* (Aristotle) [2.10]; *secundus auctorizatus*: second according to authority (of plainchant mode) [26.3]

semibrevis: semibreve [18.5] [21.6]

semidytonus/semiditonus: semiditone [1.4] [4.10] [4.15]

semitonium: semitone [4.15] [4.16] [4.17] [5.8] [7.7]

semitonus: semitone [4.10] [4.13] [5.8] [7.7] [7.8]

senarius: hexad [17.1]; *numerus senarius*: hexad number [7.7] *seneca*: Seneca [9.5]

sensibilia propria: proper sensibles [0.2]

sensitivus: sensory [0.3] [22.3]

sensus: senses [0.5], sense [43.1]

sentencia: opinion [1.2], statement [10.3], meaning [30.1] [36.2]; *sentencia aristotelis*: opinion of Aristotle [2.8]; *copia sentencie*: abundance of the message [10.6]; *sentencia litterali*: literal meaning [43.2]

Septem spiritus sunt ante tronum dei: *Septem spiritus sunt ante thronum dei* (an antiphon = intonation formula) [29.7]

septimus: seventh (plainchant mode) [26.3], seventh (plainchant tone) [26.7] [27.4] [28.3] [29.7] [30.3], seventh (psalm tone) [29.2] [29.3]

sequax: follower [5.5]

sequens: what follows [18.8], (person) following [24.1], following [29.6] [35.1]

sequentia: sequence [23.4] [34.2] [35.1] [35.2] [35.4] [35.5]

sequor: follow [28.1] [32.1] [34.1] [37.1]

sermo: discourse [9.1] [12.1] [22.5], discussion [14.3]; *sermo moralis*: moral discourse [22.1]; *sermones greci*: Greek words [31.4]

servitium: service (ecclesiastical) [23.2] [23.3]; *dei servitium*: service of God [22.5] [27.5]; *servitium ecclesiasticum*: ecclesiastical service [23.1]; *gloriosum servitium*: glorious service [23.4]

sexquialtera proportio: sesquialter proportion [1.3] [4.2] [4.16]

sexquioctava proportio: sesquioctave proportion [1.3] [4.12]

sexquitertia proportio: sesquitertian proportion [1.3] [4.3] [4.15]

sexta: Sext (little hour of the Divine Office) [23.3]

Sexta hora sedit super puteum: *Sexta hora sedit super puteum* (an antiphon = intonation formula) [29.7]

sextus: sixth (mode of measure) [17.7], sixth (plainchant mode) [26.3], sixth (plainchant tone) [26.7] [27.4] [28.3]

[29.7] [30.3], sixth (psalm tone) [29.2] [29.3]

Sicut cervus: *Sicut cervus* (a tract) [35.5]

signandus: signify [2.6] [7.2]; *ars signandi*: art of notating [15.4]

significatio: signification [18.7]

signum: sign (of notation) [7.3] [7.7] [7.8] [17.11] [18.6], sign [38.2]; *signa distinctiva*: distinctive signs [7.6]; *signa diversitatis*: diversifying signs [7.7]; *signum generale*: general sign (of notation) [18.3]; *signum pacis et concordie*: sign of peace and concord [41.1]

sillaba: (solmization) syllable [7.7] [7.10], syllable [21.6] [27.9]; *discretio sillabarum*: separation of syllables [18.6]; *diversitas sillabarum*: diversity of syllables [27.9]; *equalitas sillabarum*: equality of syllables [27.9]

sillogismus: syllogism [17.10]

simplex: simple [2.8] [4.18]; *concordantia simplex*: simple concord [4.18] [7.5] [7.7]; *simplex musica*: simple music [6.2] [14.2]; *consonantia simplex*: simple consonance [7.5] [7.7]; *corpus simplex*: simple body [8.1]; *simplex conductus*: simple *conductus* [9.4] [27.2] [37.1]; *quadrata simplex*: simple square [18.4]; *simplex cantilena*: simple *cantilena* [31.1]

sol: sun [0.4], sol (solmization syllable) [7.7] [29.2] [29.3] [29.7]; *solre*: sol-re (hexachordal mutation) [7.7]; *solut*: sol-ut (hexachordal mutation) [7.7]

sollempnitas: solemnity [34.2] [39.3], religious festival [38.1]

sollempniter: solemn [38.2]

solutio: solution [4.18]

sonans: sounding [5.10]

sonus: sound [0.2] [2.2] [2.7] [2.9] [4.11] [4.12] [5.6] [5.7] [5.9] [9.4] [12.1] [12.2] [14.1] [16.2] [16.3] [16.4] [16.5] [18.2] [18.3]; *sonus tube*: sound of the trumpet [2.9] [3.2]; *sonus tympani*: sound of the drum [2.9]; *sonus cornuum*: sound of horns [2.9]; *sonus fistu-*

larum: sound of pipes [2.9]; *in sonis*: in sounds [3.1] [3.2] [3.4] [4.1] [4.8]; *soni cum armonia*: sounds with harmony [4.9]; *sonus precedens*: preceding sound [4.14] [4.15] [4.16] [4.17]; *omnis sonus*: every sound [4.19]; *numerus relatus ad sonos*: number related to sounds [5.1]; *sonus numeratus*: numbered sound [5.3] [5.6]; *sonus armonicus*: harmonic sound [5.3]; *soni instrumentorum*: sounds of instruments [5.5]; *diversi soni*: diverse sounds [5.10]; *sonus artificialis*: artificial sound [12.1]; *sonus in instrumentis*: sound in instruments [12.1]; *soni discretio*: discernment of sound [12.2]; *sonus illiteratus*: unlettered sound [12.5] [12.6]; *minimus sonus*: smallest sound [16.3]

spatium: space (on a stave) [7.7], space [16.3]

specialia: particulars [31.2]

species: species [3.4] [9.1] [25.3]; *species proportionis*: species of proportion [2.8]; *species inequalitatis*: species of inequality [2.8]; *species dyapason*: species of *diapason* [25.3]

speculatio: theory [0.5]; *speculatio presens*: present speculation [22.5]

speculativus: theorist [0.5], inquirer [43.2]

spiritus: inspiration [1.3]; *7 dona spiritus*: 7 gifts of the spirit [4.8]; *spiritus sanctus*: Holy Spirit [30.2] [43.3]

stantipes: *stantipes* [7.8] [9.2] [9.7] [10.6] [12.3] [12.4] [12.6] [13.1] [13.4] [14.1] [14.2] [25.2] [29.6] [35.3] [40.1] [42.2]; *stantipes imperfecta*: imperfect *stantipes* [13.3]

stelle: stars [4.9]

stephanus: (Saint) Stephen [9.3]

studentes: students [9.4]

studiosus: studious [2.5]

subdupla: subduple [1.3]; *subdupla proportio*: subduple proportion [7.7]

subiecte materia: subject matter [0.3]

subtilis: subtle [4.8] [7.7] [12.2] [29.7]

subtilitas: subtlety [19.2]

subtiliter: carefully [12.1] [16.1], subtly [12.2]

superacutus: superacute (of register) [7.7]

superficies: surface [7.7] [7.10]; *superficies monocordi*: surface of the monochord [7.7]

superflua: superfluous things [18.6]

superparticularis: superparticular [2.8]

superpartiens: superpartient [2.8]

surrexit: *Surrexit* (an invitatory) [27.4]

Suscipe sancta trinitas: *Suscipe sancta trinitas* (from the offertory) [37.1]

symbolum apostolorum: Apostles' Creed [36.2]

tassynus: Tassinus [13.4]

tegni: *Tegni* (Galen) [18.7]

tempus: time [1.2] [2.2], *tempus* [16.1] [16.2] [16.3] [16.5] [17.2] [17.4] [17.6] [17.8] [17.9] [18.2] [18.5], season (of the Church year) [22.3] [32.3] [35.5]; *longus tempus*: long time [0.1]; *totum tempus*: all time [16.3]; *determinata tempora*: appointed times [22.3]; *temporum distinctio*: distinction of times [22.4]

tenor: tenor (= fundamental part in measured *cantus*) [19.1] [20.1] [20.2] [20.3] [20.4] [20.8] [21.1] [21.2] [21.3] [21.8] [27.2]

tertia: Terce (little hour of the Divine Office) [23.3]

tertia dies est quod hec facta sunt: *Tertia dies est quod haec facta sunt* (an antiphon = intonation formula) [29.7]

tertius: third (mode of measure) [17.4], third (plainchant mode) [26.3], third (plainchant tone) [26.7] [27.4] [28.3] [29.7] [30.3], third (psalm tone) [29.2] [29.3]; *tertius auctorizatus*: third according to authority (of plainchant mode) [26.3]

terminus: limit [26.7]

terra: earth [8.1]; *centrum terre*: center of the earth [0.4]; *reges terre*: kings of the earth [9.4]; *principes terre*: princes of the earth [9.4] *terrestris*: earthly [38.2]

tetragonus: square [12.2]

tetrardus: *tetrardus* (fourth modal group encompassing mode 7 ("authentic *tetrardus*") and mode 8 ("plagal of the *tetrardus*"))[26.3]

theologus: theologian [5.9] [26.2] [43.1]

de theoria planetarum: *On the Theory of the Planets* (anon.) [5.6]

thimeo: *Timaeus* (Plato) [2.5]

tonus: tone (= interval) [1.3] [1.4] [4.10] [4.12] [4.13] [4.14] [4.15] [4.16] [4.17] [4.18] [5.8] [7.7] [7.8], tone (rule of) [4.12] [24.1] [25.1] [25.2] [26.1] [26.2], (plainchant) tone [5.10] [26.5] [26.7] [26.9] [27.2] [27.3] [27.9] [28.1] [28.2] [28.3] [29.1] [29.4] [29.7] [30.1] [30.3] [33.1] [35.1] [43.2] [43.3], tone (note of unspecified pitch) [7.7] [17.2] [17.4] [17.6] [17.7] [25.1] [25.3], tone (species of *diapason*) [25.3]; *medietas toni*: half of a tone [4.13]; *tonus remissus*: diminished tone [4.13]; *tonus imperfectus*: imperfect tone [4.13]; *tonus cum dyapente*: tone plus *diapente* [4.18]; *tonus completus*: complete tone [7.7]; *tonorum modi*: modes of tones [26.9]; *diversi toni*: diverse tones [27.4]; *regule tonorum*: rules of the tones [28.2] [34.1] [37.1] [43.2]

tonicus: thunderous blow (of a hammer) [2.7]

torneamenta: tournaments [12.2]

totaliter: wholly [0.2], completely [5.10] [9.5] [21.1]

totus: whole [23.1], all [27.2] [28.1]; *tota cognitio humana*: all human knowledge [0.3]; *totus annus*: whole year [4.8]; *totus universus*: whole universe [4.9]; *tota musica*: all music [4.19]; *tota natura totius divisi*: full nature of the divided whole [6.1]; *tota civitas*: whole city [9.3] [22.5]; *tota sententia materie*: whole statement of the material [10.3]; *totus cantus*: all *cantus* [16.3] [26.8]; *totus tempus*: all time [16.3]; *totus suus*

cantus: all their *cantus* [16.5]; *totum hoc organum*: all this *organum* [19.4]

Toute sole passerai levert boscage: *Toute sole passerai levert boscage* (a round/*rotundellus*) [9.6]

tractatus: treatise [5.5] [15.1] [26.8], having dealt [7.11]; *diversi tractatus*: diverse treatises [18.7]; *tractatus musice*: treatise on music [*explicit*]

tractus: tract [35.5]; *longus tractus*: drawn-out longs [9.6]

trahendus: drawing out [27.1]

trigonum: triangle [12.2]

trinitas: the Trinity [43.3]; *trinitas gloriosa*: glorious Trinity [3.3]; *ymago trinitatis*: image of the Trinity [3.4]; *reverentia trinitatis*: reverence of the Trinity [30.2] [31.3] [35.2]

triplum: *triplum* (= part above a *motetus*) [20.1] [20.4] [21.3]

tritonus: tritone [4.18]

tritus: *tritus* (third modal group encompassing mode 5 ("authentic *tritus*") and mode 6 ("plagal of the *tritus*"))[26.3]

truncatio: truncation (of melody) [19.5]

tuba: trumpet [12.1] [12.2]; *sonus tube*: sound of the trumpet [2.9] [3.2]

tympanum: drum [12.1] [12.2]; *sonus tympani*: sound of the drum [2.9]

ultimus: finally [2.10], end [7.7] [40.1], last [8.1]

uniformis: uniform [15.2] [18.1]

unisonus: unison [4.10] [4.11]

unitas: unity [27.1]

in universali: in a universal way [21.9]

universaliter: universally [5.6] [7.9] [8.1] [18.8] [26.6] [26.9] [27.1]

universus: universe [4.9]

usus: use [6.1], practice [15.1]; *usus diversus*: diverse use [6.1] [23.5] [27.1]; *usus modernorum*: practice of the moderns [15.3]; *usus civium*: use of citizens [22.5]; *diversi usus ecclesiarum*: diverse uses of churches [27.1] [29.4] [32.5]

ut: ut (solmization syllable) [7.7] [29.2]

[29.3] [29.7]; **utfa**: ut-fa (hexachordal mutation) [7.7]; **utsol**: ut-sol (hexa-chordal mutation) [7.7] [29.7]; **utre**: ut-re (hexachordal mutation) [7.7]

ut queant lapsis: *Ut queant lapsis* (a hymn) [27.9]

utor: use [0.2] [1.4] [5.8] [15.2] [16.1] [16.5] [17.10] [18.2] [18.7] [22.3] [24.1], a use [6.1], make use of [6.2]

variationes: variations [7.6]
vario: vary [19.4] [27.9] [37.1]
velocitas: speed [19.6]
velox: swift [9.8]
veni creator: *Veni creator* (a hymn) [27.9]
venite: *Venite* [23.2] [27.2] [27.3] [27.4] [27.5] [27.7] [28.1]
venite adoremus: *Venite adoremus* (an invitatory) [27.4]
verbum: word [3.3] [35.4]
veritas: truth [0.5] [5.6] [9.3] [43.2]; **veritas increata**: truth uncreated [0.5]; **veritas prima**: prime truth [43.2]
versiculatus: *versiculatus* (mode of *cantus*) [9.2]; **cantus versiculatus**: *cantus versicu-latus* [9.2] [11.1]
versiculus: versicle [10.2] [23.2] [28.1] [28.2] [28.3] [30.3] [33.1] [35.1], little verse [32.1]
versus: verse [10.1] [10.2] [10.3] [10.4] [10.6] [27.2] [27.3] [27.6] [27.9] [30.1] [30.3] [32.1] [34.1] [35.5] [38.1] [41.1]
versus occidens: in the West [9.6]
vesperis: Vespers [23.3]
vestimenta: clothes [0.5]
vias tuas: *Vias tuas* (an introit versicle) [30.3]

viella: vielle [12.2] [12.3] [29.6]
viellator: vielle player [29.6]
virgines: virgins [30.2]
virgo: the Virgin [30.2]
virtus: virtue [0.1], force [4.9], strength [26.6]
vita: life [0.1] [9.3]
vita beati stephani prothomartyris: *Life of Blessed Stephen, Protomartyr* (a *cantus gestualis*) [9.3]
vox: utterance [2.6], syllable (solmization) [7.7] [13.4] [17.1], voice [16.2] [16.4]; **septem voces**: seven voices (= seven species of sound (A, B, C, D, E, F, G)) [7.7]; **vox humana**: human voice [9.1] [9.2] [11.2] [12.5] [18.2]; **minima vox**: smallest voice [16.3]
vulgales: common people [19.2]
vulgalis: of the people [9.1]; **musica vul-galis**: music of the people [6.2] [14.2]; **vulgalis laycus**: common laity [19.2]; **cantus vulgalis**: *cantus* of the people [25.2]
vulgaliter: like the common crowd [2.4]

ydiomata: idioms [6.1]; **ydioma greca**: Greek language [31.4] [34.1]
ymaginatio: idea [5.6]
ymago: image [3.4] [38.2]; **ymago trinita-tis**: image of the Trinity [3.4]
ypermissolidius: hypermixolydian (= mode 8) [26.4]
ypodorius: hypyodorian (= mode 2) [26.4]
ypofrigius: hypophrygian (= mode 4) [26.4]
ypolidius: hypolydian (= mode 6) [26.4]

Works Cited

Manuscripts Cited

Bamberg Staatsbibliothek, MS lit. 115
Darmstadt, Universitäts- und Landesbibliothek, MS 2663
Gent, Rijksarchief, Gaillard 12 (22 Dec. 1276–13 June 1277)
London, BL, MS Harley 281
Montpellier, Faculté de Médecine, MS 196
Paris, BnF, Arsenal 5198
Paris, BnF, fr. 33237
Paris, BnF, lat. 1085
Paris, BnF, lat. 8454
Paris, BnF, lat. 15128
Paris, BnF, lat. 16663
Paris, BnF, lat. 17296
Paris, BnF, lat. 18514
Siena, Bibliotheca comunale, L.V.30
Vatican City, Biblioteca Apostolica Vaticana, Vat. lat. 5325

Primary Sources

Aristotle. *Analytica prior*. Trans. Boethius. Ed. L. Minio-Paluello. Turnhout: Brepols, 1962.
———. *De anima*. Trans. James of Venice. Ed. Jos Decorte and Jozef Brams, ALD1. Turnhout: Brepols, 2003.
———. *De animalibus: Michael Scot's Arabic-Latin Translation*. Part 2: *Books XI–XIV: Parts of Animals*. Ed. Aafke van Oppenraaij. Leiden: E. J. Brill, 1998.
———. *De animalibus: Michael Scot's Arabic-Latin Translation*. Part 3: *Books XV–XIX: Generation of Animals*. Ed. Aafke van Oppenraaij. Leiden: E. J. Brill, 1992.
———. *De caelo*. Trans. William of Moerbeke. Ed. F. Bossier, ALD1. Turnhout: Brepols, 2003.
———. *De generatione animalium*. Trans. William of Moerbeke. Ed. H. J. Drossaart-Lulofs, ALD1. Turnhout: Brepols, 2003.
———. *De partibus animalium*. Trans. William of Moerbeke. Ed. P. Rossi, ALD1. Turnhout: Brepols, 2003.
———. *Metaphysica*. Trans. William of Moerbeke. Ed. Gudrun Vuillemin-Diem. Leiden: E. J. Brill, 1995.
———. *Physica*. Trans. James of Venice. Ed. Fernand Bossier and Jozef Brams. Leiden: E. J. Brill, 1990.
———. *Physica*. Trans. Michael Scot. *Aristotelis De Physico auditu libri octo*. Venice, 1562.
Bacon, Roger. *Communia mathematica*. Ed. Robert Steele. Oxford: Oxford University Press, 1940.

————. *Opus Tertium.* Ed. J. S. Brewer. London: Longman, 1859.

Bede. *De tabernaculo.* Ed. D. Hurst. Corpus Christianorum Series Latina 119A. Turnhout: Brepols, 1969.

————. *De temporum ratione.* Ed. Charles W. Jones. Corpus Christianorum Series Latina 123B. Turnhout: Brepols, 1977.

Boethius. *De institutione arithmetica.* Ed. Henri Oosthout and Johannes Schilling. Corpus Christianorum Series Latina 94A. Turnhout: Brepols, 1999.

————. *De institutione musica.* Ed. Godofredus Friedlein. Leipzig: B. G. Teubner, 1867.

David de Augusta. *De exterioris et interioris hominis compositione secundum triplicem statum incipientium, proficientium et perfectorum libri tres.* Ed. College of Saint Bonaventura (Ad Claras Acquas [Quaracchi]): College of Saint Bonaventura, 1899.

Engelbertus Admontensis. *De musica.* Ed. Martin Gerbert. Scriptores ecclesiastici de musica sacra potissimum. St. Blaise: Typis San-Blasianis, 1784. Repr. Hildesheim: Olms, 1963. 2:287–98.

Franco of Cologne (Franconis de Colonia). *Ars cantus mensurabilis.* Ed. Gilbert Reaney and André Gilles. Rome: American Institute of Musicology, 1974.

Galen. *De temperamentis (De complexionibus).* Ed. C. G. Kühn. Hildesheim: Georg Olms, 1964. 1:509–571.

Guido Aretinus. *Micrologus.* Ed. Joseph Smits van Waesberghe. [Rome]: American Institute of Musicology, 1955.

Guido d'Arezzo. "Epistola ad Michahelem." *Guido d'Arezzo's "Regule rithmice," "Prologus in Antiphonarium," and "Epistola ad Michahelem": A Critical Text and Translation.* Ed. Dolores Pesce. Ottawa: The Institute of Mediaeval Music, 1999. 438–530 (even).

————. "Prologus in Antiphonarium." *Guido d'Arezzo's "Regule rithmice," "Prologus in Antiphonarium," and "Epistola ad Michahelem": A Critical Text and Translation.* Ed. Dolores Pesce. Ottawa: The Institute of Mediaeval Music, 1999. 406–34 (even).

————. "Regule rhythmice." *Guido d'Arezzo's "Regule rithmice," "Prologus in Antiphonarium," and "Epistola ad Michahelem": A Critical Text and Translation.* Ed. Dolores Pesce. Ottawa: The Institute of Mediaeval Music, 1999. 328–402 (even).

Guido von Saint-Denis. *Tractatus de tonis.* Ed. Sieglinde van de Klundert. 2 vols. Bubenreuth: Hurricane Publishers, 1998.

Hascher-Burger Anon. *Tractatulus de musica.* Unpublished critical text. Ed. Ulrike Hascher-Burger. *Thesaurus musicarum latinarum.* <http://www.chmtl.indiana.edu/tml/>

Hieronymus de Moravia. *Tractatus de musica.* Ed. Simon M. Cserba. Regensburg: Pustet, 1935.

Honorius Augustodunensis. *Lucidaire.* Ed. Monika Türk. *Lucidaire de grant sapientie: Untersuchung und Edition der altfranzösischen Übersetzung 1 des Elucidarium von Honorius Augustodunensis.* Tübingen: M. Niemeyer, 2000.

Hugo of St. Cher. *Hugonis a St. Charo Tractatus super missam seu speculum ecclesiae.* Ed. Gisbert Sölch. Munich: Aschendorff, 1940.

Isidore of Seville. *Etymologiae.* Ed. W. M. Lindsay. Oxford: Oxford University Press, 1911.

Jacobus Leodiensis. *Speculum musicae.* Ed. Roger Bragard. [Rome]: American Institute of Musicology, 1955–.

Johannes Aegidius de Zamora. *Ars musica.* Ed. Michel Robert-Tissot. [Rome]: American Institute of Musicology, 1974.

Johannes de Garlandia. *De mensurabili musica.* Ed. Erich Reimer. Wiesbaden: Franz Steiner, 1972.

————. *Musica plana.* Ed. Christian Meyer. Baden-Baden: Valentin Koerner, 1998.

Johannes de Grocheio. "Ars musicae." Transcribed by Sandra Pinegar. <www.uga.edu/theme/gro-har.html>.

————. *Concerning Music (De musica).* Trans. Albert Seay. Colorado Springs: Colorado College Music Press, 1973.

————. *Der Musiktraktat des Johannes de Grocheo nach den Quellen neu herausgegeben mit Übersetzung.* Ed. Ernst Rohloff. Leipzig: Kommissionsverlag Gebrüder Reinecke, 1943.

————. *Die Quellenhandschriften zum Musiktraktat des Johannes de Grocheio. In Faksimile herausgegeben nebst Übertragung des Textes und Übersetzung in Deutsche, dazu Bericht, Literaturschau, Tabellen und Indices.* Ed. Ernst Rohloff. Leipzig: Deutscher Verlag für Musik, 1972.

Johannes Scottus Eriugena. *Annotationes in Marcianum.* Ed. Cora E. Lutz. Cambridge, MA.: Mediaeval Academy of America, 1939.

John of Damascus. *De fide orthodoxa: Versions of Burgundio and Cerbanus.* Ed. Eligius M. Buytaert. New York: Fransciscan Institute, 1955.

John Damascene. *Dialectica. Version of Robert Grosseteste.* Ed. Owen A. Colligan. St. Bonaventure, NY: Franciscan Institute, 1953.

Kilwardby, Robert. *De ortu scientiarum.* Ed. Albert G. Judy. London: British Academy, 1976.

[Lambert]. *Cujusdam Aristotelis Tractatus de Musica.* Ed. Edmond de Coussemaker. Scriptores de musica medii ævi novam seriem a Gerbertina alteram. 4 vols. Paris: Durant, 1874–76. Repr. Hildesheim: Olms, 1963. 1:251–81.

Odington, Walter. *Summa de speculatione musice.* Ed. Frederick F. Hammond. [Rome]: American Institute of Musicology, 1970.

Petrus Comestor. *Historia scholastica.* Ed. J. P. Migne. Patrologia Latina 198. Paris, 1855. Repr. Turnhout: Brepols, 1976. Cols. 1045–1720.

Petrus de Cruce Ambianensi. *Tractatus de tonis.* Ed. Denis Harbinson. [Rome]: American Institute of Musicology, 1976.

Plato. *Timaeus a Calcidio translatus commentarioque instructus.* Ed. J. H. Waszink. London: Warburg Institute and Brill, 1962.

[Pseudo] Odo. *Dialogus de musica.* Ed. Martin Gerbert. Scriptores ecclesiastici de musica sacra potissimum. 3 vols. St. Blaise: Typis San-Blasianis, 1784. Repr. Hildesheim: Olms, 1963. 1:252–64.

Seneca. *Ad Lucilium Epistularum Moralium.* Ed. Otto Hense. Leipzig: Teubner, 1898.

Siger of Brabant. *Quaestiones in Metaphysicam.* Ed. William Dunphy. Louvain-la-Neuve: Institut supérieur de philosophie, 1981.

Theorica Planetarum. Ed. Francis J. Carmody. Berkeley: University of California Press, 1942.

"The Theory of Planets." Trans. Olaf Pedersen. In *A Source Book in Medieval Science*, edited by Edward Grant, 451–65. Cambridge, MA: Harvard University Press, 1974.

Von Kalkar, Heinrich Eger. *Cantuagium.* Ed. Heinrich Hüschen. Cologne: Staufen, 1952.

Secondary Sources

Aertsen, Jan, ed. *Nach der Verurteilung von 1277: Philosophie und Theologie an der Universität von Paris im letzten Viertel des 13. Jahrhunderts: Studien und Texte.* Berlin: De Gruyter, 2001.

Anderson, Gordon A. "Magister Lambertus and Nine Rhythmic Modes." *Acta Musicologica* 45 (1973): 57–73.

Aubrey, Elizabeth. *The Music of the Troubadours*. Bloomington: Indiana University Press, 1996.

Aubry, Pierre. *Estampies et danses royales: les plus anciens textes de musique instrumentale du moyen-âge*. Paris: Fischbacker, 1907.

Baader, Gerhard. "Galen in mittelalterlichen Abendland." In *Galen: Problems and Prospects*, edited by Vivian Nutton, 213–28. London: Wellcome Institute for the History of Medicine, 1981.

Bailey, Terence. *The Intonation Formulas of Western Chant*. Toronto: Pontifical Institute of Mediaeval Studies, 1974.

Beaurepaire, Charles, ed. "Recueil de chartes concernant l'abbaye de Saint Victor en Caux." *Société de l'Histoire de Normandie Mélanges* 5 (1898): 333–453.

Beddie, James Stuart. "The Ancient Classics in the Mediaeval Libraries." *Speculum* 5 (1930): 3–20.

[Benedictines of Bouveret]. *Colophons de manuscrits occidentaux des origines au XVIe siècle*. 6 vols. Fribourg: Editions universitaires, 1965–82.

Bernhard, M., ed. *Quellen und Studien zur Musiktheorie des Mittelalters* 2. Munich: Bayerische Akademie der Wissenschaften, 1997.

Besseler, Heinrich. "Ars antiqua." In *Die Musik in Geschichte und Gegenwart: Allgemeine Enzyklopädie der Musik*, edited by Friedrich Blume, 1:687. 17 vols. Kassel: Bärenreiter, 1949–51.

———. *Die Musik des Mittelalters und der Renaissance*. Wildpark-Potsdam: Akademische Verlagsgesellschaft Athenaion, 1931.

———. "Zur 'Ars musicae' des Johannes de Grocheo." *Die Musikforschung* 2 (1949): 229–31.

Bielitz, Mathias. "Materia und Forma bei Johannes de Grocheo." *Die Musikforschung* 38 (1985): 257–77.

Brams, Jozef. "Guillaume de Moerbeke et Aristotle." In *Rencontres de cultures dans la philosophie médiévale: Traductions et traducteurs de l'antiquité tardive au XIVe siècle*, edited by Jacqueline Hamesse and Marta Fattori, 317–36. Louvain-la-Neuve: Institut d'études médiévales de l'Université Catholique de Louvain, 1990.

[British Museum, Department of Manuscripts]. *A Catalogue of the Harleian Manuscripts, in the British Museum: With Indexes of Persons, Places, and Matters*. London, 1808.

Butterfield, Ardis. "*Enté*: A Survey and Reassessment of the Term in Thirteenth- and Fourteenth-Century Music and Poetry." *Early Music History* 22 (2003): 67–101.

Buytaert, Eligius M., ed. *De fide orthodoxa: Versions of Burgundio and Cerbanus*. New York: Franciscan Institute, 1955.

Carolus-Barré, Louis. "Pillage et dispersion de la bibliothèque de l'abbaye de Saint-Denis en France." *Bibliothèque de l'Ecole des Chartes* 183 (1980): 97–101.

Carpenter, Nan Cooke. *Music in the Medieval and Renaissance Universities*. Norman: University of Oklahoma Press, 1958.

A Catalogue of the Harleian Manuscripts, in the British Museum: With Indexes of Persons, Places, and Matters. 4 vols. London, 1808–12.

"Chansons de geste—Girart de Viane." In *Histoire littéraire de la France*, 21:448–60. Paris, 1847. Repr. Nendeln, Liechtenstein: Kraus Reprint, 1971.

Christensen, Thomas, ed. *The Cambridge History of Western Music Theory*. Cambridge: Cambridge University Press, 2002.

[Colloque "Structures monastiques et sociétés en France du Moyen Age à l'époque moderne"]. *Sous la règle de Saint Benoît: Structures monastiques et sociétés en France du Moyen Age à l'époque moderne. Abbaye bénédictine. Sainte Marie de Paris, 23–25 octobre 1980.* Geneva: Droz, 1982.

Cottineau, L. H. *Répertoire topo-bibliographique des abbayes et prieurés.* 3 vols. Mâcon: Protat Frères, 1935–70.

Daly, Saralyn R. "Peter Comestor: Master of Histories." *Speculum* 32 (1957): 62–73.

Davis, Adam J. *The Holy Bureaucrat: Eudes Rigaud and Religious Reform in Thirteenth-Century Normany.* Ithaca, NY: Cornell University Press, 2006.

Delisle, Léopold. *Recueil des actes de Henri II roi d'Angleterre et duc de Normandie concernant les provinces françaises et les affaires de France, chartes et diplomes relatifs à l'histoire de France.* Paris: Imprimerie Nationale, 1920. 1:583.

Denifle, Heinrich. Ed. *Chartularium Universitatis Parisiensis.* 4 vols. Paris: 1889–97. Repr. Brussels: Culture and Civilisation, 1964.

DeWitt, Patricia. "A New Perspective on Johannes De Grocheio's *Ars Musicae.*" Ph.D. diss., University of Michigan, 1973.

Dod, Bernard. "Aristoteles latinus." In *The Cambridge History of Later Medieval Philosophy: From the Rediscovery of Aristotle to the Disintegration of Scholasticism 1100–1600,* edited by Norman Kretzmann, Anthony Kenny, and Jan Pinborg, 45–79. Cambridge: Cambridge University Press, 1982.

Dutton, Paul Edward. "Material Remains of the Study of the *Timaeus* in the Later Middle Ages." In *L'enseignement de la philosophie au XIIIe siècle: Autour du "Guide de l'étudiant" du ms. Ripoll 109,* edited by Claude Lafleur, 204–8. Turnhout: Brepols, 1997.

Eggebrecht, Hans Heinrich, F. Alberto Gallo, Max Haas, and Klaus-Jürgen Sachs. *Die Mittelalterliche Lehre von der Mehrstimmigkeit.* Darmstadt: Wissenschaftliche Buchgesellschaft, 1984.

Eske, Tsugami. "Aristoteles Musicus: Causality and Teleology in Johannes de Grocheio's *Ars musicae.*" *JTLA (Journal of the Faculty of Letters, The University of Tokyo, Aesthetics)* 25 (2000): 111–23.

Everist, Mark. "Motets, French Tenors, and the Polyphonic Chanson ca. 1300." *Journal of Musicology* 24 (2007): 365–406.

———. "Music and Theory in Late Thirteenth-Century Paris: The Manuscript Paris, Bibliothèque nationale, fonds lat. 11266." *Royal Musical Association Research Chronicle* 17 (1981): 52–64.

Falck, Robert. "*Rondellus*, Canon, and Related Types before 1300." *JAMS* 25 (1972): 38–57.

Finckh, Ruth. *Minor mundus homo: Studien zur Mikrokosmos-Idee in der mittelalterlichen Literatur.* Göttingen: Vandenhoeck and Ruprecht, 1999.

Fladt, Ellinore. "Der artifizielle Prozess im Hochmittelalter." *Die Musikforschung* 40 (1987): 203–29.

———. "Johannes de Grocheo." *Die Musik in Geschichte und Gegenwart: Allgemeine Enzyklopädie der Musik.* Ed. Ludwig Finscher. Kassel: Bärenreiter, 2003. 9:1094–98.

———. *Die Musikauffassung des Johannes de Grocheo im Kontext der hochmittelalterlichen Aristoteles-Rezeption.* Munich: E. Katzbichler, 1987.

Fontanel, Julie. *Le cartulaire du chapitre cathédral de Coutances: Étude et édition critique.* Saint-Lô: Archives départementales de la Manche, 2003.

Franklin, Alfred. "Collège du Trésorier." In *Les anciennes bibliothèques de Paris: églises, monastères, colléges, séminaires, institutions, fondations, hôpitaux des origines au moyen âge jusqu'au XIXe siècle,* 1:337–62. Paris: Imprimérie nationale, 1867.

Frobenius, Wolf. "Der Musiktheoretiker Franco von Köln." In *Die Kölner Universität im*

Mittelalter: Geistige Wurzeln und soziale Wirklichkeit, edited by Albert Zimmerman, 345–56. Berlin: De Gruyter, 1989.

———. "Zur Datierung von Francos *Ars cantus mensurabilis.*" *Archiv für Musikwissenschaft* 27 (1970): 122–27.

Fuller, Sarah. "Discant and the Theory of Fifthing." *Acta Musicologica* 50 (1978), 241–75.

Gerbert, Martin. *Scriptores ecclesiastici de musica sacra potissium.* 3 vols. St. Blaise: 1784.

Gilles, André. "*De musica plana breve compendium* (un témoignage de l'enseignement de Lambertus)." *Musica disciplina* 43 (1989): 33–51.

Glorieux, Palémon. *La faculté des arts et ses maîtres au XIIIe siècle.* Paris: Librairie Philosophique J. Vrin, 1971.

Grouchy, Marquis Emmanuel-Henri de. *Mémoires du Maréchal de Grouchy.* 5 vols. Paris: E. Dentu, 1873–74.

Grouchy, Comte de. *Notes sur la Maison de Grouchy en Normandie.* Paris, BnF, fr. 33237.

Gruchy, Guy Fortescue Burrell de. *Medieval Land Tenures in Jersey.* Jersey: Bigwood, 1957.

Haas, Max. *Musikalisches Denken im Mittelalter: Eine Einführung.* Berlin: Peter Lang, 2005.

———. "Die Musiklehre im 13. Jahrhundert von Johannes de Garlandia bis Franco." In *Die Mittelalterliche Lehre von der Mehrstimmigkeit*, edited by Hans Heinrich Eggebrecht, F. Alberto Gallo, Max Haas, and Klaus-Jürgen Sachs, 91–158. Darmstadt: Wissenschaftliche Buchgesellschaft, 1984.

———. "Studien zur mittelalterlichen Musiklehre I: Eine Übersicht über die Musiklehre im Kontext der Philosophie." In *Aktuelle Fragen der musikbezogenen Mittelalterforschung: Texte zu einem Basler Kolloquium des Jahres 1975*, edited by Hans Oesch and Wulf Arlt, 323–456. Winterthur: Amadeus, 1982.

Haas, Robert. *Aufführungspraxis der Musik.* Wildpark-Potsdam: Akademische Verlagsgesellschaft Athenaion, 1930.

Haines, John. *Eight Centuries of Troubadours and Trouvères: The Changing Identity of Medieval Music.* Cambridge: Cambridge University Press, 2004.

Haines, John, and Patricia DeWitt. "Johannes de Grocheio and Aristotelian Natural Philosophy." *Early Music History* 27 (2008): 47–98.

Hammond, Frederick F., ed. *Summa de speculatione musice.* [Rome]: American Institute of Musicology, 1970.

Handschin, Jacques. "Ein mittelalterlicher Beitrag zur Lehre von der Sphärenharmonie." *Zeitschrift für Musikwissenschaft* 9 (1927): 193–208.

———. "Über Estampie und Sequenz." *Zeitschrift für Musikwissenschaft* 12 (1929): 1–20 and 13 (1930): 113–32.

Hentschel, Frank, ed. *Musik, und die Geschichte der Philosophie und Naturwissenschaften im Mittelalter: Fragen zur Wechselwirkung von "musica" und "philosophia" im Mittelalter.* Leiden: Brill, 1998.

Hibberd, Lloyd. "Estampie and Stantipes." *Speculum* 19 (1944): 222–49.

Hiley, David. *Western Plainchant: A Handbook.* Oxford: Clarendon Press, 1995.

Hofmann, Klaus. "Zur Entstehungs- und Frühgeschichte des Terminus Motette." *Acta Musicologica* 42 (1970): 138–50.

Holmes, Urban Tigner. *A History of Old French Literature from the Origins to 1300.* New York: Russell & Russell, 1962.

Huglo, Michel. "Guy de Saint-Denis." *Grove Music Online.* Ed. L. Macy. (Accessed 16 December 2006.) <http://www.grovemusic.com>.

————. "Recherches sur la personne et l'oeuvre de Francon." *Acta Musicologica* 71 (1999): 1–18.

————. "The Study of Ancient Sources of Music Theory in the Medieval Universities." In *Music Theory and Its Sources*, edited by André Barbera, 150–72. Notre Dame, IN: University of Notre Dame Press, 1990.

————. *Les Tonaires: Inventaire, Analyse, Comparaison*. Paris: Société Française de Musicologie, 1971.

Inoue, Kimiko. "Johannes de Grocheo: Volkstümliche musikalische Formen." *Journal of the Japanese Musicological Society* 19 (1972): 73–83.

Jacquart, Danielle. "De *casis* à *complexio*: note sur le vocabulaire du tempérament en latin médiéval." In *Textes médicaux latins antiques*, edited by Guy Sabbah, 71–76. Saint-Etienne: Publications de l'Universite de Saint-Etienne, 1984.

————. "Principales étapes dans la transmission des textes de médecine (Xie–XIVe siècle)." In *Rencontres de cultures dans la philosophie médiévale: Traductions et traducteurs de l'antiquité tardive au XIVe siècle*, edited by Jacqueline Hamesse and Marta Fattori, 251–71. Louvain-la-Neuve: Institut d'études médiévales de l'Université Catholique de Louvain, 1990.

Kibre, Pearl. *The Nations in the Mediaeval Universities*. Cambridge, MA: Mediaeval Academy of America, 1948.

Knaus, Herman. "HS 2663. Johannes de Grocheo: Ars musicae." Unpublished MS description. Darmstadt Universitäts- und Landesbibliothek, n.d.

Lafleur, Claude, ed. *Le "Guide de l'étudiant" d'un maître anonyme de la faculté des arts de Paris au XIIIe siècle: Édition critique provisoire du ms. Barcelona, Arxiu de la Corona d'Aragó Ripol 109, ff. 134ra–158va*. Quebec: Faculté de philosophie, Université Laval, 1992.

————. *Quatre Introductions à la philosophie au XIIIe siècle: Textes critiques et étude historique*. Paris: J. Vrin, 1988.

Lalou, Elisabeth, ed. *Les comptes sur tablettes de cire de la chambre au deniers de Philippe III le hardi et de Philippe IV le Bel (1282–1309)*. Paris: Boccard, 1994.

Le Quesne, Walter J., and Guy M. Dixon. *The De Gruchys of Jersey: Including Their History from Norman Times and Comprehensive Trees from the Fourteenth Century to 1881*. St. Helier, Jersey: Channel Islands Family History Society, 2001.

Lebedev, Sergey. "Zu einigen *loci obscuri* bei Johannes de Grocheio." In *Quellen und Studien zur Musiktheorie des Mittelalters* 2, edited by M. Bernhard, 92–108. Munich: Bayerische Akademie der Wissenschaften, 1997.

Leftwich, Gregory V. "Polykletos and Hippokratic Medicine." In *Polykleitos, the Doryphoros, and Tradition*, edited by Warren G. Moon, 38–51. Madison: University of Wisconsin Press, 1995.

Leitmeir, Christian Thommas. "Types and Transmission of Musical Examples in Franco's *Ars cantus mensurabilis musicae*." In *Citation and Authority in Medieval and Renaissance Musical Culture: Learning from the Learned*, edited by Suzannah Clark and Elizabeth Eva Leach, 29–44. Woodbridge: Boydell Press, 2005.

Maddrell, John Edward. "Grocheo and the Mensurability of Medieval Music: A Reply to Hendrik van der Werf." *Current Musicology* 11 (1971): 89–90.

Maître, Claire. "La place d'Aristote dans l'enseignement de la musique à l'Université." In *L'enseignement des disciplines à la Faculté des arts (Paris et Oxford, XIIIe–XVe siècle)*, edited by Olga Weijers and Louis Holtz, 217–33. Turnhout: Brepols, 1997.

Marks, Richard Bruce. *The Medieval Manuscript Library of the Charterhouse of St Barbara at Cologne.* 2 vols. Salzburg: Institut für Englische Sprache und Literatur, 1974.

McGee, Timothy. "Medieval Dances: Matching the Repertory with Grocheio's Descriptions." *Journal of Musicology* 7 (1989): 498–517.

———. *The Sound of Medieval Song: Ornamentation and Vocal Style according to the Treatises.* New York: Oxford University Press, 1998.

McVaugh, Michael. "The 'humidum radicale' in Thirteenth-Century Medicine." *Traditio* 30 (1974): 259–83.

Mews, Constant J., and John N. Crossley, eds. *Communities of Learning Networks and the Shaping of Intellectual Identity in Europe 1100–1500.* Turnhout: Brepols, 2011.

Mews, Constant J., Catherine Jeffreys, Leigh McKinnon, Carol J. Williams, and John N. Crossley. "Guy of Saint-Denis and the Compilation of Texts about Music in London, British Library, Harley MS 281." *Electronic British Library Journal* (2008), art. 6, pp. 1–34 <http://www.bl.uk/eblj/2008articles/pdf/ebljarticle62008.pdf>.

Meyer, Christian. "Le tonaire cistercien et sa tradition." *Revue de Musicologie* 89 (2003): 77–91.

Moberg, Carl Allan. "Om flerstämmig musik i Sverige under medeltiden." *Svensk Tidskrift för Musikforskning* 10 (1928): 67–82.

Moon, Warren G., ed. *Polykleitos, the Doryphoros, and Tradition.* Madison: University of Wisconsin Press, 1995.

Morlet, Marie-Thérèse. *Dictionnaire étymologique des noms de famille et prénoms de France.* Paris: Perrin, 1997.

Moser, Hans J. "Stantipes und Ductia." *Zeitschrift für Musikwissenschaft* 2 (1920): 194–206.

Mullally, Robert. "Johannes de Grocheo's 'Musica Vulgaris.'" *Music and Letters* 79 (1998): 1–26.

Müller, Hermann. "Zum Texte der Musiklehre des Johannes de Grocheo." *Sammelbände der Internationalen Musikgesellschaft* 4 (1902): 361–68 and 5 (1903): 175.

Nebbiai-Dalla Guarda, Donatella, ed. *La Bibliothèque de l'abbaye de Saint-Denis en France du IXe au XVIIIe siècle.* Paris: Éditions du Centre national de la recherche scientifique, 1985.

———. "Le collège de Paris de l'abbaye de Saint-Denis-en-France (XIIIe–VIIIe siècle)." In *Sous la règle de Saint Benoît: Structures monastiques et sociétés en France du Moyen Age à l'époque moderne. Abbaye bénédictine. Sainte Marie de Paris, 23–25 octobre 1980,* 461–88. Geneva: Droz, 1982.

———. "Des rois et des moines: Livres et lecteurs à l'abbaye de Saint-Denis (XIIIe–XVe siècles)." In *Saint-Denis et la royauté. Études offerts à B. Guenée,* edited by Françoise Autrand, Claude Gauvard, and Jean-Marie Moeglin, 355–74. Paris: CNRS, 1999.

"[Nicolas du Pressoir]." *Histoire littéraire de la France* 26, 457–58. Paris, 1873. Repr. Nendeln: Kraus Reprint, 1971.

O'Boyle, Cornelius. *The Art of Medicine: Medical Teaching at the University of Paris, 1250–1400.* Leiden: Brill, 1998.

Page, Christopher. *Discarding Images: Reflections on Music and Culture in Medieval France.* Oxford: Clarendon Press, 1995.

———. "Grocheio [Grocheo], Johannes de." *Grove Music Online.* Ed. L. Macy. (Accessed 28 November 2006.) <http://www.grovemusic.com>.

———. "Johannes de Grocheio on Secular Music: A Corrected Text and a New Translation." *Plainsong and Medieval Music* 2 (1993): 17–41. Reprinted in Page, *Music and Instruments of the Middle Ages.*

———. *Music and Instruments of the Middle Ages: Studies on Texts and Performance*. Aldershot: Variorum, 1997.

———. *The Owl and the Nightingale: Musical Life and Ideas in France 1100–1300*. Berkeley: University of California Press, 1990.

———. *Voices and Instruments of the Middle Ages: Instrumental Practice and Songs in France 1100–1300*. Berkeley: University of California Press, 1986.

Parsoneault, Catherine Jean. "The Montpellier Codex: Royal Influence and Musical Taste in Late Thirteenth-Century Paris." Ph.D. diss., University of Texas at Austin, 2001.

Pattison, Mark. *Isaac Casaubon*. Oxford: Oxford University Press, 1892.

Pedersen, Olaf. "In Quest of Sacrobosco." *Journal for the History of Astronomy* 16 (1985): 175–221.

———. "The Origins of the 'Theorica Planetarum.'" *Journal for the History of Astronomy* 12 (1981): 113–23.

Peraino, Judith. "Re-Placing Medieval Music." *JAMS* 54 (2001): 209–64.

Piché, David. *La condemnation Parisienne de 1277*. Paris: Vrin, 1999.

Pietzsch, Gerhard. *Die Klassifikation der Musik von Boethius bis Ugolino von Orvieto*. Halle: Niemeyer, 1929.

Pinegar, Sandra. "Textual and Conceptual Relationships among Theoretical Writings on Mensurable Music of the Thirteenth and Early Fourteenth Centuries." Ph.D diss., Columbia University, 1991.

Piolin, Paul, ed. *Gallia Christiana* 11. Paris: Victor Palmé, 1874.

Pollard, Graham. "The Pecia System in the Medieval Universities." In *Medieval Scribes, Manuscripts and Libraries: Essays Presented to N. R. Ker*, edited by Malcolm B. Parke and Andrew G. Watson, 145–61. London: Scholar Press, 1978.

Rasch, Rudolf A. *Johannes de Garlandia en de ontwikkeling van de voor-Franconische notatie*. New York: Institute of Medieval Music, 1969.

Raynaud, Gaston. *Bibliographie des Chansonniers Français des XIIIe et XIVe siècles*. Paris 1883–84. Repr. New York: Burt Franklin, 1972.

Reaney, Gilbert. "The Anonymous Treatise *De origine et effectu musicae*, an Early 15th Century Commonplace Book of Musical Theory." *Musica disciplina* 37 (1983): 109–19.

———. "Johannes de Grocheo." In *Die Musik in Geschichte und Gegenwart: Allgemeine Enzyklopädie der Musik*, edited by Friedrich Blume, 7:95–100. 17 vols. Kassel: Bärenreiter, 1958.

Reaney, Gilbert, and André Gilles, eds. *Ars cantus mensurabilis*. Rome: American Institute of Musicology, 1974.

Recueil des historiens des Gaules et de la France 23. Paris, 1876.

Reimer, Erich, ed. *De mensurabili musica*. 2 vols. Wiesbaden: Franz Steiner, 1972.

Reynolds, L. D. *The Medieval Tradition of Seneca's Letters*. London: Oxford University Press, 1965.

Rico, Gilles. "'Auctoritas cerum habet nasum': Boethius, Aristotle, and the Music of the Spheres in the Thirteenth and Early Fourteenth Centuries." In *Citation and Authority in Medieval and Renaissance Musical Culture: Learning from the Learned*, edited by Suzannah Clark and Elizabeth Eva Leach, 20–28. Woodbridge: Boydell Press, 2005.

Rieckenberg, Hans Jürgen. "Zur Biographie des Musiktheoretikers Franco von Köln." *Archiv für Kulturgeschichte* 42 (1960): 280–93.

Rohloff, Ernst. *Der Musiktraktat des Johannes de Grocheo nach den Quellen neu herausgegeben mit Übersetzung*. Leipzig: Kommissionsverlag Gebrüder Reinecke, 1943.

————. *Die Quellenhandschriften zum Musiktraktat des Johannes de Grocheio. In Faksimile herausgegeben nebst Übertragung des Textes und Übersetzung in Deutsche, dazu Bericht, Literaturschau, Tabellen und Indices.* Leipzig: Deutscher Verlag für Musik, 1972.

————. "Studien zum Musiktraktat des Johannes de Grocheo." Ph.D. diss., Universität Leipzig, 1925.

————. *Studien zum Musiktraktat des Johannes de Grocheo.* Leipzig: Frommhold & Wendler, 1930.

Round, J. Horace, ed. *Calendar of Documents Preserved in France, Illustrative of the History of Great Britain and Ireland.* London: HMSO, 1899.

Rouse, Mary A., and Richard H. Rouse. *Authentic Witnesses: Approaches to Medieval Texts and Manuscripts.* Notre Dame, IN: University of Notre Dame Press, 1991.

Rouse, Richard H. "Manuscripts Belonging to Richard de Fournival." *Revue d'histoire des textes* 3 (1973): 253–69.

Rouse, Richard H., and Mary A. Rouse. *Manuscripts and Their Makers: Commercial Book Producers in Medieval Paris 1200–1500.* 2 vols. Turnhout: Harvey Miller Publishers, 2000.

Rüthing, Heinrich. *Der Kartäuser Heinrich Egher von Kalkar 1328–1408.* Göttingen: Vandenhoeck and Ruprecht, 1967.

Sachs, Curt. *Eine Weltgeschichte des Tanzes.* Berlin: Dietrich Reimer, 1933.

Spanow, Michail. "*Ductia* und *cantus insertus* bei Johannes de Grocheio." *Beiträge zur Musikwissenschaft* 32 (1990): 296–99.

Stockmann, Doris. "Musica vulgaris bei Johannes de Grocheio (Grocheo)." *Beiträge zur Musikwissenschaft* 25 (1983): 3–56.

————. "'Musica vulgaris' im französischen Hochmittelalter: Johannes de Grocheo in neuer Sicht." *Musikethnologische Sammelbände* 7 (1985): 163–80.

Swerdlow, Noel. "Musica Dicitur a Moys, Quod Est Aqua." *JAMS* 20 (1967): 3–9.

Tabbagh, Vincent. *Diocèse de Rouen.* Turnhout: Brepols, 1998.

Thesaurus Musicarum Latinarum. <http://www.chmtl.indiana.edu/tml/>.

Thomson, S. H. *The Writings of Robert Grosseteste: Bishop of Lincoln 1235–1253.* Cambridge, 1940. Repr. New York: Kraus Reprint, 1971.

Thorndike, Lynn, and Pearl Kibre. *A Catalogue of Incipits of Mediaeval Scientific Writings in Latin.* London: Mediaeval Academy of America, 1963.

Tischler, Hans, ed. *The Montpellier Codex.* 4 vols. Madison, WI: A–R Editions, 1978.

————. *Trouvère Lyrics with Melodies: Complete Comparative Edition.* 15 vols. Neuhausen: Hänssler, 1997–98.

Trout, John William. "The *Ars Musicae* of Johannes De Grocheio: The Unanswered Questions and a Glimpse of Medieval Culture, Traditions, and Thinking." Ph.D. diss., University of Cincinnati, 2001.

Vellekoop, Kees. "La place de la musique." In *L'enseignement des disciplines à la Faculté des arts (Paris et Oxford, XIIIe–Xve siècle),* edited by Olga Weijers and Louis Holtz, 235–37. Turnhout: Brepols, 1997.

Waite, William G. "Johannes de Garlandia: Poet and Musician." *Speculum* 35 (1960): 179–95.

Waszink, J. H. *Timaeus a Calcidio translatus commentarioque instructus.* London: Warburg Institute and Brill, 1962.

Weijers, Olga. "La place de la musique à la faculté des arts de Paris." In *La musica nel pensiero médiévale,* edited by Letterio Mauro, 245–61. Ravenna : Longo Editore, 2001.

Werf, Hendrik van der. *The Chansons of the Troubadours and Trouvères: A Study of the Melodies and Their Relation to the Poems.* Utrecht: A. Oosthoek, 1972.

Whitney, Elspeth. "Paradise Restored: The Mechanical Arts from Antiquity through the Thirteenth Century." *Transactions of the American Philosophical Society* 80 (1990): 1–169.

Wingell, Richard J. "The *De musica* of Engelbert of Admont: The Transmission of Scholastic Musical Thought." In *The Intellectual Climate of the Early University: Essays in Honor of Otto Gründler,* ed. Nancy van Deusen, 125–40. Kalamazoo, MI: Medieval Institute Publications, 1997.

Wolf, Johannes. "Die Musiklehre des Johannes de Grocheo: Ein Beitrag zur Musikgeschichte des Mittelalters." *Sammelbände der Internationalen Musikgesellschaft* 1 (1899): 65–130.

———. "Rezension von: E. Rohloff, Der Musiktraktat des J. de G., 1943." *Die Musikforschung* 2 (1949): 72–74.

Wolinski, Mary E. "The Compilation of the Montpellier Codex." *Early Music History* 11 (1992): 263–301.

Wright, Cyril Ernest. *Fontes Harleiani—A Study of the Sources of the Harleian Collection of Manuscripts in the Department of Manuscripts in the British Museum.* London: Trustees of the British Museum, 1972.

Yudkin, Jeremy. "The Anonymous Music Treatise of 1279: Why St Emmeram?" *Music and Letters* 72 (1991): 177–96.

———, ed. *De musica mensurata: The Anonymous of St. Emmeram.* Bloomington: Indiana University Press, 1990.

Index of Names, Works, and Places

Page numbers in italics indicate references to Grocheio's text. For technical terms see the Lexicon. Names of authors and works occurring only in the notes have not been included here.

Typeset in 11/13 Adobe Garamond
Designed and composed by Tom Krol
Manufactured by Cushing-Malloy, Inc.

Medieval Institute Publications
College of Arts and Sciences
Western Michigan University
1903 W. Michigan Avenue
Kalamazoo, MI 49008-5432
http://www.wmich.edu/medieval/mip

 WESTERN MICHIGAN UNIVERSITY